PROPER ISLAMIC CONSUMPTION

D1566316

DISCARD

NIAS – NORDIC INSTITUTE OF ASIAN STUDIES
Monograph Series

73. Vibeke Børdahl: *The Oral Tradition of Yangzhou Storytelling*
74. Cecilia Nathansen Milwertz: *Accepting Population Control*
75. Sharifah Zaleha Syed Hassan & Sven Cederroth: *Managing Marital Disputes in Malaysia*
76. Antoon Geels: *Subud and the Javanese Mystical Tradition*
77. Kristina Lindell, Jan-Öjvind Swahn & Damrong Tayanin: *Folk Tales from Kammu – VI*
78. Alain Lefebvre: *Kinship, Honour and Money in Rural Pakistan*
79. Christopher E. Goscha: *Thailand and the Southeast Asian Networks of the Vietnamese Revolution, 1885–1954*
80. Helle Bundgaard: *Indian Art Worlds in Contention*
81. Niels Brimnes: *Constructing the Colonial Encounter*
82. Ian Reader: *Religious Violence in Contemporary Japan*
83. Bat-Ochir Bold: *Mongolian Nomadic Society*
84. Shaheen Sardar Ali & Javaid Rehman: *Indigenous Peoples and Ethnic Minorities of Pakistan*
85. Michael D. Barr: *Lee Kuan Yew: The Beliefs Behind the Man*
86. Tessa Carroll: *Language Planning and Language Change in Japan*
87. Minna Säävälä: *Fertility and Familial Power*
88. Mario Rutten: *Rural Capitalists in Asia*
89. Jörgen Hellman: *Performing the Nation*
90. Olof G. Lidin: *Tanegashima – The Arrival of Europe in Japan*
91. Lian H. Sakhong: *In Search of Chin Identity*
92. Margaret Mehl: *Private Academies of Chinese Learning in Meiji Japan*
93. Andrew Hardy: *Red Hills*
94. Susan M. Martin: *The UP Saga*
95. Anna Lindberg: *Modernization and Effeminization in India*
96. Heidi Fjeld: *Commoners and Nobles*
97. Hatla Thelle: *Better to Rely on Ourselves*
98. Alexandra Kent: *Divinity and Diversity*
99. Somchai Phatharathananunth: *Civil Society and Democratization*
100. Nordin Hussin: *Trade and Society in the Straits of Melaka*
101. Anna-Greta Nilsson Hoadley: *Indonesian Literature vs New Order Orthodoxy*
102. Wil O. Dijk: *17th-Century Burma and the Dutch East India Company 1634–1680*
103. Judith Richell: *Disease and Demography in Colonial Burma*
104. Dagfinn Gatu: *Village China at War*
105. Marie Højlund Roesgaard: *Japanese Education and the Cram School Business*
106. Donald M. Seekins: *Burma and Japan Since 1940*
107. Vineeta Sinha: *A New God in the Diaspora?*
108. Mona Lilja: *Power, Resistance and Women Politicians in Cambodia*
109. Anders Poulsen: *Childbirth and Tradition in Northeast Thailand*
110. R.A. Cramb: *Land and Longhouse*
111. Deborah Sutton: *Other Landscapes*
112. Søren Ivarsson: *Creating Laos*
113. Johan Fischer: *Proper Islamic Consumption*
114. Sean Turnell: *Fiery Dragons*
115. Are Knudsen: *Violence and Belonging*

PROPER ISLAMIC CONSUMPTION

Shopping among the Malays in Modern Malaysia

JOHAN FISCHER

NIAS – Nordic Institute of Asian Studies
Monograph series, No. 113

First published in 2008
by NIAS Press
Leifsgade 33, DK-2300 Copenhagen S, Denmark
tel (+45) 3532 9501 • fax (+45) 3532 9549
email: books@nias.ku.dk • website: www.niaspress.dk

British Library Cataloguing in Publication Data

Fischer, Johan
  Proper Islamic consumption : shopping among the Malays in
  modern Malaysia. - (NIAS monographs ; no. 113)
  1. Consumption (Economics) - Malaysia 2. Consumption
  (Economics) - Religious aspects - Islam
  I. Title
  339.4'7'09595

        ISBN: 978-87-7694-031-7 (hbk)
        ISBN: 978-87-7694-032-4 (pbk)

.

Typeset by NIAS Press
Produced by SRM Production Services Sdn Bhd
and printed in Malaysia

To Pernille and Anton

Contents

FIGURES

Preface

I wish to explain the context in which this monograph was written. This work started as a PhD thesis that I embarked upon in 2000 and successfully defended in 2005. In 1996 I conducted fieldwork in Kuala Lumpur for my master's thesis on modernity and identity formation among the rising Malaysian middle class. This was my first visit to Malaysia and this research evoked my interest in 'proper Islamic consumption' – the central theme explored in this monograph. Initially, impressions from this stay in 1996 gave shape to the somewhat vague idea that Islam and consumption seemed to be overt and linked forces in Kuala Lumpur. It is a city with a large and growing number of modern mosques and malls; Islamic fashion and banking as well as *halal* food and a whole range of other products are ubiquitously advertised in public, and in a context of what seemed to be a Malaysian version of state capitalism.

As my doctoral fieldwork in 2001–2 progressed, more and more empirical evidence supported existing and emerging linkages between class, proper Islamic consumption, market relations, Islam and the state in contemporary Malaysia.

Of course, there is a large body of literature on Islam and Islamic revivalism in Southeast Asia and Malaysia. And by now, a growing literature on consumption in Asia is emerging. However, there has only been scattered interest in systematic explorations of the way in which middle-class consumption is understood and contested as a particular mode of Islamic practice.

It is with great interest that I have read Maris Boyd Gillette's *Between Mecca and Beijing. Modernization and Consumption among Urban Chinese Muslims* (2000) and Yael Navaro-Yashin's *Faces of the State. Secularism and Public Life in Turkey* (2002). These works have served as inspirations that helped me conceptualise and explore Islam and consumption in Malaysia. Nonetheless, these pioneering works are not capable of capturing the way in which Islam and consumption in Malaysia are being juxtaposed at different levels of the social scale, i.e. in political and religious discourses, in market relations as well as in everyday life in Malay middle-class families. It is my hope that this exploration of the linkages between Islam and consumption in modern Malaysia substantiates the particularities and complexity of this juxtaposition at intertwined levels of the social scale.

My fieldwork-based research helped me understand the distinctiveness and division between the rural, urban and suburban worlds essential to the lives of middle-class Malays. Consequently, understandings and practices of proper Islamic consumption are explored in relation to these spatialities. More specifically, the fieldwork primarily took place among Malay middle-class families in a suburb, Taman Tun Dr Ismail, outside Kuala Lumpur.

Unsurprisingly, 9/11 changed the whole context of this research. On that day, my family and I were holidaying on the island of Pangkor after our arrival in Malaysia in early September. In a beach restaurant we witnessed on television what first appeared to be a feature film about New York under attack. A couple of days later we returned to our flat on University of Malaya campus where we lived for a shorter period of time. Like most urban Malaysians, in our home we could access the Internet, to explore the immense political, religious and economic uncertainty that 9/11 had effected on a global scale. In the context of media censorship in Malaysia, the Internet had become a central medium for uncensored information accessible to the author and urban Malaysians alike. As we shall see, media consumption turned out to be a rewarding avenue for exploring not only Islam and consumption, but also 'the political' in modern Malaysia.

Soon after the attacks on the World Trade Center and on the Pentagon I found T-shirts with Osama bin Laden prints on them available in Chinatown and elsewhere in Kuala Lumpur. The attacks seemed to sharpen my focus on proper Islamic consumption among Malay middle-class families. The attacks signified a reaction against not only the materiality of the structures in New York, but also these symbols of globalisation realised through global trade dominated by the US. Political parties in Malaysia clearly understood 9/11 in quite contradictory ways and their distinctive reading and presentation of 9/11 became the basis for political mobilisation. Also, 9/11 had become a global concern reconfiguring domestic politics in Malaysia, and the state worked hard to consolidate the country's position as a 'moderate' Islamic nation.

In Faisal Devji's book *Landscapes of the Jihad. Militancy, Morality, Modernity* (2005) he argues that 9/11 has transformed Islam into both an agent and a product of globalisation, making Islam a global phenomenon that demands an opinion about itself. It will be clear how all these issues filtered into discussions with Malay middle-class informants about proper Islamic consumption in everyday life.

Acknowledgements

First of all, I would like to thank the families of my fieldwork site, Taman Tun Dr Ismail (TTDI), for their willingness to open up their homes and thus allow a glimpse into their everyday lives. The fieldwork took place amidst the immense confusion and uncertainty that came in the wake of 9/11 and it is in this context that I would like to express my gratitude for the openness with which I was met.

Likewise, I would like to thank other informants and organisations in Malaysia that patiently put up with countless questions and inquiries. I would also like to extend my sincere thanks to Kamaruddin Said who introduced me to TTDI and its people. Most of all, he provided me with specific ideas and methods applicable to the study of this locality. During fieldwork, Shamsul A. B., Abdul Rahman Embong and Sharifah Zaleha Syed Hassan offered valuable input and feedback on the project.

I would like to thank NIAS Press and the two reviewers of my manuscript for advice and encouragement. I owe thanks also to colleagues at International Development Studies (IDS) at Roskilde University for constructive advice and support. Special thanks goes to Inge Jensen who, besides her everyday commitment, skilfully masters the bureaucratic technicalities of academia. At IDS, Daniel Fleming provided me with invaluable and fair points of criticism of early drafts, which allowed me to rethink structure and content – and hence enabled me to ask new questions. Thomas Blom Hansen's expert and committed support of the project has been an inspiration and driving force in the whole process.

Last, but not least, I would like to thank my wife, Pernille, and son, Anton, for their encouragement. In fact, I am convinced that, on the one hand, the fieldwork could not have been completed without Anton's craving for playmates that to a large extent was fulfilled in the families of TTDI. On that account, numerous and lasting contacts were established. On the other hand, our experiences as a family inspired and informed a number of significant ideas central to this monograph.

Glossary of Frequently Used Malay Terms

This glossary includes local and foreign terms (e.g. Arabic) that are in common usage in contemporary Malaysia.

adat	tradition, local customary law
akhirat	afterlife
baju kurung	long-sleeved loose fitting long blouse for women
baju Melayu	traditional outfit for men consisting of shirt and trousers
Bahasa Melayu or *Bahasa Malaysia*	mother tongue of the Malays
bangsa	literally, race or nation of people
bomoh	traditional healer
bumiputera	literally, sons of the soil
dakwah	literally, salvation
dapur	kitchen
Hadith	traditions concerning the life and works of the Prophet Muhammad
haj	the pilgrimage to Mecca, which is a principal obligation of adult Muslims
halal	lawful or permitted
haram	unlawful or prohibited
jamaat	mosque committee
janggut	beard
kampung	village
kelas agama	religious class

kelas pertengahan	middle class
kenduri	feasting
kerajaan	literally, government
kopiah	skull cap
lepak	loitering
makanan Islam	proper food for Muslims
mashbooh	doubtful
Melayu Baru	New Malay
negara	state, realm, capital, court or town.
riba	interest
salat	prayer
sharia	Islamic law
solat tahajud, solat tasbih	commendable acts
sufi tareqat	mystically inclined orders
sunna	the life, actions and teachings of the Prophet Muhammad.
sunnat	optional prayer
surau	prayer house
tudung	long headscarf

Abbreviations and Acronyms

ABIM	Angkatan Belia Islam Malaysia or the Islamic Youth Movement of Malaysia
BN	Barisan Nasional or National Front
IKIM	Institut Kefahaman Islam Malaysia or Institute for Islamic Understanding
ISA	Internal Security Act
JAKIM	Jabatan Kemajuan Islam Malaysia or the Islamic Development Department of Malaysia
MCA	Malaysian Chinese Association
MIHAS	Malaysia International Halal Showcase
MPV	Multi Purpose Vehicle
NEP	New Economic Policy
NST	*New Straits Times*
PUM	Persatuan Ulama Malaysia or Malaysian Ulama Association
SMS	Short Message Service
STPM	Sijil Tinggi Pelajaran Malaysia or Malaysian Certificate of Higher Education
UDA	Urban Development Authority
UMNO	United Malays National Organisation

1

Shopping among the Malays in Modern Malaysia

From my 14th floor condominium balcony in Taman Tun Dr Ismail (TTDI),[1] a middle-class suburb about 15 kilometres west of Malaysia's capital, Kuala Lumpur,[2] I have two quite distinct views beneath me: to one side TTDI, my fieldwork site, and to the other side a view over the lush greenery of Sungai Pencala (Figure 1, overleaf). The overriding focus of this monograph is 'proper Islamic consumption' among Malay middle-class families inhabiting the suburb of TTDI (Figure 2, p. 3). Sungai Pencala has the status of a Malay reserve meaning that formally only Malays can buy land in this area.

A fence marks both the real and the imaginary boundary between the respectable middle-class suburb of TTDI and Sungai Pencala. Sungai Pencala is also the home of the commune of Darul Arqam. Darul Arqam or the House of Arqam is an Islamic group whose believers seek to follow the behaviour of the Prophet Muhammad in everyday life. Followers appear to engage in an ascetic lifestyle and deny themselves Western luxuries such as furnishings, television, radio and other amenities, rejecting what in a study of Arqam was called 'items of progress' (Nagata 1984: 113). In spite of the fact that TTDI and Sungai Pencala are quite distinct and distinctive spatialities, the physical and mental presence of Sungai Pencala and Darul Arqam is vital for Malays living in TTDI and thus for the central arguments throughout this monograph.

Established in 1971, Arqam developed into a commune comprising about 40 houses on eight acres of land. The group set up its own prayer house (*surau*), medical clinic, school and a number of workshops. Arqam members represent a unique visibility in everyday life in TTDI, in particular due to their dress style: Arab turbans for men and veiling for women. Most of the Arqam followers were middle-class university graduates sharing many of the social characteristics of the Malays of TTDI. Among Arqam devotees

1

Figure 1: Sungai Pencala and the Darul Arqam commune.

there was a small number of 'highly placed civil servants', who during the day worked as 'Western style' bureaucrats and, after office hours, returned to Arqam and transmuted into pious followers in Arab dress (ibid.: 105). The question of how divergent Islamic lifestyles or registers of consumption are shaped by and shape the 'overtly public' (subjected to the gaze of others) versus the 'covertly private' (family intimacy) are central to Malay middle-class life, as we shall see in the following.

Of the greatest interest to Malay families in TTDI and elsewhere in Malaysia, however, is Arqam's cultivation and marketing of an Islamic vision of Malay independence and prosperity through the production of a

Figure 2: Taman Tun Dr Ismail, the suburban fieldwork site.

wide range of *halal* (lawful or permitted) food products, but also products such as toothpaste, talcum powder, medication and notebooks. Ideally, this vision was to ensure the group full independence from any kind of non-Muslim (Chinese or foreign) control (ibid.: 107). Arqam successfully promoted this vision of communal self-sufficiency, and their halal goods were traded throughout peninsular Malaysia.

The Malaysian National Fatwa Council banned the organisation in 1994, reasoning that the movement and its leader, Ustaz Ashaari, believed in the imminent appearance of the Mahdi (or hidden Imam), a key idea in Shia belief. From the viewpoint of Malaysian Sunni orthodoxy, this notion implies unseen power and sectarian secrecy (Ackerman and Lee 1997: 49–51). In the everyday lingo of the state and press in Malaysia, this is labelled 'deviationism', persistently staged as an outside other threatening the nation and state nationalist visions of modernity. In the eyes of state nationalism, Arqam seemed to signify a kind of regressive, subversive and excessively ritualistic way of living. Furthermore, allegations of polygamy and sexual perversion in Arqam fuelled the hype surrounding the organisation. In other words, deviationism in Malaysia was evoked as the other of the pure and modern national Islam promoted by state nationalism.

The banning of the organisation, its lifestyle and activities were still very much of significance to the Malays in TTDI, as we shall see. Several aspects of the life of Arqam both concerned and fascinated my informants: they expressed concern over the authoritarian leadership of Ustaz Ashaari as well as rumours of polygamy and the general secretiveness of the organisation. At the same time, informants were fascinated by Arqam's asceticism and piety. Most of all, however, there was appreciation of Arqam's enterprise in promoting halal goods and successfully marketing these.

The anxiety regarding ubiquitous forms of deviationism became ever more pronounced after 9/11, when both national and international pressure intensified in order to identify so-called fundamentalists, Islamists, radicals and deviationists. Arqam is only one of numerous revivalist or *dakwah* (literally, 'salvation') organisations that emerged in Malaysia in the 1970s. Of all these organisations, Arqam most clearly represented an inclination towards Shia ideas.

I first visited the condominium, Villa Flora, next to Sungai Pencala and Arqam, to be shown the flat before starting my fieldwork in September 2001. The Chinese realtor, with a somewhat uncomfortable facial expression, referred to the view over Sungai Pencala and Arqam as 'a village view'. The Chinese owner of the apartment, who accompanied the realtor, added that 'Malays are *so* lazy'. Thus, TTDI and Sungai Pencala comprise a potent field that brings out a number of social, religious, ethnic and spatial ambiguities and conflicts in contemporary Malaysia.

Seen from the Villa Flora condominium balcony, middle-class suburbia stretches far into the horizon with its one- and two-storey terraced and semi-detached houses, bungalows and condominiums housing Malays, Chinese, and Indians (Figure 3).

In the Malaysian population of around 23 million, 65.1 per cent are indigenous Malays (virtually all Muslims) and tribal groups, also labelled

Figure 3: The stretch of suburbia.

bumiputera (literally, 'sons of the soil'), 26 per cent Chinese, and 7.7 per cent Indians (www.statistics.gov.my). Quite contrary to Sungai Pencala, TTDI is truly the space of 'items of progress'. On the surface, suburbia seems to embody extreme homogeneity (i.e. standardised and mass-produced housing types with only little visible external variation), orderliness, clear demarcations between houses and cleanliness. I shall argue that Malay households in their houses are crucial spheres in Malay middle-class formation in contemporary Malaysia: i.e. styles of Islam and styles of consumption as markers of class position, gender, ethnicity and generation.

When you reach the Nissan-sponsored welcoming sign (Figure 4) by the highway you can enter by one of two routes. You can go straight, passing the mall, One Utama, which is currently in the process of being considerably expanded to become one of Asia's largest shopping complexes (Figure 5). Before retiring in 2003, Malaysia's Prime Minister Dr Mahathir Mohamad, with perfect symbolic timing, inaugurated this new mall. After several years of careful preparation and spectacle, Mahathir resigned after 22 years as Prime Minister. Then you turn right and you are in TTDI. One Utama houses a large number of shops, supermarkets, fast food chains, restaurants and entertainment outlets such as cinemas and playgrounds. This is also the home of IKEA in Malaysia, a widely popular store for lifestyle products and

Figure 4: The Nissan-sponsored welcome sign to TTDI.

Figure 5: The expanding One Utama mall.

Figure 6: At-Taqwa mosque.

living. Nevertheless, One Utama is at the same time an object of concern to families in TTDI because of growing traffic and the pluralisation of shopping and entertainment options.

Hence, moral panic in connection with loitering (*lepak*) by teenagers is deeply felt among many families in TTDI. In addition to One Utama, there are quite a number of smaller shops, a wet market, cafes and restaurants in TTDI, testifying to the increase in the range of consumer choices in everyday life.

The other route to TTDI, if you turn right by the Nissan welcoming sign and follow Jalan Tun Mohd Fuad, takes you past the largest of the mosques in TTDI, the At-Taqwa (Figure 6) – the primary mosque of choice of the majority of my informants and Malays more generally in TTDI. There is, however, one more mosque in TTDI, Balai Islam, and a third one on the fringes of TTDI. While the At-Taqwa is ideologically as well as financially dependent on the state and the United Malays National Organisation (UMNO), the dominant political party in Malaysia since independence from Britain in 1957, the Balai Islam mosque is 'independent' (of direct state intervention) in relative terms, and therefore requires private funding for its operation and activities. This funding is to a large extent covered through donations, advertising Islamic products, and services such as seminars, excursions and hotels that are marketed as living up to Islamic requirements. Lastly, the Al-Mujahideen mosque situated between TTDI and One Utama is largely influenced by the Islamic political party PAS (Parti Islam Se-Malaysia). In October 2001 in this mosque, I found an announcement that encouraged boycotting American goods because of the war in Afghanistan and American support of Israeli oppression of the Palestinians. Most graphically, the announcement included a fake picture of an Israeli plane crashing into the *Kaaba*.[3] The site of TTDI is in this sense encircled by mosques of the different religious and political orientations conditioning the lives of the Muslim residents of TTDI.

In the micro-social context of the homes of the Malays of TTDI, squeezed in between the mosques and the mall, the choice of which mosque to attend thus also reflects these broader religious and political issues. This monograph explores a field of contradictory Islamic visions, lifestyles and debates articulating what Islam is or ought to be. These controversies frame the everyday organisation and justification of consumer behaviour within Malay middle-class households. The mall and the mosques in TTDI are signs of two central spheres of modern suburban life in which identity performances and politics are staged.

THE TEXTURE OF THE PROBLEM

Quite literally, the homes of Malay middle-class families squeezed in between the mosques and the mall make up the stage on which the central theoretical and empirical problematics of this monograph are played out. Mosque and market in Malaysia are not only 'stages for the acting out of preordained parts; they are rather potentially "fields of force," highly charged and full of social energy' (Gilsenan 2000: 173). Malay middle-class identity formation, I argue, should be examined in the interfaces between these highly symbolically charged domains: on the one hand, the invocation of Islam as a worldview and a performance of acts of piety; on the other hand a range of consumer practices and lifestyle choices made by, and within, families.

One specific research question informs and shapes the entire monograph. *How is Malay middle-class consumption understood and contested as a particular mode of Islamic practice?* Due to intense political, religious and social contestation, Islam in Malaysia is increasingly being transformed into a 'discursive tradition'. The central question is this tradition's capability to construct, maintain and identify 'proper Islamic'

8

practices. Thus, the primary argument is that controversies over what Islam is, or ought to be, are intensifying the more cultures of consumption assert themselves. As new consumer practices emerge, they give rise to new discursive fields within which the meanings of Islam and Islamic practice are being debated.

In scholarly literature, radical Islamic groups and discourses, e.g. Arqam, are conventionally seen as rejecting consumption *per se*. On the contrary, I argue that modern Malay Muslim identity in Malaysia is unimaginable outside the context of the emergence of a wide range of conflicting understandings and practices of consumption. Consequently, the question of what constitutes a typical Malay Muslim consumer is infused with confusion and uncertainty. Contested understandings, legitimations or valorisations of the morally proper and socially appropriate forms of consumption inevitably evoke the problem of excess or when what is excessive to whom.

The above problematics may appear to refer only to a private and micro-social context. However, I will show how the state, or more precisely, a particular state nationalist vision of a high-consuming yet Islamic modernity is omnipresent as an authoritative discourse in contemporary Malaysia. The state's attempt at moulding a modern form of Malayness is intimately linked to challenging Islamic discourses or *dakwah*, each with particular ideas and standards of how to combine consumption and Islamic practice. In order to pre-empt these confrontations, the state aggressively engages in a re-conceptualisation of consumption that envisions the amalgamation of Malay ethnicity, consumption practices and Islam. This ongoing project, which started in the early 1970s, is intensifying in the context of economic growth and globalisation. It will be clear how nation-building and conflicting types of nationalism emerge as products of these immensely potent, but also confusing and ambiguous developments. All these transformations are of acute concern to the rising middle class in Malaysia, and particularly to the Malay middle class. This new middle class has actively been produced by the state and is promoted as a class of modern entrepreneurial, hard-working and consuming Malays.

In all this, a critique of the generally held idea that consumption essentially is intimate and 'beyond the state' is unfolded. In fact, I argue that the Malaysian state's presence in consumption is not only ubiquitous, but also constitutive of the everyday compliance with, and the authority and authenticity of, state reach and power. This line of reasoning contradicts, for example, the contention that through the privatisation of everyday life, material consumption to a large extent is beyond regulatory measures of the state, suggesting relatively free choices in this private sphere (Chua 2000a: 18). On the contrary, the privatisation, domestication and individualisation of proper Malay Muslim consumption is intricately linked to 'effects' of the state. I shall call this relationship of overlapping and overspilling loyalties, compliances and dependencies 'shopping for the state', i.e. ways in which particular forms of consumption have come to represent novel modes of state reverence and domination on the one hand, and, on the other, state delivery of spending power and privileges to some Malays.

Supportive of what I shall call patriotic consumption in Malaysia shopping has become a patriotic duty in mass culture (Zukin 2004: 14). Therefore, a number of moral imperatives involved in shopping link the shopping of individuals and groups with national sentiments and discourses. Our decisions about where and what to shop separate us from others, but at the same time, shopping exposes us to the presence and gaze of others (ibid.: 2). In this sense, shopping as a public activity is inescapably linked to the performance and spatial context of proper Islamic consumption. This study takes seriously the insight that shopping is 'the zero point where the whole economy of people, products, and money comes together' (ibid.).

CONSUMING SUBURBIA

Urbanisation in contemporary Malaysia and the growth of its capital city, Kuala Lumpur, encompasses a relatively overlooked transformation: the expansion of suburbs surrounding the city, extending suburbia into new territory. Traditionally, urban monumentality is associated with public architectural representations of modernity. Conversely, I argue that the middle-class suburb functions as a symbolic monument embodying imaginaries of the authentically quotidian core of the nation. In the eyes of informants, the middle-class suburb is distinctly different from the 'rural' and the 'urban'. Consequently, suburban Malay middle-class identities come into existence in a negotiation between precisely suburb, village (*kampung*) and city. The suburb may be monumental in its physical organisation, but, contrary to the monuments of the city, it is intimately private and 'familistic', i.e. designed so that families can turn in on themselves as the primary model of social and moral identification. In this section, suburbanisation is discussed from a more generalised perspective, while the question of how a suburb such as TTDI is understood and practised in the everyday lives of middle-class Malays is taken up in greater detail in Chapter 4.

TTDI is located as an outpost on the frontier between the Federal Territory on the one side, and on the other the state of Selangor, stretching all the way to the Strait of Malacca. On the TTDI Residents' Association's homepage (http://ttdi-ra.com.my) it is outlined how the history of the development of TTDI started in 1974, when a government body for urban planning and a private developer who owned this old rubber estate joined forces. It was pivotal for the above-mentioned planning bodies to conceive a distinct suburban design – a 'social statement':

> If Malaysians of various races are brought together in pleasant communities, with plenty of opportunities for neighbourly interaction, they will come to be more aware of the things they have in common and less conscious of the aspects in which they differ. If their children grow up together, and mix freely in schools and on the playing fields, they will think of themselves and of each other as Malaysians rather than Malays, Chinese or Indians (http://ttdi-ra.com.my/index.htm).

TTDI was intended to accommodate the diversity of these ethnic groups. But it was not only the question of race and ethnicity that was of significance in this new community. Ideally, TTDI should provide model housing for what I shall call the new 'national Malaysian family':[4]

> ... with the belief that it is not good sociology to group families of differing means into separate enclaves, the pattern of development was based on the neighbourhood concept with each neighbourhood containing a mixture of house types spanning a wide price range, served by a local commercial centre and having its own landscaped park (http://ttdi-ra.com.my).

As is evident from the above, planning visions have obvious centrality in ordering the space that came to be TTDI. TTDI in many ways embodies the idealised middle-class suburb at a safe distance from urban noise, crime, pleasures, excess and crowds. A suburb like this is planned to be clean, constructed around family values, and focused on recreational facilities such as parks and playgrounds. This type of modern and affluent suburb monumentally symbolises the progress of the Malaysian nation in a post-colonial context, the celebration of the growth of the middle class, and the ordering of space into manageable and exploitable form. Moreover, the suburb is distinctly different from the 'rural' (Sungai Pencala, Arqam and the *kampung* from which many of the suburban residents migrated) and the 'urban' (Kuala Lumpur with its spectacular and even vulgar architectural symbols of urban modernity hyped as *the* national signifier in the national and global media).

The nature of the suburb is 'deep' in the sense that it is intimately private. It is in the private realm of suburban nuclear family houses that the spirit of the modern suburb is produced. The emergence and proliferation of suburbia as the specific style and form that the expanding city produces in the Malaysian context should therefore be examined as a particular urban form in its own right. As previously mentioned, TTDI enjoys the convenience of modern local mosques and shopping facilities, and, eventually, has come to experience the tension that arises between Islam and what is seen as excessive consumption in this local context.

In Taman Tun Residents' Association's monthly (No. 2, October 1998), the Chairman explains on the front page that TTDI generally is considered 'a well laid out residential estate for mainly upper middle income residents'. This remark points towards two broader features of suburban life. Firstly, that a spatiality such as TTDI is the aesthetic product of careful planning and entrepreneurial intervention in the ordering of space. This point is crucial in understanding the nature of the middle-class suburb vis-à-vis its spatial others, the *kampung* and the city. Secondly, that the suburb is a place where class is essential to the way space is practised.

Kuala Lumpur in many ways embodies the quintessential (conception of a) modern and prosperous Asian metropolis. The standard view of Southeast Asian urbanisation takes as its natural starting point the 'urban' as mirroring ambivalent hypermodernity. For one, Gullick (1994: 73) argues that the transformation of Kuala Lumpur is most visible in the form of the appearance of a skyline in the city centre and the massive rise in private transportation and thus pollution. Within the past 30 years, industrialisation, urbanisation and economic growth have produced a city that expands both vertically and horizontally. Skyscrapers are, indeed, a very visible manifestation of the Malaysian miracle of the Tiger Economies essentialised in and through monumental and visible urban and national hypermodernity. Horizontally, however, Kuala Lumpur is expanding in the form of suburbanisation, creating vast new residential areas.

The nation is embodied in and embodies the spaces of the city as a primary national symbol. Architects, developers and the state all attempt to embed the national in the urban and vice versa. The negotiation between city and nation seems to be preconditioned on representation of architecture and urban design. This negotiation, in turn, produces ways in which 'the nation imagines its body – the shape of the people it rules, the legitimacy of its age, and the geography of its domain'. Urban design thus works as a 'technique for turning cities into fields of social, cultural, and national identity production' (Kusno 2000: 97).

The effect of the monumental form of architecture in central Kuala Lumpur is that the urban is equated with this particular form of visibility. I shall argue that the private sphere of the household in Malay middle-class families as an optic for understanding the city and urbanisation more accurately highlights how the city is lived and transformed in everyday contexts. Moreover, in the majority of cases studies of house culture in Southeast Asia are carried out in the *kampung*. The interplay between the imaginary and real Malay house in the *kampung* and the suburban house intimately links urban growth and migration from *kampung* to Kuala Lumpur as an almost mythical narrative of mobility for the middle class. Focusing on the intimate space of Malay nuclear families in their houses in the suburb puts an emphasis on how urban space and its transformations, and even the nation, is produced and understood in contemporary Malaysia.

O'Connor (1995: 45) rightly argues that '[t]he myth is that the city is just what practicality wants and not what a culture constructs'. Especially when looking at suburbs, there is a tendency to see that this type of locality is associated with universal features such as extreme homogeneity, ubiquity, sterility, or rigid planning deriving its form from Europe in a colonial context.

Kuala Lumpur developed from being a tin mining village in the 1850s to a modern metropolis of economic growth and trade, and to a major population centre. From 1860 onwards, Kuala Lumpur became an administrative, commercial, political and institutional node in the Malaysian nation. This status has been further consolidated within the last 30 years.

Kuala Lumpur, in Bahasa Melayu or Bahasa Malaysia, the mother tongue of the Malays, meaning muddy river junction, began as a minor settlement between the rivers Klang and Gombak. As early as the 1820s, sources mention Malay villages in the area (Gullick 1994: 1–2). Until the middle of the nineteenth century, the Klang Valley, in which Kuala Lumpur is situated, was scantily populated by the indigenous Malay population. Not until alluvial tin was first commercially exploited and a profitable business emerged around 1860 did in-migration from especially southern China commence. To this population of Malays and Chinese were added Indian labourers, who arrived at the end of the century, primarily as a workforce in the rubber plantations.

The in-migration of Chinese and Indians and migration from rural areas caused Kuala Lumpur to grow from a population of 3,000 in 1880 to about 100,000 in the 1920s. The population in the 1980s was 1.2 million, reaching 1.7 million in 1990 (Forbes 1996: 86). As a consequence of the importation of labourers from China and India, at the turn of the twentieth century the population of the Klang Valley had become multi-ethnic (Brookfield et al. 1991: 9).

In 1896, Kuala Lumpur was made capital of The Federated Malay States (FMS), encompassing the states of Selangor, Negeri Sembilan, Perak and Pahang (Andaya and Andaya 1982: 82). The FMS were administered by the emerging European dominated bureaucracy in Kuala Lumpur (Roff 1994: 93), giving impetus to Kuala Lumpur's newly acquired status as the country's administrative capital. The status as capital of the country was confirmed at independence in 1957 and, finally, in 1974 when Kuala Lumpur was given the status of Wilayah Persekutuan or Federal Territory. The urban fabric of the Federal Territory was broadened and diversified to include new specialised shops and supermarkets, high-rise office buildings and hotels, educational facilities and industrial estates. Most importantly perhaps, Kuala Lumpur has developed into the intellectual centre of the nation (Brookfield et al. 1991: 10).

Industrial growth and large-scale manufacturing supported by government policy, which started in the 1950s and has been accelerating since 1970s, is vital to the development of the Klang Valley. The contemporary landscape of this urban region is generated by industrial estates developed by government agencies and private companies (Forbes 1996: 86).

There is a long tradition of maritime trade between Southeast Asia, China, India and Europe, and this is clearly reflected in the emergence of Kuala Lumpur as a historical market city in Malaysia. Writing about the emergence of Kuala Lumpur, Sardar (2000: 76) argues that '[i]n a city and a country formed by trading connections, shopping is the connective tissue, the lifeblood and essential ingredient that makes all apparent and comprehensible'.

Furthermore, there is an intimate relationship between trade and the spread of Islam in island Southeast Asia, as in the case of peninsular Malaysia in the thirteenth century (Andaya and Andaya 1982: 52). Kuala Lumpur's status as a market city and commercial centre is today more evident than ever before. At the same time, Kuala Lumpur is a centre for religious, educational and political institutions in Malaysia. To my knowledge, however, no study so far seriously addresses the question of Malay Muslim identities in the suburban context of growth and transition.

Kuala Lumpur is the stage for powerful Islamically inspired symbolism such as: the National Mosque or Masjid Negara[5] representing the merging of state, nation and Islam, embedded in architectural and monumental modernity as a specifically public form produced by and producing what I shall call the nationalisation of Islam; the massive Menara Dayabumi (literally the tower of native strength or ability), the government complex in central Kuala Lumpur that also houses the Central Post Office; the Menara KL (KL Tower) as a focal point for mass communication and globalisation; and Petronas Towers and KLCC, arguably the highest buildings in the world with Kuala Lumpur's most luxurious mall below them.

These monuments are standard signifiers of the modern, bustling Asian metropolis to such an extent that instead of seeing these constructions as signs of unambiguous progress, they can be seen by some urban Malaysians as misrepresenting Malaysian identity as overt, materialistic, ahistorical and shallow.

In previous fieldwork in Kuala Lumpur (Riese, Koefoed and Fischer 1997), identity strategies and modernity were explored in the Malaysian middle class. Informants in this study felt that modernity and modern life were not something external or monumental. Rather, the modern was signified as an intimate feeling one not only lives in, but something that resides inside of one as nationalised culture.

Centralised planning through government intervention has not been able to control the rapid urban growth fulfilling visions of the importance of Kuala Lumpur in processes of nation building and structured urbanisation. Early British colonial governments did little to control or plan Kuala Lumpur's growth and expansion and were far more interested in centralising economic growth as well as social and administrative functions in the city (Lee 1983: 76).

As early as the 1890s, affluent groups of all ethnic communities were leaving the city for the surrounding areas as Kuala Lumpur now was 'crowded, noisy, and sometimes smelly' (Gullick 1994: 22). About 100 years later, massive urban expansion in the Klang Valley and consequent traffic congestion together with housing and environmental problems had led to the general deterioration of the urban environment (Lee 1989: 156). This deterioration was a primary reason behind the creation of suburbs around central Kuala Lumpur and new forms of urban expansion, encroachment, lifestyles and types of planning.

The first attempts to control the growth and formation of the city were made in 1931 with the first simple zoning plan, followed by the General Town Plan in 1939. In the post-independence context of the mid-1960s, it was realised that the expansion by now had got out of hand. In 1970, it was clear that the Comprehensive Development Plans had been relevant in controlling and guiding the development of Kuala Lumpur. However, these were not sufficiently comprehensive, with only limited focus on the element of time or objectives. In effect, the plans consisted of three sets of maps that could by no means accommodate the massive in-migration supported by industrial job opportunities in the post-1970s (Lee 1983: 77–8). In 1974, Kuala Lumpur extended its territory from 93 to 243 square kilometres, which was now called the Federal Territory. The inadequacy of the Comprehensive Development Plans necessitated the writing of the Draft Structure Plan in 1982, establishing the broad policy framework for the planning of the Federal Territory from 1980 to 2000 (ibid.: 78). According to the Draft Structure Plan, the city core is to provide specialised metropolitan services; national and international commercial, administrative and central government activities; and specialised shopping for city-centre residents.

Other activities were to be relocated to alternative peripheral self-contained areas such as Sungai Pencala, bordering on TTDI. The Draft Structure Plan envisioned that planning should weaken ethnic segregation, but in most areas it actually encouraged social and ethnic enclaves. Thus, through centralised planning the state expanded the city towards the frontiers of the Federal Territory bordering on the state of Selangor. In the case of TTDI, which is situated on this frontier in the North Eastern corner of the Federal Territory, the ideal of ethnic diversification did come into existence.

The body of literature on suburbanisation in Malaysia sees this type of development from different perspectives. The new towns such as Petaling Jaya, in which TTDI is situated, were designed according to the concepts of the British new towns or frontier towns that emerged in the 1970s. Petaling Jaya, the first new town of its kind, began, firstly, as a response to the 'overcongestion' of Kuala Lumpur (Lee 1987: 166). Secondly, new towns were developed 'to enable more *Bumiputra* participation in the activities of the urban areas and to pioneer the modernization and urbanization of the backward region' (ibid.: 166). As we shall see, a suburb such as TTDI is a quintessential example of how proper Islamic consumption of housing, food, clothing and cars, for example, is being practised in this type of middle-class universe.

In a wider perspective, there is an 'intimate relationship between cultural identity processes, spatial transformations and modernist aspirations in Malaysia' (Goh Beng Lan 2001: 159). Simultaneously, cultural politics and spatial transformations should be explored with reference to larger processes of modernity in the Malaysian context so that 'cultural dynamics rooted in the contest over changing notions of nation, ethnicity, and class connect urban processes to recent economic restructuring and identity reconstruction in the push to turn Malaysia into a fully industrialized country by the year 2020'[6] (Goh Beng Lan 2002: 12).

In the 1990s Kuala Lumpur and the urban region in which it is situated were exposed to 'unprecedented attempts by federal authorities to discursively and materially reconstruct urban space and subjectivities in "global" ways' (Bunnell 2003: 65). This fascination with global ways includes increased access to the electronic media such as satellite television and the Internet as well as the availability of a wide range of consumer goods due to expanding markets. Moreover, 'The constitutive work of space may be understood in terms of the role of urban planning and architectural design as technologies of bodily disciplining and routinisation' (ibid.: 84). Much like Malaysia, in the case of middle-class estates outside Jakarta in Indonesia, these emerged in an era of public and proactive planning by the state. This is a modernist, social and social democratic form of urban planning 'adopted and adapted in the entirely novel settings of Southeast Asian cities' (Hogan and Houston 2002: 252) in order to 'engender the creation of new social relations that arise from healthy spaces and forms' (ibid.: 258). The design of TTDI and its housing styles is anything but a unilinear process of metropolitan promotion and colonial emulation (Kusno 2002). As I shall show, the powerful linkages between class, consumption, market relations, Islam and the state in modern Malaysia tend to come together in a suburb such as TTDI.

17

DISCOURSES OF PROPER ISLAMIC CONSUMPTION

Islam in Malaysia has been and increasingly is subject to not only intense political, but also cultural and ethnic transformation and contestation individually, socially and collectively. In John R. Bowen's monograph *Muslims Through Discourse: Religion and Ritual in Gayo Society* (1993) on Islam among the Gayo in highland Sumatra, Indonesia, he employs an approach to the diversity of Islam that draws attention to the debates about what Islam is or ought to be and the divergent responses produced by these controversies. Bowen's focus is 'on the field of debate and discussion in which participants construct discursive linkages to texts, phrases, and ideas held to be part of the universal tradition of Islam' (ibid.: 8). He applies discourse to stress its centrality in regard to 'social pragmatics' in the Gayo context, namely 'speech events; the cultural importance of commentary on those events; and the heterogeneous, "dispersive" quality of religious discourse' (ibid.: 9) he finds in Foucault.

In much the same manner, I take Islam in current Malaysia to be a discursive tradition, especially with regard to the way Malay consumption is contested and debated in everyday life. The observation that the religious perspective is mostly adopted, even by religious experts, sporadically in the everyday world of practical and down-to-earth terms is valuable in this context (Geertz 1968: 107). The discursiveness of tradition and practice within modernist Islam is, in fact, constitutive of the dynamics and vitality of the *umma* or community of Muslims. The logocentrism of modernist Islam encompasses modern, sensible and socially contextualised readings of the Koran and the Hadith.[7] Consequently, discourse in the highly educated Malay middle class is a way of coming to terms with and legitimating Islamic ideas and practices of modern life that are constantly subjected to contestation and distinction.

The idea of Islam as a discursive tradition is not recent, but rather an immanent feature of the history of Islam. Asad (1986: 14) argues that an anthropology of Islam should be built on the central concept of Islam as a discursive tradition. This tradition involves diverse interpretations of the Islamic past and future with a reference to a particular Islamic practice in the present. Consumption as a point of debate in current Malaysia can be seen to constitute such a new domain of contestation.

The contestation of Islam is highly visible in party politics in Malaysia, as reflected in the intense controversies between UMNO and PAS over being the true defender of the faith. UMNO accuses PAS of wrong teachings while PAS blames UMNO for giving in to Western values and materialism. These two parties have been and still are integral to the post-colonial political, economic and cultural trajectory of Malaysia. However, none of my informants indicated that they had ever been, were presently or intended to become members or active supporters of either UMNO or PAS.

At the time of UMNO's foundation in 1946, the party was communal in nature and mainly served to protect Malay interests (Crouch 1996: 36). Ever since, UMNO has insisted on the inescapable bonds between nation, state, Islam and Malayness on the one hand and an ideology built on Malay privileges and domination on the other.

Essentially, the ruling political coalition, Barisan Nasional (National Front or BN), is dominated by UMNO and a number of peripheral parties of which the Malaysian Chinese Association (MCA) is the most prominent. Since its formation, UMNO within the BN alliance has strived to maintain government control exercising combined 'repression, manipulation, and responsiveness to popular demands' (ibid.: 246). It is essential to grasp this deep-rooted ambivalence in order to understand the rise of proper Malay middle-class consumption in its historical and institutional context.

In societies where a culture of consumption is developed or developing shopping can be identified as the driving factor behind a turn away from collective deference to authority and reason:

> If royal authority was the moral keystone of premodern society, and reason played the same role in parliamentary democracy, then the source of morality in today's public sphere is the self – implying, at best, our right to both selfish satisfaction and human equity. (Zukin 2004: 33)

It is exactly this coupling of materialism with individualism that PAS sees promoted and practised by UMNO's state nationalism in contemporary Malaysia. Under the heading 'Battle for Islam. UMNO and PAS are locked in a struggle for the Malay soul. The outcome may irrevocably change Malaysian society' an article in *Asiaweek* 16 June 2000 describes the latest development in the ongoing rivalry between UMNO and PAS. In the general elections held on 29 November 1999, PAS won a large segment of the Malay vote, which traditionally is the basis for UMNO's power:

> PAS views UMNO as a waning party that has sold out to materialism and Western values; UMNO accuses PAS of deviationist teachings. The battle lines have been drawn and the fight is on to determine who is the true defender of the faith. (*Asiaweek* 16 June 2000)

The above is an example of a standardised view of political and religious conflict and its causes in contemporary Malaysia. Moreover, the question of ethnicity is distinctive in the fact that PAS has accused UMNO of selling out to Indians and Chinese as well as foreign capitalism, leading to Malaysia's 'underdevelopment and ongoing dependence on foreign markets and to its decadence and spiritual bankruptcy' (Peletz 2002: 10).

There has been a marked radicalisation of PAS's discourse from the 1980s. The discourse in the 1980s and 1990s was radicalised due to the state's policies to nationalise Islam, as we shall see in the subsequent section, as well as to events abroad, such as the Iranian revolution in particular. Moreover, the radicalisation of PAS's discourse and its politics of identity were fuelled by expanding consumer markets and globalisation intensifying from the 1980s onwards. A central object of otherness within both PAS and Islamic revivalist discourses is the construction of Western influences as 'Westoxication' (Stivens 1998b: 91), inspired by Ayatollah Khomeini's ideas. My study will seek to illustrate the way in which moral, political and religious models of ideas and practices within these more authoritative discourses may filter down to be contested and given more dispersed forms in everyday life.

ABIM (Angkatan Belia Islam Malaysia or the Islamic Youth Movement of Malaysia) is the major *dakwah* group in Malaysia. In spite of this fact, none of my informants indicated that they had ever been, were presently or intended to become members or active supporters of ABIM or any of the other *dakwah* groups. The organisation was formed in 1971 and has traditionally retained its strongest support among students in the campuses of the larger universities in Malaysia. ABIM is a 'fairly "this-worldly", universalistic religious organization, transcending national and some ethnic boundaries at the level of its leadership' (Nagata 1984: 104). The central message of the organisation is that Islam is a self-sufficient way of life that contains the answer to all human universal problems (Shamsul 1994: 104). The ritualistic aspects of the faith are not of vital importance so that it is acceptable for the men to wear Western-style shirts and trousers. In comparison with earlier generations of revivalists, ABIM emphasises a direct engagement, in line with the modernist tradition, with holy texts, bypassing the received wisdom of religious functionaries (*ulama*) (Ong 1995: 174).

During fieldwork in 2002, I visited ABIM's headquarters in Kuala Lumpur. The President of ABIM had worked for the organisation since

1991. He held degrees in public administration and business administration from universities in the US and had worked for two years for the Malaysian government. One particular question dominated our discussion of Islamic revivalism and consumer culture in contemporary Malaysia. The President posed this question in the following manner: 'How do you transform ABIM, the movement, into a modern one with all the latest management techniques and tools, and at the same time ensure it is rooted in religion and traditional values?' (Interview 24 January 2002.) Within this modernist position, 'balance' is a keyword that reflects the relative compatibility of modernity and Islam – i.e. that there is no insurmountable barrier between Islam and modernity. The more complex question, however, is how to work out or translate this compatibility into proper Islamic consumption in everyday life.

While *dakwah* has mainly been described as a more or less homogeneous movement, it seems more productive to adopt a diverse view because *dakwah* are highly diverse with quite different objectives. Nevertheless, they share the concern to 'revitalize or reactualize (local) Islam and the (local) Muslim community by encouraging stronger commitment to the teachings of the Koran and the Hadith to effect a more Islamic way of life' (Peletz 2002: 10). It is, however, by no means clear how this Islamic way of life is put into practice, and *dakwah* devotion has undergone relatively unnoticed processes of individualisation and domestication, which are most often expressed through certain consumer practices.

Dakwah is both an ethnic as well as a political phenomenon, which has transformed Malaysia for both Muslims as well as non-Muslims and actively drawn the country into 'the center of the Islamic social movement, economic innovation, and political activism in the world today' (Shamsul 1994: 100). While Islamic political and moral force has intensified over the past three decades, reshaping Islam into becoming a religious signifier or ethnic 'identity marker' (ibid.: 113–14) with immense effect on all Muslims, the outcome has been intense debating over the true nature of Islamic doctrine and practice.

Dakwah is intricately linked to higher educational institutions in particular. Kuala Lumpur is a centre for educational institutions in Malaysia. The country's largest university, the University of Malaya, is situated close to the city centre. It has a number of other universities including the International Islamic University Malaysia. Traditionally, the Malay middle class has been supportive of *dakwah*. Once again, to take Darul Arqam as an example, middle-class university lecturers, academics and students founded this organisation as a study group.

In connection with this fieldwork and previous fieldwork conducted in Kuala Lumpur, I lived on the University Malaya campus. In this setting, Islam is an immensely public and visible influence on all aspects of campus life. Practically all female Malay students and lecturers wear the long headscarf (*tudung*), and a large number of their male fellow students wear the skullcap (*kopiah*) and grow a beard (*janggut*), symbolising piety. These public manifestations have all become signifiers of modern Islamic identity in the urban campuses and elsewhere. The role of ethnic identity on the campuses, furthermore, seems to play a significant part in inter-ethnic relations. For example, on the University Malaya campus you rarely see Malay students socialising with Chinese and Indian fellow students, who mingle with each other more freely. A key feature in the construction of these boundaries is the deepened Malay Muslim concern with halal against that which is seen as *haram* or impure, and directly or indirectly associated with non-Muslim groups.

I shall argue that diverse Islamic understandings and practices of consumption should be embedded in a framework of performance and performativity. In Turkey, for instance, secularists' fantasies about Islamists in public life have actively produced and maintained versions of Islamism (Navaro-Yashin 2002: 7). Consequently, Islamists' compulsions to gender segregation and veiling are not essential features of Islam. Instead, Islamists 'began to know themselves and to take action upon the world in assuming, internalising, reversing, and upholding what secularists had demonized' (ibid.: 42).

The politics of identity within these groups has been deeply influenced by an expanding consumer market in the context of the globalisation of the 1980s and 1990s. Consumerism developed into a mantra or 'politics of culture' (ibid.: 79) that 'organized, expressed, and mediated' political conflicts. In this context, Islamists moulded an Islamic consumer ontology emerging in this new market for identities (ibid.: 111). This study perceptively captures the public dynamism of social group constitution. To my mind, however, there is a danger in merely accepting the commodification of public appearance, e.g. the deepened significance of the veil, its production and marketing, as the face value of the production and maintenance of stable and uncontested identities.

To sum up, I have argued that Islam in Malaysia is being subjected to various forms of contestation as a discursive tradition. Within modernist Islam in Malaysia and elsewhere, modern and socially contextualised readings of the Koran necessitate constant valorisation and legitimation of novel forms of consumption in order to define what is proper and improper from divergent Islamic perspectives. What is more, this type of contestation is evident in Malaysian party politics, where proper Islamic consumption is being intensely debated as 'materialism' or Westernisation. As the dominant political party in Malaysia since independence from Britain in 1957, UMNO has tried to secure Malay interests and privileges as well as the amalgamation of nation, state, Islam and Malayness. Since independence constitutionally Malays have only been Malays if they are Muslims. In spite of UMNO's hegemonic position, PAS has retained considerable support from Malay groups, and, most importantly, it is in the interfaces between the political rhetoric and mobilisation of PAS and UMNO that proper Islamic consumption is being debated most intensely.

THE NATIONALISATION OF ISLAM IN MALAYSIA

In James Siegel's monograph *Fetish, Recognition, Revolution* (1997) on Indonesia, he argues that the nation's capacity through the state to confer national recognition essentially transcends persons. National recognition 'seems to come, mystically enough, from the nation itself' (ibid.: 9). The nation seems to have found the subject and then a profound mode of belonging arises. Histories of postcolonial nations such as Malaysia come into being as products of the effects of complex connections between colonialism, nationalism and emergent communication systems. The complexity of these connections forges identities that emerge from confusions and contradictions. As the sum of all these influences there arises what Siegel calls the 'fetish of appearance'. This fetish signifies the desire for a power that 'cannot be appropriated but which, nonetheless, one feels one possesses' (ibid.: 10). The fetish as a magical instrument 'claims false relation to an origin' (ibid.: 91), and at the same time it is a 'fetish of modernity' (ibid.: 93).

Modernity in Malaysia makes itself felt as the foreign element that has been domesticated – the process of Malaysianising foreign influences. The most powerful quality of the fetish depends on its ability to compel someone to recognise 'within "me" something I did not know I had and making me think it might be possible to have a new identity' (ibid.: 245). All this poignantly echoes the whole Malaysian national project of producing new identities amidst the confusion over expanding markets, state formation, nationalism and revivalist Islam. In other words, to identify what is properly Islamic is all about guiding or disciplining the excess of possibilities.

In 1991, Mahathir unveiled Vision 2020, imagining Malaysia as a fully developed nation by the year 2020. At a later stage, Vision 2020 was defined as

> First, establishing a united Malaysian Nation made up of one Bangsa [literally race or nation of people] Malaysia. Second, creating a psychologically liberated, secure and developed Malaysian society. Third, fostering and developing a mature democratic society. Fourth, establishing a fully moral and ethical society. Fifth, establishing a mature, liberal and tolerant society. Sixth, establishing a scientific and progressive society. Seventh, establishing a fully caring society. Eighth, ensuring an economically just society, in which there is a fair and equitable distribution of the wealth of the nation. Ninth, establishing a prosperous society with an economy that is fully competitive, dynamic, robust and resilient. (Kassim 1995: 68)

The ubiquity and grandeur of this vision ironically enough masks its central idea that a uniquely moulded Malaysian modernity can only materialise as an intimately mental project in the form of instilling proper ethical and moral values in Malaysian citizens. This type of re-cognition evokes Siegel's point that the power in the nationalist ethos lies fundamentally in the nation's own mystical recognition of national subjects. In turn, this recognition incites a profound sense of national belonging. On a larger scale, national and global recognition of Vision 2020 was one of its main objectives. Moreover, the recognition, support and success of such a vision can only be forged in the context of 'guided' or disciplined political stability as the price that has to be paid for progress.

Almost universally, the national recognition and education of subjects is essential to greatness and self-perfection. These ideas are strongly resonant with the German philosopher Johann Gottlieb Fichte's idea that the de-votion of national subjects must be internalised as a form of national culture:

> [N]ational education is that of "the whole man" [...] sensible and spiritual, physical and intellectual, in the perspective of an identification of patriotism with pure morality, or of each individual's interiorization of the patriotic community as the community of human freedoms, the site of the moral progress of generations. (Balibar 1994: 82–3)

24

Nationally as well as globally, in the hierarchies of nations, the growing middle class embodies all these qualities and fantasies of a self-made national modernity. In spite of these attempts to recognise and realise national subjects, Malaysia is imagined (Anderson 1991) on the basis of a multitude of particularistic visions or 'nations-of-intent' (Shamsul 1998b). The trouble with the authoritative state nationalist imagination of the Malaysian nation is that in nature it is fundamentally an expression of Muslim Malay ethnic interest masked as ethnic unity in diversity. As a consequence, the new Islamic ethos in Malaysia is tied to allegiance to the state, evoked as a form of cultural kinship through religion (Ong 1999: 226).

However, the nationalisation of Islam in Malaysia is an uneven and subtle process of linkages, loyalties and dependencies between the micro-social, the state and the nation. Islam, or more accurately the social and moral meaning of proper Islamic practice, is contested and there are competing attempts to incorporate it into both state institutions, but also into a multitude of everyday practices. It is these diverse forms of transformations that together comprise the nationalisation of Islam, meaning the increased centrality of Islam as a national and ethnic signifier in Malaysia. The logic of this nationalisation is to see Islam equated with Malayness being the naturalised core of the Malaysian nation. Balibar (1991: 95) explains the logic of this nationalisation as the fusing of national and religious identities. He argues that

> ... national ideology involves ideal signifiers (first and foremost the very name of the nation or 'fatherland') on to which may be transferred the sense of the sacred and the affects of love, respect, sacrifice and fear which have cemented religious communities; but that transfer only takes place because another type of community is involved here. The analogy itself is based on a deeper difference. If it were not, it would be impossible to understand why national identity, more or less completely integrating the forms of religious identity, ends up tending to replace it, and forcing itself to be "nationalized".

At the core of the nationalisation of Islam lies the question of proper Islamic practice. Especially with regard to the explosion of everything considered halal, proper Islamic practice has taken on equal significance as signifier in the nationalisation of Islam in Malaysia.

To my mind, the nationalisation of Islam more accurately than simply evoking 'Islamisation' covers the processes crucial to this monograph. Islamisation has come to be a ubiquitous and elusive expression of Islamic

25

fundamentalism. The main trouble with the concept of Islamisation driven by 'Islamists' is the inference that a globalised and homogeneous Islamic force is emerging. This notion of a unified Islamic tradition and practice that clashes with anything else clouds the existence of national, ethnic, social or religious diversity, which may be the single most vital impetus in Islamic thinking and practice. Most of all, however, the nationalisation of Islam specifically targets the Malaysian context while keeping broader issues and perspectives in mind.

Systematic examinations of consumer behaviour in the nationalisation of Islam have been neglected. Similarly, in scholarly literature, there exists a clear tendency to isolate studies of identity to focus exclusively on identities emerging in connection with either consumption or religion. By now, Asian consumption and the construction of middle-class identities have been explored in an extensive and expanding body of literature.[8]

However, an intriguing exception to this tendency to disconnect studies of consumption from religion is Gillette's exploration of the way in which the consumption of commodities among urban Chinese Muslims 'showed that they wanted to modernize and were capable of modernizing them-selves' (2000: 223). In this analysis, attention is paid to how consumption activities effect possible changes in production, distribution, ownership and resource generation produced by Deng Xiaoping's economic reforms. In the post-Mao era, the state was no longer the central and monopolised provider of consumer goods and this fact changed the relations between objects, people and state. Consumers now consumed in order to modernise themselves on an individual basis instead of allowing the state to dictate or impel a particular form of modernisation (ibid.). To that end, 'Islam provided an index of civilization that differed from the state's paradigm' (ibid.: 227), and that index was signified by the purity of Islamic civilisation – a purity affecting all kinds of consumption and social practices in general. More specifically, urban Chinese Muslims increasing-ly desired goods and fashions of the Islamic heartland, bringing consumers closer to this sacred centre as they inscribed commodities with Islamic authenticity (ibid.: 233). While many of Gillette's findings are comparable to the developments in Malaysia, proper Islamic consumption in Malaysia is becoming increasingly regulated by the interventions of the state, but, ironically, these interventions take place in the context of intensified globalisation and neoliberal capitalism.

In trying to bridge the gap between studies of religion on the one hand, and consumption on the other, I will show how modern forms of capitalism materialise in the interfaces between class formation, religious revivalism and consumer culture. In a comparative religious perspective, Islam seems to invite the formation and consolidation of religious consumption, as it is the case in contemporary Malaysia.

There are observable overspills between state nationalist and *dakwah* discourses. This is obviously the case with regard to the demonisation of the pre-Islamic past. Mahathir depicts the inception of Islam and the radical break with the pre-Islamic past as turning away from the dark ages:

> And so the animistic ancestors of the Malays embraced Islam with such enthusiasm and faith that they destroyed all their old idols and temples. Today, Malays are constitutionally only Malays if they are Muslims. The progress of the Malays after conversion and presently owes much to Islam as a way of life. There had been lapses of course but by and large Malay civilisation and its progress in the arts and sciences, in the systems of government, the concept of justice and the rule of law, have been the result of attempts to adhere to the teachings of Islam. (Mahathir 2001: 161)

This break was total in its disavowal of the sacred sites symbolising the superstition of the past, and the rejection of a Malay cultural heritage to turn to Islamic modernity and enlightenment. This is a precise replay of Balibar's idea that national ideology encompasses signifiers on to which the sacred is transferred.

A nation is subject to myths of origin and national continuity, and this is particularly evident in the case of young nations emerging with the end of colonialism (Balibar 1991: 87). These myths function as an effective ideological form in which the national is constructed on a daily basis in the form of historical imaginings (ibid.). The inception of Islam in Malaysia marked such a mythologisation. Through emphasis on the paradigmatic break the inception of Islam represented, the nation is now open to a particularly deep and unbreakable type of imagining. The nationalisation of Islam thrives on this imagining, providing the nation with a specific and unambiguous trajectory. The construction of the essentially national operates at a symbolic level positioned in the interfaces between the traditional and the modern (Nairn 1977). Of specific significance in constructing the national is the imagining of the shared past and the birth of the nation. Nairn's notion of the 'Janus-headed' nature of the nation symbolises a safe passage away from the paganism and superstition of the pre-Islamic past into modernity in certain Islamic imaginings. The nationalisation of Islam in the sense of bureaucratisation and institutionalisation through state control moulds and orders the imagining of the Malaysian nation wielded through common history.

The nationalisation of Islam in Malaysia has incited a broader fascination with the proper and correct 'Islamic way of life'. For example, this Islamic way of life entails consuming specific halal goods, which are seen to have a beneficial impact on domains such as family, community[9] and nation. An example of this could be to prefer certain locally or nationally produced goods, e.g. Darul Arqam's locally produced halal products. For example, a male informant from TTDI, Yasir, admired Arqam's promotion and pro-duction of halal products:

> Everything is produced and consumed in their houses. They started a very good economic model for the Muslims, actually, and until today, they followed that. They produce halal fish balls, ketchup, tomato sauce, drinks. 20 years ago these things did not exist. So, they came out with that good model.

Conversely, other types of goods on ideological grounds are perceived as protective of the above domains. In general, political and Islamic discourses are deeply involved in the daily question of getting consumption right or buying into what can be considered the properly Islamic in Islam.

In contemporary Malaysia, a powerful state nationalism seeks to balance and amalgamate mass consumption in all its forms against the forceful revitalisation of Islam. Indeed, Malaysia qualifies as a *Consumers' Republic* (Cohen 2004). The Consumers' Republic embodies a post-WWII strategy, emerging in order to reconstruct the nation's economy and to reaffirm its democratic values through promoting the expansion of mass consumption. Policymakers, business, labour leaders and civic groups all try to put mass consumption at the centre of their plans for a prosperous nation. The health of the economy itself is measured according to indicators such as consumer confidence, spending and housing starts (ibid.: 401). Even more interestingly, the state in the Consumers' Republic recognises individuals as both consumers and citizens so that in the twentieth century we have witnessed the intertwining of the rights and obligations of citizenship. In this century, citizens in developed countries 'merged their aspirations for an adequate material provision and a legitimate place in the polity expecting the two to go hand in hand or the former to encompass the latter' (ibid.: 408). Consequently, political citizenship was about the entitlement to material enjoyment (ibid.). I will show how some of these developments and tendencies are being localised and given actual shape in Malaysia, i.e. how the state sees certain forms of consumer behaviour as either desirable or unwanted, patriotic or unpatriotic.

Islamic consumption in Malaysia has been subjected to state and business intervention in the form of extensive market research and the political institutionalisation of consumption, e.g. the setting up of the Ministry of Domestic Trade and Consumer Affairs in 1990. Clearly, this is a sign of the state's bid to become an apparently 'honest broker' of consumption (Zukin 2004) that protects the entitlements of Malaysian consumers against what the state and consumers increasingly see as confusing and excessive consumer culture. Consumers' trust in and dependence on the state as an honest broker in consumption legitimates state intervention regarding the right ways to shop as well as guidance in terms of public debates about value (ibid.: 32). This type of market research is aimed at the classification and definition of segments. Lastly, the state now recognises and institutionalises the power residing in commodities. It seems as if the idols and idolatry of the animistic and Indianised traditions of the pre-Islamic past, abandoned and demonised, have been purified and sanitised to return in state-recognised form as part of the nationalisation of Islam. Indeed, this can be said to qualify as a new and powerful 'language of stateness' (Hansen and Stepputat 2001: 37) that helps shape state, governance, effects and subjectivities.

FROM HALAL TO HALALISATION

In their most basic definitions *halal* is that which is permitted and *haram* is that which is prohibited by Allah (Azimabadi 1994). From this straightforward definition halal and haram in food and drink consumption are filtering into all aspects of human life. The halal/haram binary informs and controls ideas and practices such as the wearing of gold and ornaments; wigs and hairpieces; statues; paintings; photographs; keeping dogs; cleanliness; industries and crafts; sexual appetite; spreading the secrets of conjugal life and innumerable other areas (ibid.: v–ix). One point specifically highlights the arguments of this monograph – disliking excesses:

> We have now come to the conclusion that Islam likes the middle path in all the functions of life. Good appearance is no exception. One is asked to keep clean, wear nice garments and beautify oneself within a limit. Whether it is a matter of cleansing or beautifying, one is not allowed to alter one's

physical features and appearance. One should be as Allah, the Almighty has created. Alteration is clear forgery and deception and hence an act of Satan. (Ibid.: 121)

In this understanding, more and more is taken in, valorised, and then subjected to a normative halal/haram judgement. The central concern is to modify the consumption of commodities that may exactly compel personal recognition of new, unnatural and un-Islamic forms of identities.

The Koran and the Sunna[10] exhort Muslims to eat the good and lawful God has provided for them, but a number of conditions and prohibitions are in existence. Muslims are expressly forbidden from consuming carrion, spurting blood, pork and foods that have been consecrated to any being other than God himself. These substances are haram and thus forbidden.[11] The lawfulness of meat depends on how it is obtained. Ritual slaughtering entails that the animal is killed in God's name by making a fatal incision across the throat. In this process, blood should be drained as fully as possible. Another significant Islamic prohibition relates to wine and any other intoxicating drink or substance that is haram in any quantity or substance (Denny 2006: 279). The origin and nature of halal as a food taboo has been discussed in classic texts by Mary Douglas (2004), Marvin Harris (1997) and Frederick J. Simoons (1994).

Muslim dietary rules have assumed a new significance in the twentieth century as some Muslims strive to demonstrate how such rules conform to modern reason and the findings of scientific research. Another common theme in the revival and renewal of these requirements seems to be the search for alternatives to what is seen to be Western values, ideologies and lifestyles. The understanding and practice of halal requirements, however, vary among import countries and companies producing halal food. This is the point made in the book *Halal Food Production* (Riaz and Chaudry 2004: vii). This book by two US scholars is a popularised guide to promoting, marketing and producing halal foods for professionals in an expanding global food market. To my knowledge, this is the only book of its kind and it is widely used by companies worldwide that try to understand and comply with the current transformation of halal. In connection with my research on halal I have learned that this book is being studied carefully by e.g. food producers and pharmaceutical companies.

For Muslims it is obligatory to consume only halal food as established in the Koran and Sunna (ibid.: 2). Three sets of ideas guide the permissibility of foods. Firstly, impurity and harmfulness as reasons for prohibitions that follow divine definition: 'A Muslim is not required to know exactly why or how something is unclean or harmful in what God has prohibited' (ibid.: 6). Secondly, the permitted is that which is sufficient and conversely the superfluous or excessive is prohibited (ibid.). Lastly, 'Doubtful things should be avoided. There is a grey area between clearly lawful and clearly unlawful. This is the area of "what is doubtful." Islam considers it an act of piety for Muslims to avoid doubtful things' (ibid.: 6–7). The doubtful or questionable is expressed in the word *mashbooh* (ibid.: 7), which can be evoked by divergences in scholars' opinions or the suspicion of undetermined or prohibited ingredients in a commodity (ibid.).

Modern ideas and practices of halal apply to more than just foods, e.g. to cosmetics and care products (ibid.). In the modern food industry, a number of requirements have taken effect, e.g. to avoid any substances that may be contaminated by porcine residues or alcohol such as gelatine, glycerine, emulsifiers, enzymes, flavours and flavourings (ibid.: 22–5). The problem in certifying food and other products with regard to these substances is that they are extremely difficult to discover. In sum, to determine whether a foodstuff is halal or haram 'depends on its nature, how it is processed, and how it is obtained' (ibid.: 14). Besides these relatively clear requirements regarding food, there are far more abstract, individual and fuzzy aspects of context and handling involved in certification. The interpretation of these *mashbooh* areas is left open to Islamic specialists and state institutions such as JAKIM (Jabatan Kemajuan Islam Malaysia or the Islamic Development Department of Malaysia) as we shall see in greater detail below. In the end, it is concluded that 'Although these explanations may or may not be sound, the underlying principle behind the prohibitions remains the divine order' (ibid.: 12).

Knowledge of the above requirements is, of course, essential to innovative food companies that try to establish themselves in an expanding global halal market. The increased demand for halal products by conscious and educated Muslim consumers has urged developed countries to export halal products. In this way, developed countries have entered a market that was previously dominated by Muslim countries (ibid.). Moreover, the proliferation of Western franchised food has changed the international food market and subjected it to new standards of halal certification (ibid.: 29–30).

I shall call the above transformations of halal understanding and practice *halalisation*. It will be clear how halalisation signifies a powerful and growing preoccupation with the proliferation of the concept of halal in a multitude of commodified forms. What is more, halalisation has helped shape whole new forms of aesthetic Malay communities based on different taste preferences in various middle-class sections. This proliferation of halalisation has incited new and elaborate ideas of the boundaries and authenticity of halal purity versus haram impurity.

THE MATERIAL OF MALAYNESS

This section discusses how the post-colonial state in Malaysia has promoted the twin goals of rapid development fuelled by mass consumption and the nationalisation of Islam. I shall show how this ethnicised state with specific reference to shopping for the state and halalisation has tried to incorporate a particular version of state nationalist Islam into the everyday lives of Malays. The research question addressed is this. *Why and how has the question of Malays' proper Islamic consumption become a key concern for state nationalism in Malaysia over the past three decades?* This section pinpoints the intimate and subtle relationship between state responsiveness/authoritarianism, ethnicity, Islam and material identity.

I shall argue that state responsiveness through ethnic policies in Malaysia addresses two modes of desire in the Malay middle class. The first mode is that of 'state deliveries' fulfilling demands for a multitude of commodities constitutive of ethnic Malay material identity. As will be discussed below, these deliveries of the state are intimately linked to the expanding state monopolisation of the certification and standardisation of a plethora of halal commodities. Closely related to this, the second pressing endeavour of the state is the symbolic and discursive project of delivering a meaningful version and vision of a Malaysian nation in response to and pre-emption of revivalist Islamic counter-visions often strongly focused on the demand for an Islamic state.

In his book *The Malay Dilemma*, Mahathir wonders how racial tension between the 'major races', Chinese and Malays, could explode into violence the way it did in the riots in Kuala Lumpur and its environs on 13 May 1969 (Mahathir 1970: 4). In these riots about two hundred mostly Chinese and Indians were killed and about four hundred injured. These events fuelled both the authoritarianism of the state and a responsiveness in the form of a new type of ethnic politics most strongly associated with the Malaysian Prime Minister to come, Mahathir.

To Mahathir, the answer lies in Malay frailty and backwardness as against Chinese resilience. The social formula for alleviating Malay inferiority is through 'Urbanization, acquisition of new skills and the acceptance by the Malays of new values which are still compatible with their religion and their basically feudal outlook' (ibid.: 114). These visions were translated into the major scheme of state social engineering – the New Economic Policy (NEP).[12] Mahathir became the proponent of this policy, devised to improve the economic and social situation of the *bumiputera* through the manufacturing of an urban, educated, entrepreneurial, shareholding and high-consuming Malay middle class. This piece of grand social policy is essential in the everyday lives of my informants – who are the embodiment of this class.

The NEP was instigated to improve the economic and social situation of the *bumiputera* vis-à-vis particularly the Chinese. More specifically, the NEP encompassed two major goals. The first was the reduction and eventual eradication of poverty by increasing income levels and employment opportunities for all Malaysians. The second aimed at 'accelerating the process of restructuring Malaysian society to correct economic imbalance, so as to reduce and eventually eliminate the identification of race with economic function' (Second Malaysia Plan, 1971–5, quoted in Crouch 1996: 25). In actual fact, the NEP generated a number of benefits for the Malays and other indigenous groups such as increased ownership of production and quota access in the educational system. The number and proportion of Malays engaged in the modern sector of the economy rose significantly as a product of these policies.

Ideologically, the overall objective was to manufacture an urban, educated, entrepreneurial and shareholding Malay middle class (Second Malaysia Plan, 1971–5, quoted in Crouch 1996: 25). So the expanding Malay middle class can to some extent be seen as a product of ideological work on behalf of the state (Milner 1998; Embong 1998, 2002). In the eyes of every single Malay informant, the NEP is felt, even today, to be vital for the social and ethnic progress of the Malays and to have a crucial impact on their performance as Malay consumers. Informants time and again referred to themselves as New Malays. The coining of this term by Mahathir signifies the concretion of a hard-working and entrepreneurial urban Malay middle-class mentality. Rightfully, this new class of Malay consumers was entitled to enjoy the fruits of their work.

The ideological blueprints of the NEP and the New Malay, however, would have been unimaginable without the steady economic growth Malaysia has experienced since 1970.[13] The launch of the NEP and general economic growth has transformed Malaysia's class structure, producing an urban Malay middle class and the decline of agricultural occupations (Crouch 1996: 181). 1990 statistics show that the Malay middle class's share in middle-class occupational categories constituted 48.1 per cent and that Malay white-collar middle-class professions doubled from 12.9 in 1970 to 27.0 per cent in 1990 (ibid.: 184–5). Urbanisation after 1970 represented a serious challenge to UMNO, which could no longer rely on its largely passive rural base (ibid.: 192–3). The party now had to pay attention to other and more demanding sections of the urban Malay community. A similar effect was noticeable in PAS, which in 1980 was taken over by well-educated leaders who downplayed the rural-Malay ethos and stressed its Islamic foundations.

The middle class now had a 'material stake in the social order' (ibid.: 195) and was equipped to practise what I call shopping for the state. Shopping for the state encompasses the transformation of more traditional and symbolic types of reverence for authority in the form of Islam, royalty and Malayness promoted through colonial policy (Nagata 1994: 66). Instead, the state now demands the patriotic consumption of subjects in return for various forms of responsiveness, most clearly through delivering economic growth and spending power. In other words, the economic transformation of Islam in Malaysia has displaced Islam as a source of traditional legitimacy of Malay rulers. Their historical mode of articulating Malayness based on universal Islamic authority and *adat*,[14] local customary law (ibid.: 45), has been seriously destabilised. The NEP has unquestionably actively drawn Islam into the economic sphere through the proliferation of a multitude of Islamic institutions starting in the 1980s. Simultaneously, the NEP transformed Malay dominance into Malay hegemony within the notion of a plural society so that Malay culture became synonymous with 'national culture' (Shamsul 1998a: 146).

Under the heading 'Think practically, Dr M Advises ulamas' in *The Star*[15] 4 December 2001, Mahathir attacks the Malaysian Ulama Association (PUM or Persatuan Ulama Malaysia) for their call to boycott American goods in the wake of the US attack on Afghanistan: 'We should not be emotional, we should think practically, things that we can do, we do, things that we cannot, we don't talk about it, the Prime Minister told reporters after breaking fast and performing *terawih* prayers.'[16] An anonymous representative from PUM in the same article replied that 'It's unfair to ask the government to boycott [American goods], we do it on our own, things that we don't need, we don't use.' The representative added that the call was difficult to implement and cited American-made Boeing aircrafts being used to fly Malaysian pilgrims to the haj[17] as an example. The state soon elaborated its criticism of boycotting further by saying that such a boycott would have either no effect or a damaging effect on US–Malaysian relations. This view was outlined under the heading 'Goods boycott will only hurt us' (*New Straits Times* 8 December 2001).[18]

The global economic downturn and insecurity following 9/11 moderated consumer sentiments in Malaysia. Consequently, the government launched a campaign in the media aimed at boosting the consumption of domestically produced goods especially. Under the heading "'Tis season for spending, consumers told', the article encouraged patriotic shopping for the state. As a consumer you are advised not to be 'stingy about spending for the festive season as this will not help to stimulate the economy', the Trade and Consumer Affairs Ministry parliamentary secretary explained. He continued: 'As we prepare to celebrate Deepavali,[19] Hari Raya, Christmas and Chinese New Year, let's not be too rigid in our expenditure, which could lead to over saving.' With the US and global markets slowing down after 9/11, spending was the only reliable way to spur growth (*The Star* 13 November 2001). The state and nation depend on this type of patriotic consumption.[20] These ideas are directed against what the state sees as the decline of Islam due to the arrogant rejection of secular knowledge by *ulama* (Milne and Mauzy 1999: 84). Finally, the state's call to consume is in line with the neoliberal dogma that consumption is the primary source of value. The need, of course, is to examine how consumers in reality negotiate and practise this kind of discourse.

The above debate shows that in Malaysia mass consumption is subjected to intense political and religious contestation. Most importantly, the issue of proper Islamic consumption is now inseparable from the way in which the state seeks to incite feelings of reverence, loyalty and patriotism in its citizens. In all this, halalisation stands out as the most striking example of these new forms of loyalties that find their everyday concretion in the forms of commodities. Halalisation as ideas and practices has multiplied in certification, commercialisation, standardisation and promotion by the state and private enterprise. For Malay consumers, this trend encompasses a concern not only with food products, but also with an increasing number of non-food halal products.

The Ministry of International Trade and Industry's mission is to promote halal products and the institution of halal is outlined as follows:

> The goal is to introduce the institution of halal to manufacturers, educators and regulatory bodies, to develop an awareness of halal among all consumers, to make halal foods conveniently available and to provide halal solutions to consumers' needs. In support of our mission and goals, we engage in the following activities: Supervising the production of halal products; Certifying the production of halal; Leading discussion about topics affecting the halal consumer; Finding solutions for ever-evolving challenges; Publishing relevant information; Maintaining 'best in class' producers for halal production. (http://www.miti.gov.my/miti-halalhub.html)

This information is backed up by a guide to the practicalities pertaining to halal certification in a folder (n.d.) issued by JAKIM entitled *Application for a Halal Certificate and Logo*. In the folder's introduction it is stated that in order to certify halal food, 'the Halal Endorsement Certificate will be issued to manufacturers of food and products who have complied with all the conditions as stipulated according to JAKIM's Guidelines on Food, Drinks and Products for Muslims'. In this procedure, 'Inspection and analysis of products and manufacturing premises will be conducted on every application of the Halal Endorsement Certificate.' Following these procedures, final approval, renewal of certificates and follow-up inspections all take place according to specific guidelines.

At the same time, the expansion of the halal market on a global scale has pluralised, legitimised and confused consumer choices involved in everyday consumption in a relatively affluent country such as Malaysia. After coming to power in 1981, Mahathir in 1982 set off the wave of institutionalising and regulating halalisation. In all this, he was clearly a tactical visionary blending calculated and coordinated state responsiveness and authoritarianism.

The Malaysian political system since the 1970s has been subjected to processes of simultaneous authoritarianism and democratisation:

> On one hand, the state exercised strong authoritarian powers to preserve political stability and the continued domination of the Malay elite. On the other hand, it was faced with countervailing forces in society that limited its power while regular competitive elections, although loaded against the

opposition, forced the government to be sensitive to popular pressures. (Crouch 1996: 5)

Thus, Mahathir actively Malaysianised the international proliferation of halal and concentrated its certification in the realm of the state where it has remained. In other words, in order to pre-empt pressure from *dakwah* groups such as Darul Arqam and PAS, the state combined authoritarianism and responsiveness in the nationalisation of Islam as well as halalisation.

Malaysia is described as a model country in terms of complying with halal standards. Malaysia, along with a number of other countries, has strong halal activity in food processing and the export/import trade as reflected in its systematisation and standardisation of halal certification. Moreover, halal certificates for imports of meat, food and kindred products are mandatory (Riaz and Chaudry 1994: 35). In response to the expansion of food service establishments and the opening of international restaurants in Malaysia from the 1970s onwards, a thorough enactment of laws, diverse procedures and guidelines was worked out:

> The passage of the Trade Description (use of expression 'halal') Order of 1975 made it an offense to falsely label food as halal, and the Trade Description Act (halal sign marking) of 1975 made it an offense to falsely claim the food to be halal on signs and other markings. (Ibid.: 54)

The Malaysian state in 1982 set up a committee to evaluate the certification of halal commodities under the Islamic Affairs Division (later JAKIM) in the Prime Minister's Department (ibid.). Mahathir was a driving force behind these moves. Exclusively, this committee was responsible for 'instilling halal awareness amongst food producers, distributors, and importers'. Another responsibility was mandatory halal certification of all imported meat. More specifically, the Islamic Affairs Division of the Prime Minister's Department and the Department of Veterinary Services should approve all meat plants exporting to Malaysia (ibid.: 52). Consequently, a company that 'wishes to use the official Malaysian halal logo, the processing facility in the country of origin has to be inspected and evaluated for halal certification by a team of two auditors from JAKIM' (ibid.: 52–3).

The Malaysianisation of halal requirements strongly reflects the heightened sensibilities involved in new forms of consumption. At the same time, the centralisation of certification procedures parallels the Malay ethnicisation of the state. In a way, halalisation purified and legitimised the expansion of imported commodities. Formally, certification assured anxious consumers of the purity and validity of commodities. Indeed, these measures established shopping for the state as pure practices of mass consumption.

In this picture of the roots of halalisation, there is no requirement that halal food should be produced or prepared by Muslims. But in JAKIM specifications of halal requirements, there seems to be a presumption of this specific point. Regarding 'Devices and utensils' in halal production it is stated that:

> Premises and facilities such as devices and utensils (machines) should only be used for processing halal food. The same premises and facilities are not allowed to be used for processing both halal and non-halal food, although they can be washed and cleaned properly as required by the Syriah law. (Ibid.: 213–14)

In terms of storage, display, and serving. 'All halal products that are stored, displayed, sold, or served should be categorized and labelled halal at every stage so as to prevent it from being mixed or contaminated with things that are not halal' (ibid.: 214). In practice, the correct Islamic handling of commodities is crucial in bringing out their halal qualities as against those which are considered haram or *mashbooh*. Only Muslims are able to fulfil these practices that are extremely prone to pollution. Most of all, these formal procedures signify a celebration of JAKIM's authority to market halal as a brand or logo of the state and nationalised Islam. Consequently, halal products for some Malay informants can even take on an ethnic significance, as this group will only buy food that is produced by Muslims. These commodities are considered pure in contrast to non-halal products, most often produced by non-Malays.

The immense confusion in processes of halal production, marketing and consumption is addressed in the handbook *Halal Food. A Guide to Good Eating – Kuala Lumpur* (Azmi 2003a). In the book, over a hundred restaurants, take-away counters and cafés are listed and reviewed. Much more than strictly traditional halal requirements are involved in guiding Muslim consumers: the spatial context (atmosphere/feel/ambience) of food consumption as practice may be just as significant as the intrinsic qualities of the food and its ingredients. The various establishments are classified according to their halalness, e.g. whether alcohol is sold or food is produced/served by Muslims/non-Muslims. Explicitly, it is stated that the authors refer to and rely on the official channels of Malaysian halal certification and not their personal preferences.[21] All this is expressive of new formations of meta-industries that are beyond the strictly religious focus on halal/haram dichotomies and halal's certification, but instead target the marketing, pluralisation and promotion of halalisation as a brand or logo of state capitalism: *Halal*™.

Branding takes place at two concurrent levels, i.e. in the sphere of institutional relations and in material objects. In both these spheres, branding concentrates on 'techniques of packaging, positioning and promotion which together serve to reshuffle constantly the separate and linked relations among and between institutions and commodities' (Moeran 1996: 279). In terms of definition, 'brand' qualifies as that which 'is well known for being well known!' (ibid.: 280). In the end, as shown in the case of halalisation, advertising puts forward a structure of belief that is akin to that of religion (ibid.: 287).

To sum up, we can say that state deliveries fulfilling the demand for a wide range of commodities were expressive of the Malay ethnicisation of the state. The NEP and the steady economic growth over the last three decades shaped and consolidated the urban Malay middle class personified by the New Malay. This class was now able to perform patriotic shopping for the state, and this type of practice largely displaced more traditional forms of reverence tied to Islam and Malay rulers. Local, national and global halalisation proved to be a prime example of how these new forms of loyalty are concentrated in modern mass consumption. Forms of authoritarianism accompanied mass consumption as the state's privileging of the Malay middle class and, conversely, the resilience of state nationalism depended on *bumiputera* support. Halalisation became integral to manufacturing and sustaining modern forms of state power and patriotic shopping for the state as a particular Malaysianised form of millennial and neoliberal Islamic capitalism.

MALAYSIANISED MILLENNIALISM

In their discussion of millennial capitalism, Comaroff and Comaroff (2000: 294) argue that consumption presently works as '*the* factor, *the* principle, held to determine definitions of value, the construction of identities, and even the shape of the global ecumene'. Thus, consumption in all its forms 'animates the political impulses, the material imperatives, and the social forms of the Second Coming of capitalism'. These points were obvious in the above example of the state nationalist rejection of challenging

Islamic sentiments of boycotting. At the same time, this second coming of capitalism or millennial capitalism both feeds into and is fed by new religious ideas. Malaysia is an example of the emergence of such a complex, and often highly ambiguous, millennial capitalism.

In the age of neoliberal millennial capitalism, the 'chiliastic urge emphasizes a privatised millennium, a personalized rather than communal sense of rebirth; in this the messianic meets the magical' (ibid.: 315). In the Malaysian context, Arqam, for example, was a sign of this form of messianic, secretive and sectarian type of capitalism. Their production and marketing of halal in the seclusion of their commune embodied this second coming of capitalism. Symptomatically, the Malaysian state's ban on Arqam reflects both the authoritarianism and responsiveness already discussed: firstly, an authoritarian form in the banning of the organisation; secondly, a responsive form in the state's move to institutionalise and monopolise the certification of everything halal. Taussig (1992: 117) writes that it is the concentration of reason-and-violence in the State that produces 'the bigness of the big S'. This is exactly the kind of repression-responsiveness that reflects the ambiguity of Malaysian nation-building.

In all this, religious consumption is becoming a core idea and practice in Malaysian millennial capitalism. In fact, halalisation has entered the Malaysian market as a brand or logo of the state, which is nevertheless virtually unverifiable, and thus boundless, in the context of production or consumption. This points to the inherent intangibility in millennial capitalism.

In a historical perspective, the imprint of European economic and political power in Malaysia unfolded in three successive phases (Said 1993: 24). Firstly, Portuguese and Dutch mercantilism from early 1600 to late 1800 and, secondly, the establishment of free trading marked by the 'opening' of the island of Penang in 1786 by the British. The Straits Settlements (the Island of Penang, Singapore and Malacca) thus safeguarded British trade in the Peninsula. This period terminated in 1874 in connection with the Pangkor Treaty that portended the coming of colonialism. This third phase, the expansive colonial-capitalist economy and the modern market and forms of exchange, effectively subsumed Peninsular Malaysia. Thus, the visions of an Islamic economy have basically co-existed with the rationality of capitalism for over a century (ibid.: 29).

In contemporary Malaysia, capitalism is more than ever before inseparable from and subjected to elaborate Islamic ethics and standards, as shown in the case of halalisation in production, certification and consumption. The present effects of consumer capitalism may even be promising material paths to redemption and divinity (Lee 1993: 36). As a consequence, the religious market transcends international boundaries and expands within a framework of advertisement and accessibility to the public. In other words, millennial capitalism in Malaysia is infused with much more than Westernised market rationality critiqued by diverse groups of Muslims.

To a large extent production has been superseded by less tangible ways of generating values by controlling 'the provisions of services, the means of communication, and above all, the flow of finance capital' (Comaroff and Comaroff 2000: 295). Again, the marketing, production and consumption of halalised commodities are prime examples of controlling and categorising that which is fundamentally elusive and unverifiable.

In line with the Comaroffs' ideas, Malaysian millennial capitalism is flavoured with 'casino capitalism'. Historically, this type of capitalism was seen as a pariah in the mindset of the Protestant ethic and populist morality. Today, however, state institutionalised gambling has become an essential metaphor that has transformed the morality of everyday life (ibid.: 295–6). At the core of this metaphor there are cravings for 'abundance without effort, of beating capitalism at its own game by drawing a winning number at the behest of unseen forces'. In all this, there is an 'invisible hand' at play (ibid.: 297). This invisible hand is ubiquitous in the expanding type of halal certification and capitalism discussed above.

The local variant of capitalism in Malaysia emerges as highly ambiguous in several respects. Mahathir promoted the New Malay Protestantised work ethic as a cornerstone of modern state nationalism. These official ideas of a New Malay work ethic were to set new standards for the realisation of national modernity. This work ethic was aimed at curbing the desire for 'instant riches' that can be transmuted unproblematically into material status. Mahathir writes that

> One weakness of the Malays is they are impatient to become rich. Therefore they will sell every opportunity and allocation given to them. Shares, licenses, permits, contracts and others specially allocated to them were immediately sold to others to gain instant profit. (Mahathir 2001: 21)

In support of these ideas, a heading in *The Star* (30 March 2002) read 'Wealth disparity because of greed. Mahathir slams people who yearn for instant riches'. This is an example of a strategic critique of the excess, extravagance and greed of ordinary Malays. Mahathir's critique indirectly targets greedy Malays who put *bumiputera* reserved privileges on the market for the Chinese capitalist to buy.

In reality, quite contradictory interests and activities flavour the Malaysian version of capitalism. The channelling of privileges and funds through ethnic party corporatism has been systematically institutionalised in Malaysia (Gomez 1994). UMNO dominance of the state has enabled Malays to effectively curb what is seen as the excessive economic influence of foreign and Chinese capital (ibid.: 21). What came into existence in Malaysia was a form of party political capitalism controlled by the Malay elite that produced major class inequalities (ibid.: 22).

The NEP was a means to establish new forms of reverence for the UMNO-led state through what I have called patriotic shopping for the state. However, every single informant agreed that the NEP was indispensable as a provision for material Malayness. Obviously, there are a number of moral dilemmas involved in this kind of ethnicisation of state privileges. The NEP has brought about a 'marked propensity of the Bumiputera electorate to lean heavily towards the state for solutions to their problems' (ibid.: 290). Another reason for the emergence of a Malay elite group is Mahathir's personalisation of political patronage in encouraging *bumiputera* capitalism (ibid.: 291).

This type of capitalism is effectively promoted as a capitalism that adheres to Islamic standards. At the same time, it is fundamentally organised as business that is subservient to politics (ibid.: 293). Of crucial importance to the formation and consolidation of a particular Malaysian capitalism was the way in which Islam became a cornerstone of the Malay ethnicisation of the state and its policies. In other words, the state and Islam together effected the invisible hand of millennial capitalism in Malaysia – shopping for the state as a neoliberal dogma.

The responsiveness of the state was accompanied by the deepening of authoritarian powers in the post-1969 emergency context. Concretely, this new state ethos entailed the centralisation of powers in order to counter in particular the causes that were seen to have led to the riots. There was a limitation of the legal challenge to detention under the Internal Security Act (ISA), which was an emergency legislative measure of preventive detention from 1960. For example, the leader of Arqam mentioned above was detained under the ISA. Other types of legislation controlled the content of political debates, challenging political activity and the freedom of the press. In reality, all major newspapers were owned by BN interest groups (Crouch 1996: 94–5) and it was not only the written press that was owned by these groups. As part of the larger NEP project, the state established a great number of *bumiputera* corporations such as the Urban Development Authority (UDA)[22] in 1971, which was to provide assistance and land for Malay businesses in Chinese-dominated areas (ibid.: 201).

From the 1970s onwards, the state was ethnicised to become a signifier of Malayness and unambiguous Malay identity. Moreover, *dakwah* movements challenged Malay state nationalist authority for its overemphasis on material development. More specifically, *dakwah* activists criticised the NEP for its emphasis on materialism and Western capitalist models of development (Zainah 1987: 94). Against this type of critique, state institutionalised halalisation proved to be an elaborate and effective measure for assuaging *dakwah* sentiments.

The state's employment of combined authoritarianism and responsiveness was intended to curb the challenge from a multitude of Islamic discourses. In respect of authoritarianism and especially ISA together with other legislative measures, this ensured some degree of state control over *dakwah* and what was identified as deviationism. Most importantly, however, the state embarked on a wide range of measures symbolising its dedication to Islamic values. The economy thus fused with a politics of ethnicity that in itself was defined in terms of religion (Shamsul 1999b: 43).

The growing centrality of Islam in Malaysian society is also reflected in the materialisation of an Islamic bureaucracy or the bureaucratisation of Malay ethnicity (Ackerman and Lee 1997: 33). The Islamic clergy and bureaucrats hold a central position within this political and bureaucratic establishment (ibid.: 22). An example of an Islamic bureaucratic body set up by the state is IKIM (Institut Kefahaman Islam Malaysia or Institute for Islamic Understanding), established in 1992 by the Prime Minister's Office. One of its main objectives is the message not to fear the afterlife (*akhirat*) alone, but the needs of the here and now are stressed (Nagata 1994: 75). IKIM, together with other Islamic foundations, has taken on the role of a national 'public moral councillor' (ibid.: 76) that constantly addresses questions of proper Islamic thought and practice. Of special significance to state organisations such as IKIM is guiding Malays on correct and rightful Islamic practice in everyday life against challenging views.

In the Malaysian post-colonial context, UMNO in the Mahathir era re-signified its role as protector of the Malays. UMNO and its leader in many ways came to replace and embody the unquestioned loyalty or reverence accorded to leadership in the form of sultans and the *kerajaan* (literally meaning government) in return for protection – especially against the non-Malays (Muzaffar 1979). Consequently, 'unquestioning loyalty is something that a Malay protector expects from the Malays and from UMNO in return for what he sees as the political, economic, cultural and psychological protection provided to the community and the party' (ibid.: 129–30).

After independence money politics and patronage were common practices in the ruling political party in Malaysia. There are recognisable continuities involved in the way in which the ruler–ruled relationship produces and maintains certain forms of political culture. In all this, Mahathir performed the role of the concerned yet harsh national educator seeking to compel Malay subjects to achieve greatness, self-perfection and devotion, internalised as it were as national culture. In other words, at all times, the protection of a plethora of Malay privileges was accompanied by an unswerving critique of their laziness and traditionalism. Apparently, proper Islamic consumption in the Malay middle class has been and still is instrumental to the modern workings of the political.

To sum up, the forging of Malay identities through consumption has become the central focus of the ethnicised state in Malaysia. New forms of mass consumption have displaced older forms of loyalty and provided the state with new technologies of constructing loyalty, reverence, contingency and dependence. Forms of authoritarianism and constant calls for moral correction meticulously balance these types of state deliveries of a wide range of privileges and rights of *bumiputera*. Ironically, the success of state nationalism is entirely dependent on the steady delivery of these privileges, without which their *bumiputera* support would be seriously endangered. In all this, halalisation stands out as an extremely elaborate avenue for manufacturing and sustaining modern forms of state power. Thus, patriotic shopping for the state appears to be a particular Malaysianised form of millennial capitalism. While Mahathir rhetorically promoted a modern state nationalist work ethic for the Malays, in actuality UMNO centralised power with an elite of state beneficiaries. This type of authoritarianism and bureaucratisation was accompanied by capitalism promoted as a capitalism that adheres to Islamic standards.

A NOTE ON METHODOLOGY

The larger argument of the fieldwork is explored mainly on the basis of narratives of Malay middle-class families. These narratives are plotted storylines, narrations, or sequences of events in the lives of informants. Narratives, however, are not neatly informing and structuring practices in everyday life. Instead, narratives are performed and given meaning by informants in the presence of the researcher and his inquiries. The scene where these narrations emerged was predominantly the intimacy of the suburban middle-class house. Family narratives emerging in this homely realm also embraced the history of the family – the 'larger picture' in terms of narratives of migration and urbanisation. Hence, these narratives were 'spatial trajectories' (de Certeau 1984: 115).

Narrative knowledge can be seen as a legitimate form of reasoned knowing (J. Bruner 1986) and arguably the principal property of narrative is its sequentiality in terms of events, mental states, or happenings (Bruner 1990: 43). The insight within social science that people 'narrativise' their experiences has subjected the research interview to more than merely extracting information – it is also aimed at capturing the narrations of the informants.

Narratives are performed as changeable expressions of how we as individuals narrate everyday life. It is a story or narration that delineates our life trajectories in respect of past, present and future. For example, the legitimation of consumption in a multitude of forms and contexts among suburban Malay middle-class families is an essential storyline or narration in this monograph. The narrative comes into being through autobiographical accounts of wider temporal and spatial transformations. In the end, ethnographies can be seen to be guided by implicit narrative structures in the form of stories told about the people studied. As a tool, narrative more constructively than, for example, metaphor or paradigm captures order and sequence for the study of transformations and life cycles (E. M. Bruner 1986).

In October 2001, the central part of the fieldwork started. But the context of the fieldwork had changed dramatically since my arrival in early September. The aftermath of the attacks on the World Trade Center in New York and on the Pentagon on 11 September was felt strongly in Malaysia. Here, as everywhere else, speculations and reflections dominated the media completely. Politically, religiously, economically, and, not least, consumption-wise the context was suddenly another. Less than one month after the attacks I found T-shirts with Osama bin Laden prints on them available in Chinatown and elsewhere in Kuala Lumpur.

The question was what impact this would have on the focus and methodology of the fieldwork. Obviously, the attacks signified a reaction against not only the materiality of the structures in New York, but also against these as symbols of globalisation realised through global trade. Furthermore, when the US government decided to invade Afghanistan in search of Osama bin Laden during Ramadan, this had severe repercussions in Malaysia as in most Muslim countries. These issues obviously filtered into discussions with informants and, ironically, seemed to highlight the actuality of the study, e.g. the debate about boycotting US products.

The initial stage of the fieldwork was quantitative in outlook. Informants were carefully selected on the basis of the TTDI survey. The design of the survey primarily served to specify in particular the ethnic composition of the households, indicators such as family size, income and consumer behaviour, and served as an introduction to the theme of consumption and my general purpose in the project. (At a later stage, this information served statistical purposes in order to broaden the perspective regarding the anthropological outlook of the project.) In this early stage of the fieldwork, the material from the questionnaires, impressions from meeting informants and their residential environment enabled me to formulate qualitative interview guides. The specific data obtained in the survey were thus translated into a more qualitative format.

On the basis of the survey, adults in ten Malay families were selected for interviewing and participant observation. Altogether, fourteen adults in these households were interviewed. Three interviews were carried out with each of these families. The first round of interviews served a number of purposes. Firstly, it established a relationship of confidence between the families and the researcher. Secondly, the questionnaire outlined both very specific questions pertaining to consumer behaviour as well as social and demographic indicators such as occupation, education and trajectories of migration. The focus here was on consumer priorities and budgeting, i.e. priorities concerning the house and its decoration, cars, electronics, food, clothes/fashion, savings/credit, children's education and mass media. In the interview, the stress was on what was important to members of the families in terms of these consumer decisions and how these priorities were played out in everyday decisions and practices. We discussed which objects/goods/things are preferred and avoided and the rationales behind these choices. As such, this first interview introduced the researcher and the topic of research, and it simultaneously provided in-depth knowledge of the family and gave me an impression of the household, its decoration, furnishing and utilisation.

The second round of interviews was designed to elaborate on points of interest from the first interview with the informants. I carefully read the transcript of every first interview to extract themes for further discussion. In this way, the second interview was personalised in accordance with the informants' narratives in the first interview. In order to make the fourteen interviews in the second round comparable and to bring in more abstract and theoretical points for discussion, an interview guide structured the interviews. In this way, the second interview was personalised while at the same time retaining its comparative outlook regarding the other interviews conducted. The third and final interview served the purpose of complementing and elaborating the themes of the two first interviews. If anything was missing, this final interview could cover these issues.

These fourteen Malays became the key informants of the study. As you would expect, participant observation among these informants and families varied in intensity and nature. Participant observation took place not only while the three rounds of interviews were conducted in these households, but also in the form of visits on the occasion of celebrations, festivals and social visits. Moreover, I kept one detailed fieldwork diary for each of the families selected and a general one for the entire fieldwork. Photographs, some of them included in this monograph, were used as documentation to support the participant observation since the monograph focuses on the dialectic between visibility in public and the private sphere of the home. Participant observation was crucial in order to capture any discrepancies between the intentionality and practice involved in everyday consumption.

Informants were chosen on the basis of two criteria: first, their relative statistical position in the survey; and second, their appearance and dress, and style of decoration of the house, which I could observe when visiting families. Interviews and participant observation almost always took place in the living room, the most presentable, decorated and semi-public site: both the primary site of intimate family living and the location where guests, neighbours and relatives are entertained.

Moreover, this in-depth knowledge of the private realms of families enabled me to compare their ideas and practices to those expressed in public when I accompanied them on their shopping sprees or encountered them in my ten months of fieldwork in TTDI. Crossing back and forth between these blurred boundaries allowed me to explore the interconnectedness of what I shall call the semi-public or semi-private. In this manner both survey material and ethnographic methods informed the selection of the single family for in-depth interviewing. Often teenage children participated together with their parents. In many cases, my son of three accompanied me to the homes of the informants, especially if there were children his own age in these households.

In addition to the interviews with the key informants in TTDI, interviews and participant observation with four younger Malay informants from other suburban residential areas were conducted. These informants were included (a) because of difficulties in covering this younger age group in TTDI, (b) in order to put the material from this residential area into perspective, and (c) to discuss the themes of the monograph with younger informants without their parents being present.

Other methodological concerns include that of language skills. I acquired a fair level of oral proficiency in Bahasa Malaysia. Nevertheless, one characteristic of the middle class in Malaysia is their high level of oral proficiency in English. Hence, discussions took place both in Bahasa Malaysia and English, often in the company of my Malay research assistant. In fact, the Malay middle class in the Klang Valley is among the most anglicised in Malaysia and the majority of these Malays prefer to use English frequently in their daily communications as compared to Malay (Embong 2002: 124).

The primary purpose of interviewing was to ensure that these empirical inputs covered the overall thematic and theoretical arguments of the monograph. To a large extent, these ideals were met during the fieldwork in TTDI and Kuala Lumpur. Moreover, the combination of quantitative and qualitative methods proved to be a highly rewarding approach to addressing this particular field of study.

A second type of interview was background interviews with scholars, newspapers, the TTDI Residents' Association, representatives from government organisations, Islamic organisations, and members of the mosque committee (*jamaat*) at the At-Taqwa mosque in TTDI. I contacted Taman Tun Dr Ismail Residents' Association and attended their meetings, and I followed their work, and the issues they addressed in the local context. The association also contributed material such as historical documents covering the development of the area and older issues of their newsletter, *Masyarakat TTDI.*

To sum up on the processes of interviewing, three levels were covered: firstly, the intimate level of the informants in their houses; secondly, the local level in TTDI involving the Residents' Association, local Islamic organisations, and the mosques; and thirdly, the more authoritative discourses of Ministries and other national organisations. A general experience during the fieldwork was great openness when interviewing both organisations and individuals.

The fieldwork scope was, however, not confined to TTDI. The particularity of the empirical evidence from TTDI was contextualised and supplemented with material from newspapers, magazines and websites. Through examining the above sources of information, it was apparent that the material from TTDI represents broad tendencies and logics in contemporary urban Malaysia.

ORGANISATION OF THE MONOGRAPH

Chapter 2 introduces my informants in order to familiarise the reader with their lifeworlds, e.g. family trajectories, migration, housing types, education, occupation and income. A central argument is that class in modern Malaysia should be treated as an emic or performative category, i.e. I analyse how objective parameters of class are involved in class practices or performances. I argue that the historical emergence of the Malay middle class should be explored within a national Malaysian framework as the stage where being middle class is performed. Similarly, I show that the ambiguities and confusions involved in particular classing strategies must be situated in their local Malaysian context. The chapter ends with a discussion of the informants' ideas of class and the way in which these inform practices in everyday life.

Chapter 3 discusses the emergence of a Malaysian 'ontology of consumption' driven by consumer desires as well as heartfelt social anxieties about the moral and social integrity of families. This chapter is an exploration of the way in which the proper in Malay Muslim consumption is understood and practised in suburban middle-class homes. Malaysian bodies are subjected to halalisation on the one hand and theoretisation on the other and this aspect is essential in my discussion of proper Islamic consumption. Above all, it is food and dress that are exposed to elaborate ideas about proper Islamic consumption and hence these forms of consumption are examined in depth.

Chapter 4, 'Housing suburban halalisation', shows how the homes of middle-class Malay families work as semi-domains into which a wide range of ideas and commodities are imported, consumed, understood and contested. This analysis of suburban domesticity embraces issues such public and private cleanliness as a fundamental aspect of everyday life; informants' migration narratives and cycles; the aesthetic of security; how the ethnic other is given shape through proper Islamic consumption; and ways in which cars figure prominently in narratives of physical and social mobility.

In Chapter 5, I shall examine how the 'national family' in Malaysia at different levels of the social scale (e.g. in powerful political discourses of Asian values as well as in the suburban universe) has come to work as the primary model of social and moral identification in the lives of middle-class Malays. Moreover, this chapter explores malls as dominant and contested domains of status as well as moral panic in suburbia. The chapter ends with an examination of the private sphere of middle-class Malays as a site for manufacturing new gender and kinship/generation identities in the interfaces between Islam and consumption.

Chapter 6, 'The excess of possibilities', investigates the concept of excess in two ways. Firstly, how moderation and excess are binaries giving shape to understandings and practices of proper Islamic consumption in Malay middle-class families. What is more, halalisation has also spread into services such as Islamic banking and finance, pushing the boundaries between moderation and excess. This chapter also re-examines 'performance' and 'the body' in the light of previous discussions. Secondly, I explore excess together with the concepts of authenticity and fetishism in a wider theoretical framework.

In Chapter 7, I shall analyse ways in which 'the political' in contemporary Malaysia endeavours to condition certain understandings and practices of proper Islamic consumption among Malay middle-class families. Moreover, it will be clear how modern rituals evoked by the state in Malaysia conflict with more traditional and personal forms of ritual in Islam. Ultimately, the contested issue of ritual between state and individuals feeds into imaginings of the Malaysian nation.

The final chapter, 'Consumptions, conclusions and the wider picture', ties together the findings of the monograph and it also addresses a number of wider questions. One issue taken up is how Malaysian Islam seemingly is expressive of a distinct materiality or 'thingness'. This Malaysianised materiality or 'thingness' is now fuelling or filtering into Malaysian visions of halal networks on the global stage. Hence, halalisation in the nationalisation of Islam in Malaysia may be entering a new phase in which the state tries to market and globalise its visions of the compatibility of Islam, consumption and modernity.

NOTES

1   The word *taman* literally means 'garden'. This word 'attempts to project an identity for the area, not only as green and beautiful, but more importantly, as constituting a peaceful community suitable for family living' (Embong 2002: 130). Tun Dr Ismail was Malaysia's first ambassador to the US and a Malaysian representative to the UN before he became Deputy Prime Minister in Malaysia.

2   Locals mostly refer to Kuala Lumpur as 'KL'.

3   The *Kaaba* is the square building inside the great mosque in Mecca, containing a sacred black stone.

4   The term 'family' in the singular here denotes national and ideological essential-isations. In the discussion of Malay families later on, I am well aware of the contested, deconstructed and discursive nature of the term. Consequently, families are discussed as primary sites for the contestation of gender, generation, class and ethnicity.

5   *Negara*, however, signifies a wider range of meanings. According to Geertz, *negara* can embody '[s]tate, realm, capital, court, town. A general term for superordinate, translocal political authority and the social and cultural forms associated with it' (Geertz 1980: 262). Interestingly, the state translates Masjid Negara into National Mosque in spite of the fact that literally its name means 'state mosque'.

6   Below, I shall return to Vision 2020 in greater detail.

7   Traditions concerning the life and works of the Prophet Muhammad.

8   At least two book series (The Consumasian Book Series and The New Rich in Asia Series) address these issues. Also see, for example, Chua Beng-Huat's *Consumption in Asia. Lifestyles and Identities* (2000), and Richard Robison and David S. G. Goodman's *The New Rich in Asia. Mobile Phones, McDonald's and Middle-Class Revolution* (1996). With respect to the formation and consolidation of middle-class groups in Brazil, see Maureen O'Dougherty's *Consumption Intensified: The Politics of Middle-class Daily Life in Brazil* (2000), and Mark Liechty's *Suitably Modern. Making Middle-Class Culture in a New Consumer Society* (2002), a discussion of new sociocultural patterns in modern urban life in Kathmandu.

9   An example of this type of idealisation is the contention that 'Islam regards a Muslim community as an essential social and economic entity where individuals who constitute the community are economically interdependent of each other' (Nik 2001: 20).

10 The life, actions and teachings of the Prophet Muhammad.

11 These four prohibitions parallel the Jewish prohibitions that include a number of additional prohibitions, e.g. a number of marine species. Contrary to halal, kosher

51

requirements have a longer history of systematic institutionalisation, certification and standardisation.

12 In the 1990s, the NEP was replaced by its downscaled version called the NDP (National Development Plan).

13 Real per-capita income doubled in the period between 1970 and 1990, and this significantly reduced the number of families living below the poverty line (Crouch 1996: 189). On two occasions, in the mid 1980s and late 1990s, economic growth was slowed down due to economic instability and recession.

14 A discursive element within Islam in Malaysia is the tension between modernist Islam and adat, which, according to Geertz is defined as 'something half-way between "social consensus and moral style"' (Geertz 1983: 185). The tension between this tradition and modernist Islam materialises for example in connection with traditional healers (*bomoh*), whom the comparatively more authoritative tradition of Islam sees as representing superstitions of 'folk religion'.

15 *The Star* is one of Malaysia's two leading newspapers in English enjoying widespread popularity.

16 The *terawih* prayer is a special prayer only performed at Ramadan to mark the breaking of the day's fast.

17 The haj is the pilgrimage to Mecca, which is a principal obligation of adult Muslims.

18 *NST* is one of Malaysia's two leading newspapers in English. Many Malaysians consider *NST* a somewhat conservative pro-government paper.

19 *Deepavali* is the Hindu Festival of Light.

20 For a more detailed discussion of this debate see Fischer (2007).

21 In this publisher's pendant to the Kuala Lumpur guide, *Halal Food: A Guide to Good Eating – London* (2003), it is stated in the introduction that '[t]he city of London does not have a specific all-encompassing authority that acts as the central or sole halal certifier for all restaurants. However, the city has several empowering bodies and councils who give certifications to food suppliers and outlets.' (Azmi 2003: 11) Consequently, for Malays or Muslims in general living in London and elsewhere, halal certification is even more complex, confusing and blurred. In the end, this competition over asserting oneself as a producer, authority or trader in the halal market most likely deepens and widens halalisation.

22 UDA was strongly involved in the development of TTDI (http://ttdi-ra.com.my). This is an example of the way state *bumiputera* bodies attempted to both control and liaise with Chinese entrepreneurial capitalism. Other areas of state enterprise involvement were trading, engineering, real estate, mining and security (Crouch 1996: 201).

2

Becoming Middle-Class Malays

On the basis of survey data from 241 households in TTDI,[1] the following is intended to give the reader an idea of ethnicity, migration, and social differentiation in the neighbourhood. In terms of ethnic composition the survey showed that 49 per cent of the households in TTDI are Chinese, 43 per cent Malay, 5 per cent Indian and 3 per cent other. TTDI as such is a clear example of an ethnically mixed residential area. Below, Indians are not included as they are statistically insignificant. Only when significant differences between indicators of the various ethnic groups materialise is this indicated. Migration patterns show that the vast majority of residents moved to TTDI between 1980 and 1999.

Most respondents listed that their primary motivation for moving to TTDI was employment and family. Other reasons for moving were buying a house, friends living in the area and education. Respondents typically, in this order, had migrated from the bordering state of Selangor, Kuala Lumpur, Johore, and the island of Penang. The remaining respondents had migrated from all over Malaysia, including the East Malaysian states of Sabah and Sarawak and in a few cases from abroad. The statistics testify to the fact that migration into TTDI largely takes place from an urban or semi-urban environment, while direct migration from rural areas to TTDI takes place rarely.

Sample data supported Embong's (2001: 88; 2002: 2) quantitative research on middle-class income in the Klang Valley in which metropolitan Kuala Lumpur is situated. Embong's data showed that new middle-class groups are relatively affluent in that they have on average a monthly income above RM 4,000.[2] 60 per cent of the Malays in TTDI earned a high monthly income ranging from RM 4,000 to over RM 10,000. More Chinese than Malays fitted into middle income groups, while Malays dominated in the category above RM 10,000 in which the Chinese were virtually absent.

In terms of educational level, the vast majority of respondents listed that as their highest level of education, they had received either A-levels or tertiary education. While more Chinese than Malays listed A-levels[3] as their highest level of education, Malay respondents were far more prominent in respect of tertiary education. We can say that Malays in TTDI possessed the highest level of education. There were relatively more business owners among the Chinese, while more Malays than Chinese worked as professionals.

Summing up on the socio-economic strata and differentiation, TTDI is composed of ethnically mixed and diverse age groups whose primary motivation for migrating was employment and family. Above all, and especially in case of the Chinese, residents have moved directly from an urban or semi-urban environment. Income distribution shows that while the Chinese are most prominent in the middle to high income groups, Malays dominate in the highest income group. Malays have the highest level of education and this fact may explain why Malays relatively more often are employed as professionals. The Chinese possess a lower level of education and are more often business owners. Despite the informants' stress on ethnicity and distinctions throughout the interviewing process, ethnic discrepancy in the above indicators was relatively narrow. In other words, ethnic distinctions are far more pronounced in the ethnographic material when this is compared to the sample data.

PRESENTATION OF INFORMANTS

The informants are introduced in greater detail below in order to familiarise the reader with their lifeworlds and narratives. This introduction includes informants' self-presentation. Throughout this book, these informants are of vital significance to the wider discussions and arguments. The presentation of informants is structured according to their particular type of housing in a middle-class suburb such as TTDI – bungalows, condominiums and one and two-storey terraced houses. Firstly, key informants from TTDI are introduced and then younger informants are presented. All names of informants have been changed.

Mascud

Mascud: *My wife and I both came from the same state, Kelantan. East coast of Malaysia. We were married in 1977. We have seven children.*

Figure 7: A bungalow in TTDI.

Mascud and his wife are in their mid-forties. The family lives in a large bungalow. They moved from a *kampung* to Kuala Lumpur and then to TTDI in 1986. He holds a bachelor's degree in economics and after working in a bank, he started his own business specialising in security printing. The monthly income of the household is above RM10,000.

Izura and Yusof

Izura: *I come from a family of six, three brothers and two sisters. My husband and me are from Kelantan. I have four kids, two boys and two girls. They are all overseas trained or graduate. All of them are working.*

Izura and her husband are in their fifties. In 2001, they moved from their bungalow in TTDI to a newly built house in a prestigious estate outside Kuala Lumpur. Izura was in Malay Girls' College after which she went to Teacher's College before starting to teach. Yusof went to Military College and was educated in England in Electrical Engineering. After that he came back and worked for a while before doing his Master's degree in Australia. The monthly income of the household is above RM10,000.

Figure 8: A condominium in TTDI.

Yasir

Yasir: *My name is Yasir. I am thirty-seven years old. I am married and we have one child. I received my primary education in Singapore up to primary six. I finished my O-levels in Kuala Lumpur. In terms of work, my force is marketing and sales. At the moment, I am holding a position of head of business development of an IT company.*

The family moved into their condominium flat in 1998. Besides this business, Yasir works for an Islamic organisation in TTDI. The monthly income of the household is RM5,001–10,000.

Siti

Siti: *My parents are from Kedah. My husband's family is from Ipoh. I retired about ten years ago, I was teaching all over the place. I was in eight schools because my husband was posted in Penang, Ipoh, Malacca.*

Siti is in her forties, married with one adult son, who is studying in Australia, and has lived in this condominium flat since moving to TTDI from the state of Ipoh in 1992. She was educated as a teacher in Malay Girls' College. Siti's husband holds a senior position in a bank. The monthly income of the household is above RM10,000.

Ahmad

Ahmad: *I was born in Perlis. Now I'm working as a Business Development Executive. I'm an accountancy graduate from University of Hull, UK.*

Ahmad is in his late twenties, and moved to TTDI around 1996 to live with his sister, her husband and children in their one-storey terraced house. Ahmad hopes to advance in terms of career so that he can establish a home of his own. The monthly income of the household is above RM10,000.

Udzir and Nur

Udzir: *My name is Udzir. I grew up in Kota Bharu. I did my primary and secondary school also in Kota Bharu.*

Nur: *My family originally is from Alor Setar, Kedah, but we have lived here all my life. My parents migrated to KL in the early 70s.*

Udzir and Nur are a couple in their thirties. They moved into their one-storey terraced house around 1995, and live here with their two young boys. They moved to TTDI because they wanted to live closer to relatives already living in TTDI. Udzir is educated as an architect in both Malaysia and the US, and now teaches architecture. Nur holds a degree in mass communication and works as a Public Relations Consultant. The monthly income of the household is between RM5,001–10,000.

Henny and Azmi

Henny: *I'm thirty-nine years old. I'm a fulltime housewife. I have four kids, two boys and two girls. My hobbies are gardening, serving and cooking.*

Azmi: *I'm forty-five years old. I'm from Kuala Langat, Selangor. I was educated in building construction. That's why I started working as a supervisor in a developer company.*

The family moved into the one-storey terraced house in 1999 to live with Henny's mother. They plan to find a place of their own in the near future. Henny took a part-time secretarial course, worked as a secretary in a company, but now she is at home taking care of the kids. Azmi is currently unemployed. The monthly income of the household is RM1,001–1,500.

Sardi

Sardi: *I grew up in a village. Then I attended Malay school until standard four. I didn't have a chance to attend boarding school because of financial problems. My wife and I have one girl and four boys.*

Figure 9: A one-storey terraced house in TTDI.

The family have lived in this one-storey terraced house since 1980, having moved from Kuwait where Sardi was posted for three years as a civil servant for the government. Altogether, he has worked for the government for thirty-six years. After retiring, Sardi was offered a position as a contract officer. Sardi's wife is a housewife. The monthly income of the household is RM1,501–2,000.

Binsar

Binsar: *I was born in a kampung in Pahang. I grew up and got my education there. Then I went for my secondary school in Temerloh. After that I continued doing my diploma in Koran studies. My wife is from Butterworth, Penang. She was a teacher in a religious school under the government for about eight years. Then we opened this school together.*

Binsar and his wife, in their thirties, moved into the one-storey terraced house in 1997. The couple have three children. Binsar moved to Kuala Lumpur to attend Maahad Tahfiz, an institute for Koran studies. The monthly income of the household is RM4,001–5,000.

Irfan and Murni

Irfan: *I did my degree in Kuala Lumpur, mechanical engineering.*

Figure 10: A two-storey terraced suburban house in TTDI.

Murni: *I was schooling in KL. And after O-levels I got a scholarship to further my studies in the UK. After that I did my degree in accountancy. Then I came back and worked for fourteen years. I resigned to take care of my four young kids.*

Irfan and Murni are in their forties, and live in a two-storey terraced house, which they moved into in 1986. Irfan is actively engaged in missionary work with the At-Taqwa mosque in TTDI, and together with his wife they travel extensively both in Malaysia and abroad. Their monthly income is above RM10,000.

Below, the reader meets four younger Malay informants who supplemented material acquired from key informants in TTDI.

Jeti

Jeti: *I come from a family of seven. I've got 5 brothers and sisters. My parents still live in Terengganu, but I live in a family house in Kajang. My dad is a lecturer.*

Jeti is a woman in her early twenties. She moved into the two-storey terraced house she is living in now with her family in 1986. At that time they had returned from Scotland, where her father taught. Jeti holds a bachelor's degree in English and linguistics, currently works as a research assistant, and was going to London to do her MA. The monthly income of Jeti's household is above RM10,000.

Hazan

Hazan: *I was born in Terengganu. I grew up in a small fishing village. I got my education, primary and secondary education there. I moved to KL in 1992, purposely pursuing my studies.*

Hazan is a twenty-five-year-old man. He moved into the flat where he is living now a couple of years ago. He holds a master's degree in Southeast Asian Studies and an advanced master's degree in history. He now works as a researcher. Both his parents live in the state of Terengganu. His monthly income is RM2,001–3,000.

Jomono and Maslina

Jomono: *I came from Batu Pahat, Johore. We lived there since 1954. And then after that I went for further studies in KL.*

Maslina: *I'm from Penang. My father is an ex-prison officer. My mother is still working. She's a clerk. I have seven siblings. Before I studied here, I worked as an instructor in a school in Lumut for one year and now study here for a degree in computer science.*

These two informants lived in the same building and attended the same university. They are both in their early 20s. Jomono is a man who shares a flat with 8 fellow students. In the same complex, Maslina lives with five female fellow students. Their monthly income is RM1,001–1,500.

CONCEPTUALISING CLASS IN MALAYSIA: HISTORY, CAPITAL, STATE AND PERFORMANCE

Obviously, there is no immanent conceptualisation of class in Islam, but class, or more precisely classing practices, are essential in order to explore how Malay Muslim consumption is understood and practised in contemporary Malaysia. When asked about self-definition in terms of class, all informants without exception, but for different reasons, referred to themselves as 'middle class' (*kelas pertengahan*). This point is supported by sociological evidence (Embong 2002: 125).

To informants the term 'middle' appeared to be a convenient way of signifying social mobility attained through education, occupation and family background. At the same time, 'middle' was a workable expression of a rather indistinct or intermediate class-belonging in an objective sense.

Informants would agree that fixed class distinctions should have no place in Islam, and being middle class seemed to indicate a somewhat pious position before God. The logic of this internalisation of middle-classness in self-definition so obvious among informants necessitates an empirically detailed analysis that systematically links class understandings, experiences and practices.[4]

I argue that while the growing number of studies on the middle class in Malaysia so far assume that class is something etic or *an sich*, class should also be treated as an emic and performative category. Thus, this exploration of classing focuses on how objective parameters of class are involved in class practices or performances.

According to international practice, Malaysian statistics analyse the evolution of class structure in Malaysia on the basis of seven main occupational categories. Firstly, 'upper or solid' middle class: 'professional and technical' and 'administrative and managerial'. Secondly, lower middle class: 'clerical' and 'sales' workers excluding the 'services' category. Thirdly, working class: 'production, transport and other'. Finally, 'agricultural': agricultural workers and fishermen. At the time of independence, 56.4 per cent of the work force was employed in the agricultural sector with a very small urban middle class except within professional and technical categories such as schoolteachers, nurses, and higher-level civil servants, bringing their share to 35.1 per cent. 1990 statistics show that the Malay share in the middle-class categories was 48.1 per cent: 'By 1990 less than two in five Malays were involved in agriculture while one in four was employed in a white-collar middle-class occupation.' (Crouch 1996: 181–2).

Inspired by Erwin Goffman's *The Presentation of Self in Everyday Life* (1971), I take performance to be particular kinds of reflexive and strategic practices. The iterability of performances is highly formative of social relationships such as class (ibid.: 27). The force of the dramaturgical metaphor of performance lies in its applicability along three axes:

(1) *Intentionality versus practice.* An example of this is the way in which some Malays articulate or stage a fascination with and modelling of the pious lifestyle of the Prophet as described in Hadith or the embodiment of the Islamic way of life that is unattainable and almost impossible to put into practice.

(2) *The complex element of spatiality*, in Goffman conceptualised as front and back regions. The performance of different parts is premised on

61

these two types of regions. First, a front region referring to the place where the performance is given, a setting where different types of fixed 'sign-equipment', e.g. the *tudung* or the *kopiah* are in place in order to convey the idea that the performer's activity in the region maintains and embodies distinct standards (ibid.: 110). Second, a back region or stage where performances are produced and illusions and impressions constructed (ibid.: 114). While public manifestations or representations may appear overt and demonstrative, such practices cannot be analytically divorced from their preparation in the back region. The public domain or the front region, I maintain, is inconceivable without its social base in the back region, secluded from the direct gaze and power of the state. Cultural intimacy works as 'the recognition of those aspects of a cultural identity that are considered a source of external embarrassment but that nevertheless provide insiders with their assurance of common sociality' (Herzfeld 1997: 3). It is in the 'intimacy of a nation's secret spaces' we should look for the 'original models of official practice': 'People recognize as familiar, everyday phenomena some of officialdom's most formal devices, and this generates active scepticism about official claims and motives' (ibid.: 4). It is in the intimate sphere of the home that the potential to escape and rework state power can arise.

In multicultural Malaysia, cultural intimacy provides a constructive way of comprehending the linkages between the public and private. It is in public that Malays most visibly perform class and status according to certain internalised moral, social and religious scripts. This is also the sphere in which consciousness of ethnic and class distinctions become most pronounced. At the same time, the public is a field of latent exposure, i.e. a space where you are most vulnerable to being unveiled as excessive, and thus 'materialistic', or to falling through as being hopelessly unfashionable. In essence, performing in public is altogether about delivering the proper impression to meet the real and imaginary gazes of the ethnic other – the front region as the space of inter-ethnic exposure. Finally, the public is where performers practise divergent understandings of the nationally proper. Conversely, the back region, the essentially intra-ethnic domain, works as a haven in which the audience for performances is the family itself or occasional guests and relatives. There is no clear-cut, functional or workable way of distinguishing between these two interconnected or parallel spheres, which may thus most fruitfully be seen as both semi-private and semi-public.

(3) *Consumption of fronts* as 'expressive equipment' in Goffman's phrase, e.g. houses, cars, or dress, works as the setting for performances. Fronts function in general and fixed ways to define the specific situation for observers.

Divergent groups seem to be constituted on the basis of different performances and staging. In other words, in the eyes of different Malay middle-class groups, Islam should ideally be internalised as a national-cultural consciousness or as deeply embedded beliefs manifest in a distinct lifestyle. Halalisation is an example of embedding Islam in a series of everyday practices that necessitate reference to fundamental principles or a moral codex. Obviously, the inner coherence of such principles is fragile and therefore calls for constant reiteration and intellectual elaboration.

I show that even though a certain correlation between social indicators and religious stance exists, quite a number of consumer practices escape existing theories and conceptions of consumption. For instance, I was surprised when the informant Maslina, who had received her education in a respectable Islamic school, told me that her favourite movies of all times unquestionably were the horror movies 'Nightmare on Elm Street, Parts 1–5'. Often theories of consumption seem to be sociologially reductive: if you consume A that will lead you to construct identity B.[5] Instead, I will capture the complexity, even arbitrariness at times, involved in Malay consumption and how this contributes to individual and group identity formation. In the discussions to come I found that dramaturgical metaphors, and performance in particular, proved to be analytically useful in order to explore proper Islamic consumption in Malay middle-class families.

Class experiences are also given substance by specific practices in everyday life, and hence class can be conceptualised as something that occurs in human relationships (Thompson 1963: 9). Class happens when people due to common experiences 'feel and articulate the identity of their interests as between themselves, and as against other men whose interests are different from (and usually opposed to) theirs' (ibid.: 9). Class consciousness is the product of the way in which the above experiences are handled culturally, in traditions, value-systems, ideas, and institutionally (ibid.: 10).

Moreover, it seems sensible that 'the "substantial" identity of the classes was only ever a secondary effect of the practice of classes as social actors' (Balibar 1991: 180). As I shall show, explaining class has everything to do with making sense of class and personal class experience (Kessler 2001: 35). This form of making sense of class and class experience is a precondition for being able to perform class in social space.

Debates over proper modes of Malay consumption are of particular significance amongst the Malay middle class, as it is within this inter-mediate group that the nature of what Islam is or ought to be is most strongly contested. This contestation, nevertheless, does not assume the character of overt conflict or controversy in contemporary Malaysia. Rather, the contestation takes the form of doubt regarding their belief and not its validity (Geertz 1968: 61). The question of proper Malay Muslim consumption and halalisation evokes a new range of doubts and ambiguities. Thus, the emerging ontology of consumption in Malaysia is all about 'getting Islamic consumption right' – what informants referred to as 'balanced consumption'. Ideally, balanced consumption signifies modes of Malay consumption that convey social mobility and status without being excessive.

This study substantiates that various styles or registers of consumption work as expressions of different interpretations and orientations of Islam in everyday life. Scholars (see e.g. Kahn 1996) have noted that a conceptual framework that can capture the diversity involved in the constitution of the middle classes should be conceived. This exploration of Malay Muslim consumption tries to provide such a framework.

There seems to be a paradoxical blurredness and imprecision of the middle-class concept on the one hand, and on the other its ability to explain the origins of the modern world (Wallerstein 1991: 143). Hence, the middle class occupies a mythical place in the advent of development and modernity – the emergence of this class 'expanded the realm of monetary transaction and unleashed thereby the wonders of the modern world' (ibid.: 143). The explanatory validity and value of this myth may be limited. It is, nevertheless, obvious that for a developing economy such as Malaysia, the emergent middle class has become an almost mythical national signifier of mental and material development.

This myth is very much alive and has been internalised as a significant point of self-understanding amongst the Malaysian middle class and political elites. The state elite views the creation of such a class as a necessary prerequisite for economic, national and social cohesion (Embong 1998: 85). More specifically, the coining of the new term *Melayu Baru* or New Malay by Mahathir should be seen as an attempt at manufacturing an entrepreneurial vanguard of Malay middle-class modernity. The New Malay embodies an aggressive, entrepreneurial, and global 'we can' mentality (Khoo 1995), abandoning feudalistic values of traditionalism, excess, luxury and privilege. In this way, the New Malay can be seen as a product of an emerging Protestantised middle-class work ethic. These new middle class Malays are modern individuals and groups acutely aware of practising middle-classness through Islam, consumption and legitimate taste.

More specifically, their knowledge of manners or styles as symbolic manifestations constitutes one of the key markers of class and is an ideal weapon in distinctions (Bourdieu 1984: 66). The concern for the symbolic, appearance, pretension and bluff are all genuine marks of the middle class (ibid.: 253). Thus, the Malay middle class is being performed as a class *für sich*. Time and again, informants would refer to themselves and their children as New Malays, meaning that in terms of education and occupation, they were the living sign of this New Malay entrepreneurial spirit. This again enabled these individuals to practise New Malay consumption.

Moreover, the ambiguities and confusions involved in classing strategies must be situated in their local context. The Comaroffs point out that class contrasts 'are mobilized in a host of displaced registers, its distinctions carried in a myriad of charged, locally modulated signs and objects' (Comaroff and Comaroff 2000: 306).

Before entering into the particular classing strategies of informants, I will briefly discuss the historical emergence of the Malay middle class within a national Malaysian framework as the stage where middle class is being performed. Before the British colonial era, the three major classes were the aristocracy, the peasantry, and a merchant class (Embong 1998). From the beginning of the twentieth century under British economic domination, rudiments of new classes began to appear. These new class formations consisted of a 'European bourgeoisie, Chinese compradors, Indian moneylenders, a small group of European officers, junior Malay administrators, Asian white-collar employees, and a growing proletariat (mainly Chinese and Indian)' (Embong 1998: 91).

With the exception of the Malay administrative elite and non-Malay white-collar and technical workers, other groups materialised as a consequence of the demands of expanding colonial capitalism. Eventually, class formation became more pronounced in the post-independence context (Embong 1998: 92). While the state may be a major ideological driving force behind the manufacturing of a Malay middle class, the force of the market and capitalist relations of production should not be downplayed (ibid.: 86). Similarly, it has been demonstrated that the British middle class emerged in and through the market place that provided proper moral and religious lives for middle-class families. With regard to production and consumption, middle class was a function of the market (Davidoff and Hall 1987: 21).

I now proceed to the question of class taste and preference in a micro-social context. The relationship between practice and social origin is caused by two effects – effects exerted by the single family and wider social trajectories (Bourdieu 1984: 111). He argues that the 'trajectory effect' blurs the 'relationship between social class and religious or political opinions, owing to the fact that it governs the representation of the position occupied in the social world and hence the vision of its world and future' (ibid.).

This blurring effect is most pronounced in the middle class, and in particular in its newer groups or grey areas composed of individuals with highly scattered trajectories (ibid.: 112). Aesthetic choices are significant markers of this intra-class struggle. It is mainly against the groups closest in social space that the struggle for recognition through legitimate taste is most fierce (ibid.: 60). Social identity, Bourdieu maintains, is defined, asserted, and practised through difference (ibid.: 172). The 'practice-unifying' and 'practice-generating' principles are both internalised types of class conditionings and themselves conditioners. It is these principles that comprise the class *habitus* (ibid.: 101).

A number of different types of capital (economic/cultural/social) and social factors (residence/gender/age/marital status) make up the 'specific logic of the field, of what is at stake and the type of capital needed to play for it, which governs those properties through which the relationship between class and practice is established' (ibid.: 112–3). The above factors constitute the objective building blocks of classness with its inherent cultural, social and economic logics.

Middle-class identities may be shaped in the interfaces between the luxury/excess of elites and the economic necessity of the lower classes. This type of negotiation is reflected in the discussion over balanced or proper Islamic consumption. The cultural predicament of the Malay new rich is materially motivated through questioning the 'excesses of the Malay royalty', who are represented by the Malaysian king and the sultans of nine peninsular states (Shamsul 1999a: 105).

To my mind, classing processes in Malaysia cannot exclusively be reduced to stringent sociological reasoning à la Bourdieu. Surprisingly, more intangible effects of class such as religion and ethnicity are excluded from Bourdieu's analyses. In Malaysia, class distinctions between Malays and Chinese in particular often materialise in the grey zones between religion, ethnicity, the state and modes of consumption.

Classing in Malaysia is obviously not reproduced in a strictly de-terministic, symmetrical or functional universe as put forward in some Marxist inspired analyses. In Jomo's classical account of class formation in Malaysia, *A Question of Class. Capital, State, and Uneven Development in Malaysia* (1986), class contention is the 'main motive force of history. [...] The existence of class contention does not always involve collective self-consciousness, nor does it necessarily entail organized activity' (ibid.: 283). To understand class formation in Malaysia, Jomo argues, one must look at the 'relations of production which arose as a consequence of colonialism, from Malaya's integration into the world economy' (ibid.). In this type of conceptualisation, class is something strangely deterministic, distinct, objective, stable and etic that seems to escape direct human influence or practice. Only through radical breaks (revolution) with the forces of class production and reproduction can class contention be re-conceptualised, i.e. mainly as fixed 'scripts' rather than agency or performance conditioning classing.

The paradox is that 'Classes are certainly for Marxism historical *agents*; but they are structural, material formations as well as "intersubjective" entities, and the problem is how to think these two aspects of them together' (Eagleton 1994: 187). In essence, the class analysis suggested here is one that aims at capturing what Geertz (1993) called 'deep play', i.e. connecting specific social actions in the local context to wider structural processes and transformations. Class experience in Malaysia is informed by a myriad of changeable and intangible factors that do not seem to be reducible to sheer economic or sociological reasoning. Goffman's dramaturgical metaphors, most notably performance, precisely capture all this elusiveness, the strategies and the ambiguities involved in Malay middle-class practice.

BECOMING MIDDLE-CLASS MALAYS:
EDUCATION, FAMILY, INCOME AND CONSUMPTION

I now turn to informants' ideas of class and the way in which these inform practices in everyday life. I will not apply a stringent and neat graduation of class groups as Bourdieu does according to socio-occupational categories, but instead explore the way in which informants map the full range of middle-class practices and then plot themselves in.

The performance of class in the first type of narrative starts with *education and family background.* Combining academic education within social science and the humanities and a family background of economic and social capital promises a safe passage to middle-classness. This is the logic in the case of Jeti and Hazan, who both worked in academic positions at University Malaya. While Hazan saw himself as lower middle class, Jeti as the sole informant described herself as 'At least middle class because I can afford many things and have a lot of privileges.' This exceptional feeling of being higher than middle class in social space can be related to the fact that Jeti's father, a university lecturer, is the parent with the longest education among all informants.

The general tendency by far is that the younger generation has advanced in terms of social and economic capital in comparison with their parents. In spite of the significance of education in the self-understanding of the above informants, there is another and deeper narrative that permeates virtually all accounts. This narrative encompasses consumption and distinction as tangible effects or conditioners of classing through education. Consequently, education provides one with an income that allows one to perform in a middle-class way through consumption of a multitude of commodities. Distinctions in terms of education are crucial to Hazan, who remarked that

> People see you according to education. It plays quite an important role now in Malaysia to classify which group you belong to. And then, I guess, it's quite natural as a human being you try to associate yourself with the same group, communicate with others.

Education, consumption and distinctions together with the ideal of Islamic piety is the stuff Malay middle-class identities are made of. Jeti explained that 'I know people with my background who tend to live a more lavish lifestyle than I do.' Accordingly, Jeti felt that she was probably not seen as excessive or materialistic by others. Sardi likewise fitted into this group, associating education with income that could be invested in consumption as the prime class conditioner. The logic here was that a good education will give you a good income that can be invested in goods so that others can tell that you are 'middle class'.

Another idea about class points to *income* as a class determinant. Ahmad is the most apparent informant in this type of account encompassing the young, aggressive and entrepreneurial New Malay accountancy graduate who plots himself into the class map strictly according to income:

> At my age I should earn around RM3,000, that's lower middle class. But I have a plan, it's a ten-year, maybe fifteen-year plan. I want to stop working for people by the age of 45 and build my wealth on property. I started already.

Moreover, Islam has a central place in Ahmad's entrepreneurial vision: 'In Islam, it's the same way. You have to find your wealth. It's like you're not going to die. But you know that you're going to die. Be moderate and create wealth.' Ahmad thus negotiated the division between this world and the next in terms of the moral acceptability of becoming wealthy. Ahmad, however, did not believe that hard work in itself would provide wealth – there was an invisible hand involved in economic success. Therefore, he repeatedly said approved prayers hoping to be blessed with divine wealth. Hopefully, the invisible hand would shortly place him comfortably in the New Malay middle class.

To Ahmad, TTDI was a typical middle-class area in terms of education, income and social background, but eventually also mentality of especially the upper class: 'They don't want to mix, maybe because of attitude.' Ahmad's mother was a housewife not working away from home, his father a retired teacher. The grandparents came to Malaysia from Sumatra, Indonesia, as poor immigrants: 'We want to live a better and more secure life than our parents and grandparents.'

The vast majority of understandings of class, however, emerge as far more material *consumption* narratives in class mapping. Typically, informants would evoke suburbia as the quintessential stage for excessive upper-class consumption against which they practised balanced middle-class consumption. One example of this type of distinction is Mascud's account. He describes himself as 'Middle class. Middle middle.' Moreover, his class affiliation matched his spending, he felt. Against this image Mascud, living in his large bungalow, assessed that 'My neighbour is upper class; he is very rich and owns a publicly listed company.' Thus, the house was the most prominent object into which class belonging through distinction was inscribed.

Correspondingly, Yusof, who had just moved from TTDI with his wife, Izura, to a mansion in an estate further away from Kuala Lumpur, argued that 'We are just middle class, lower middle class.' In Malaysia, more generally, he saw the middle class stratified into 'lower middle class', 'middle middle class', and 'upper middle class', and added that 'We cannot become upper class.' He explained that Malaysia has a dual class structure. On the one hand, royalty and Malaysian titles are institutionalised by the state. On the other hand, there are competing classes determined by one's wealth. Yusof pointed to an even larger mansion than his own across the street inhabited by a Chinese businessman: 'When you're wealthy you are on top of everything, like this fellow over there.' To Yusof, he was situated in this latter category where social mobility is determined by hard work: 'We struggled. Even now we are struggling. Life is a struggle. Depending on your social and material success others will eventually try to classify you.' These social class inscription practices are ultimately tied to consumption, ethnicity and lifestyle. Yusof's father-in-law worked in the government service collecting taxes and revenues, but started his own business building houses and as a goldsmith at a later stage. His mother was a businesswoman, but had received no formal education.

Udzir, for example, plotted his family in as lower middle class because they lived in a relatively modest one-storey terraced house. Another class set of ideas encompasses the intricate links between residence and consumption in constituting class. Murni explained that

> Taman Tun would be slightly in the upper class, but we are more in the middle. Maybe because we live in a link house. The middle is mostly in the link houses. The upper more in the semi-d or maybe the condos. It has more to do with religious attitude. We don't have Mercedes. And most importantly, our lifestyle is very simple; we don't have branded goods, go for expensive hotels or restaurants.

Against this image, upper-class Malaysians are excessive, wearing branded goods to maintain status. The distinction between middle and upper class strata Murni also linked to the choice of car. Irfan added that

> Our way of living is moderate. So, even if we were earning much more I don't think that our lifestyle would change. We want to be just like this.

And anything extra it is our duty to give others as we have been asked to do. Otherwise, we are not just. So, even though we would want to earn much more, then we are still at this level.

This is an account articulated through Islam as a model guide in everyday life.

Siti's self-definition of class emerged almost exclusively in contra-distinction to the excesses of the upper class:

We are mostly middle class. If you're a wage earner, you should be middle class. We cannot be upper class. Because the upper class they earn so much. They live in a bungalow. They go on holiday overseas most of the time. I don't put myself into that group. I think I'm classless. Not up, down or middle.

Regarding class positions in TTDI, she stated that 'I think Taman Tun is more mixed. If you want to see people who are really upper class, Damansara Heights and Ampang are the places to go.' Informants generally associated certain residential areas with particular classes, with their type of consumption contributing to the emergence of quite specifically bounded and demarcated geographies of spending.

Yasir and Azmi/Henny of all informants were most explicit about defining middle-class identity through material distinctions. When asked about his personal class affiliation, and after recovering for a second, Yasir replied:

Wow... I think we belong to the middle class, it's not nice to say this. Everybody in our salary group belongs to the upper class. RM5,000 and above is considered upper class, am I right? But we try not to show it. Nothing wrong there. We still mingle around also; people I don't know, I say hello to. People working in the streets, I say hello to them. Instead of me expecting them to say hello to me. I still practise that in order to downturn where I belong. If not, you feel like everybody needs to respect you instead of you respecting the rest of the people.

To my mind, this is the ultimate performance of a pious and morally intact middle-class identity. Yasir's strategy is to play two parts simultaneously: firstly, that of a well-to-do middle-class individual overly conscious of the family's place in social space; secondly, escaping the traps of materialism, showing-off and indifference, which to him as a pious Muslim go hand in hand with the former part. These contested parts are negotiated through material distinctions. For TTDI, Yasir explained to me that

The upper class in the bungalows is the elite, really untouchable. When they come to the shop they walk like that ... [showing-off] then we know that, oh, this person is from up there. They drive Mercedes. You park your car wrongly, they horn like mad. Then there are people who live in the one-storey terraced houses. They probably earn about RM3,000–4,000.

The excesses of the other that guide informants and their families in classing are to a large extent dependent on visible, even overt, consumption of houses and cars. Perhaps more importantly, as we saw with Yasir, certain materialist identities are seen to emerge from the excesses of the other. This is evident in the case of Azmi and Henny, who in their present situation as relatively disadvantaged financially and professionally, were very explicit about the shopping habits of the upper class and the political elite. Henny:

> They'll tell us to buy Malaysian products. So, all these middle-income people will buy Malaysian products, but they themselves go to buy Italian sets; they go all the way overseas to do their shopping. But when they come back again they will say buy Malaysian products.

According to Henny, the resourcefulness of the upper class produced a fake patriotism through consumption of foreign goods in urban overseas destinations. This group of affluent cosmopolitans in actual fact reject patriotic consumption for materialism and excess. The tendency towards stratification, according to Azmi, is even further pronounced in the national context where the class gap is obvious and growing due to government complicity.

In sum, the strategies involved in classing take consumption in all its forms as the starting point of material, ethnic and religious distinctions in the suburban universe. Inscribing the other with excess in social space is maybe the most pervasive factor of individual and group class constitution. At the same time, one's class identity is constructed through the gaze of others. Interestingly, conventional parameters such as income and education alone are not prime conditioners of understandings and practices of class with informants. What is more, there is a clear tendency to see that both men and women have received a higher level of education, and thus often higher income, compared to their parents' generation. More exactly, informants' ideas reflect a deep-rooted fixation on how social and financial resources as forms of surplus are invested in terms of consumption as material evidence of social standing. The main objection of all informants alike to the improper or excessive consumption of other class groups is that these groups more or less convincingly perform a false and unmerited role.

Naturally, defining the other as excessive has the effect of identifying oneself as a balanced and moderate Malay Muslim consumer in the context of the nationalisation of Islam. Interestingly, Islam does not seem to be expressive of class in these class narratives. Some Malays, however, seem to adopt a more concerned attitude towards consumption as a class conditioner. The question, of course, is to what extent they invest or translate this anxiety into specific everyday conceptualisations and practices of consumption. Several informants explained that overt and unambiguous consumption against such formal parameters as education or occupation is 'what you can see'. Therefore, consumption works as the most lucid indicator of the way in which (licit/illicit) incomes are invested in social status through consumption. Consumption in all its forms has materialised as the most pervasive narrative or script in class narratives in contemporary suburban Malaysia.

NOTES

1   In 2003, there were an estimated 5,300 households in TTDI (*Masyarakat TTDI* No. 4, December 2004).

2   On 18 November 2004, one Malaysian Ringgit (RM) equalled US$0.26.

3   In Malaysia, A-levels equal 'Sijil Tinggi Pelajaran Malaysia' (STPM) or Malaysian Certificate of Higher Education, which is a necessary qualification to enter public universities.

4   See, for example, texts on women and class processes by Maila Stivens (1998a) for Malaysia and Nirmala PuruShotam (1998) for Singapore.

5   An example of this type of theory is the argument put forward by Mary Douglas: 'The basic choice that a rational individual has to make is the choice about what kind of society to live in. According to that choice, the rest follows. Artefacts are selected to demonstrate the choice. Food is eaten, clothes are worn, cinema, books, music, holidays, all the rest are choices that conform with the initial choice for a form of society.' (Douglas 1996: 82)

3

Halalisation in and on Malaysian Bodies

The most significant transformation over the last three decades in Malaysia may have been the mass availability of commodities. All aspects of everyday life for Malaysians are affected by the advent of a vast range of commodities. Unsurprisingly, this mass availability of commodities has produced inequalities and distinctions between those able to buy and those unable to do so. In the domains of housing, transportation and communication, foodstuffs, dress and the way daily time is structured (Lee 2000: xiiii), radical changes are taking place. Hence, a Malaysian 'ontology of consumption' has emerged, which is split between individual consumer desires in the market for identities on the one hand, and heartfelt social anxieties about the moral and social integrity of the 'national' family on the other.

Another point of tension is between, on the one hand, everyday consumer choices and practices, and, on the other, articulations of halalisation within the wider process of creating a national Islam. In this multitude of everyday decisions and debates, there is a marked tension between notions of excess and balance. Understandings of proper Islamic consumption are determined by constant attempts to resolve this tension. As one would expect, the commodity form itself is central to the above problems. I shall argue that this construction of commodities as fetishes compels two sets of contradictory actions and feelings.

Common to both these sets is the search for authenticity and identities in the form of commodities. The first type of search is associated with the quest for material status and social mobility through consumption practices. The second manifests itself as a desire for commodities and/or practices in accordance with the ever widening process of halalisation –

whether certified by the state or not. Each of these two sets of desires tries to inscribe commodities with a wide range of intrinsic dual qualities, e.g. purity–impurity, halal–haram, familiar–alien or balanced–excessive. This fetishisation of the commodity form makes possible a mapping of the moral, religious and social dimensions of everyday practices of consumption, and thus provides, in turn, a guide to consumers in their everyday choices.

In everyday understandings and practices of consumption in Malay middle-class families, however, it is not so much the intrinsic qualities of the commodity form itself that shape identities. It is rather the ritual and performative context in which commodities are consumed that is constitutive of individual and social identity formation. Such performances seek to forge Malay middle-class identities by displaying proper and advanced taste that is religiously legitimate, respectable and sophisticated at one and the same time. Halalisation, as will be dealt with in detail, is, in other words, strongly focused on re-signifying commodities as what I shall call non-commodities *qua* their cultural and religious markings. This process requires a massive investment in targeting ever more commodities that are open to this type of ritual cleansing. Purification, moreover, involves a constant balancing of notions of intrinsic (and powerful) properties of commodities that can be bracketed, negated or amplified by the context of handling, style and display.

The overriding concern in this and the subsequent chapters is an exploration of the way in which the proper in Malay Muslim consumption is understood and practised in suburban middle-class homes. In order to provide the most ethnographically 'thick' descriptions of how halalisation is played out in everyday life, I examine a number of object domains (Miller 2000: 117) such as food, dress, interior decoration, cars, services and cultural consumption. All these object domains have to varying degree been subjected to the elaboration and expansion of halalisation. At the same time, halalisation is a controversial and contested field of meaning in diverse Malay middle-class groups.

These chapters explore how understandings and practices of consumption both inform and are informed by political and religious discourses. The contention is that Malay middle-class identities are moulded through negotiations between two levels of social reality: the official or 'authority-defined' social reality of individuals within dominant power structures on the one hand and the 'everyday-defined' social reality on the other (Shamsul 1997: 208).

With the extension of consumer goods markets and their advertising around the globe, a complex ideology or social ontology of global consumption was required (Mazzarella 2003: 12). In Malaysia, the emergence of such a new ontology of consumption was felt most forcefully in the advertising of images that reflected the desire of individual consumers and simultaneously presented 'a generalized sounding board for the national community, now reconceptualized as an aesthetic community' (ibid.: 13). This type of aesthetic community with its own social ontology of consumption is distinguished by its taste preferences, which are most clearly pronounced in the emerging middle class – being a social person or possessing a certain identity through sets of proper Malay Muslim consumption. As I shall show, the aesthetic community among the Malays emerged through halalisation. This process can be seen to encompass a particular form of Malaysianising foreign brands in a national setting. In effect, this works as 'glocalising' local marketing and an appropriation of the global (Robertson 1992).

In this exploration, it is suggested that the constitution of public distinctions between two Malay middle-class groups is a highly uneven process full of ambiguities and contradictions. What is appearing, then, are two Malay registers of modern lifestyles. Firstly, one group performs proper Islamic consumption as a localised form of purism. Secondly, another group of middle-class Malays are more orientated towards a pragmatic approach to the performance of consumption.

This distinction between the more puristically and pragmatically inclined middle-class Malays materialised from the empirical material in the course of the fieldwork. Naturally, this distinction is the researcher's categorisation or ordering of the chaotic reality of proper Islamic consumption in the Malay middle class. These categories, nevertheless, capture everyday distinctions in the lives of middle-class Malays. Most of all, the applicability of this particular form of distinction in the Malaysian context lies in the recognition, by the researcher and informants alike, that taste and lifestyles are formative of everyday difference. Distinction can refer to difference or recognition of difference between, firstly, objects or people or, secondly, excellence in quality, talent, honour or respect (Bourdieu 1984). I shall show how these two groups reflected on class and Islamic consumption through the desire to construct a wide range of material and mental everyday distinctions. In other words, rather than being deep-rooted or fundamental conflicts, distinctions give shape to the understanding and handling of proper Islamic consumption.

As could be expected, there is internal variation in the two registers, and everyday straddling among these groups is not uncommon – this type of straddling is for the most part conditioned by context and performance, as I shall return to below. Nonetheless, the stability of these groups was recognizable, i.e. informants possessed the necessary capability to recognise distinctions between self and other according to taste distinctions involved in proper Islamic consumption.

Pragmatic Malays seek to reshape and reform Islam in order to make the religion more compatible with an individualised and pluralistic type of Malaysian modernity. In Indonesia, more pragmatically oriented Muslims'

> ... main intention seems to be to reconcile a revised Islam with state, regime, and nationhood, mainly by shaping Islam in the image of an 'inner religion' which is entirely compatible with the initiatives and demands of a modern nation directed by rationalism. (Kolig 2001: 33)

In a similar vein, the style of the more pragmatic Muslims in a Persian village

> ... is to concentrate on the this-worldly pertinence of religious symbols, conceiving of God as the Good Provider, the afterlife as an intangible issue, worldly defects as man's own fault rather than God's, and ritual as a means to secure health and welfare. (Loeffler 1988: 287)

Conversely, the more puristic Muslims embody 'a re-spiritualisation rather than an effective "purification" of Islam' (ibid.: 37).

The following example illustrates a specific point of tension or distinction between a pragmatic and puristic orientation. While halalisation is morally given among the latter group, the former either reluctantly accepts the imposition of halalisation or simply rejects it as a material and thus shallow display of belief – as Islamic materialism or excess. The informant Azmi, who clearly represented the more pragmatically inclined group, explained the distinction between her personal position and 'the other group'. She emphasised that Islamic consumption in all its forms had become expressive of an unbearable moralism among those who through proper Islamic consumption tried to perform the role of perfectly pious Muslims. In other words, to Azmi, this moralistic attitude was merely a public performance intended to display proper and balanced consumption and taste. Indicative of her more pragmatic stance, she concluded that 'Islamic belief alone should be fine.'

These two styles or registers of Islamic consumption may materialise as relatively stable groups through sets of distinctions, but cannot be reduced to strict cultural logics on the basis of 'Islamism' and 'secularism'. These conceptualisations sit uneasily with the complexity of Islam as a discursive tradition in Malaysia and elsewhere. Most of all, perhaps, 'Islamism' versus 'secularism' appear to be analytically convenient, but empirically vague categories, especially in terms of everyday performances taking place both in front and back regions. For example, in the monograph *Sacred Tensions: Modernity and Religious Transformation in Malaysia* (Ackerman and Lee 1997), 'secularists' and 'traditionals' seem to embody smooth and functional characteristics that, in turn, are taken to be constitutive of the ideas and practices of these groups. I suggest that puristic and pragmatic Malays should be regarded as performative registers by means of which each in their way understand and practise proper Islamic consumption.

MALAYSIAN BODIES IN HALALISATION

At a more aggregate level, this section serves the purpose of exploring the way in which Malaysian bodies have been subjected to halalisation on the one hand, and theoretisation on the other. In other words, a number of broader arguments and assumptions pave the way for more detailed examinations of the two object domains in which halalisation has been felt most forcefully, i.e. food and dress, to be explored in the two subsequent sections.

The growing preoccupation with the body and bodily functions is perhaps linked to at least one ideological transformation of the present, namely 'the urge to aestheticize modern life. The body as image – in advertisement photographs, on television, and in the flesh' (Asad 1997: 43). Today, the body may well operate as the prime site for conceptualising, practising and critiquing consumption. Within consumer culture itself, images of the body are dominant, and the consumption of these images constitutes the inner logic of this culture (Featherstone 1991: 178). In the Malaysian context, this new visibility and these phantasmagorical qualities of the body come into being as what I call a new ontology of consumption, tightly linked to the advertising, promotion and marketing of an ever growing range of commodities and services. In all of this, bodies in Malaysia have been subjected to a number of moral, political and religious discourses.

The *habitus* can be understood as habits that vary between individuals, societies, education, property, fashion and prestige. The habitus, then, emerges as 'the techniques and work of collective and individual practical reason' (Mauss 1973: 73). Practices are highly dependent on education and 'imitative action' so that there is no 'natural way' for adults (ibid.: 74). These techniques of the body make it both a technical object and a technical means (ibid.: 75). Mauss concludes by commenting that 'I think that there are necessarily biological means of entering into "communication with God"' (ibid.: 87). Halalisation and the new ontology of consumption in the Malay middle class encompass a type of habitus that is informed by the daily habits of Malay consumers. This type of habitus is inseparable from a multitude of religious and political discourses through which all seek to discipline Malaysian bodies. Techniques of the body are part of performances that ideally balance the display of class while covering/ dressing the body properly.

Human bodily existence can be seen as both the basis and the 'model' of the constitution of the subject or the self. The body is essential in consumption as it is the site for often involuntary and revealing display. Bourdieu (1977: 72–82) developed the concept of habitus further, referring to the existence of social reality in individuals, and the social and material world outside. Habitus encompasses principles of practice in interaction between social structures, systems and actors. For Bourdieu, the most significant process of embodiment is the interaction that takes place between the bodies, on the one hand, and the space structured around myth and ritual on the other (ibid.: 89).

The rise of institutionalised and standardised Islamic consumption in Malaysia has produced bodies that are less given and more open to multiple choices and interpretations. An obvious example is that of dress in connection with the fusing of Islamic requirements and fashion in contemporary Malaysia. Arguably, the *dakwah* movements have been subject to a Western feminist stereotypisation of veiled women, portraying these as repressed and anti-modern (Nagata 1995: 103). What is often left out is that many of these women are prominent in the middle class, highly educated and cosmopolitan. These Malay middle-class women actively pursue an Islamic worldview and lifestyle that makes *dakwah* fashions compatible with popular and foreign-influenced trends (ibid.: 112). Islamic meaning is inscribed into the attire in a way that retains modesty and control while simultaneously signalling experimentation. Hence, *dakwah* dress symbolised de-peasantisation, the exploration of modern Malay class mobility, and gender identity (Ong 1995: 181).

Ritualisation produces distinctive forms or types of bodily actions in different contexts. Therefore, different situations and events address and activate different perceptions of bodies. The economy of managing these, often conflicting, conceptualisations and practices of the body, its responsibilities and performances, may call for routine control of the body. Both Islamic revivalists and state nationalism, on the background of the emergence of novel forms of consumption and consumer practices, have created images of the body as a key element in their competing visions of the Malaysian nation (ibid.: 183).

These conflicts reflect different positions within Islam in Malaysia as a discursive tradition. State nationalism and Islamic revivalism, each following relatively distinct moral logics, 'have incited and intensified concerns and ambivalence about female sex, space, and actions, and more generally, how competing knowledge-power schemes deployed to patrol the borders between races and classes have affected women in different classes in different ways' (ibid.: 159). The crisis of national and moral uncertainty is most visible in the middle class as an intermediate class, subject to resurgent Islam and the idealisations of pious embodiment.

I propose to see these ideological manifestations and articulations of the body as critically absorbed, handled and negotiated within families as a primary influence on the way in which different ideas and practices of bodies come into being. In fact, the tension of the commodity discussed above has a parallel in the body. Like the commodity, there is a tension between its intrinsic properties or dispositions, due to 'blood' or gender. Most of these dispositions would be assumed to be 'evil' or 'base', especially in the case of women. Consequently, practice emerges through the way in which these things can be disciplined, amplified or mitigated through learned behaviour, adornment or comportment.

In an enlightening discussion of the 'political nature of symbols and practices surrounding the body politic and the human body' (Ong and Peletz 1995: 6), the body politic involves entangled 'cross-referencing inscriptions of power' or ways in which society and its diverse articulations of values, expectations or demands are symbolically mapped onto the body. Intrinsic to these articulations of embodiment, generally and more specifically in the Malaysian context, is the ability of regimes to perform relatively simple inscriptions of ideology and power onto the subject. In much the same vein, Khuri (2001) outlines a fairly fixed body ideology of Islam that does not seem to be open to transformation. In the Malaysian context, the conditions of embodiment have changed dramatically over the past thirty years due to the emergence of urban consumer ontologies in the wider nationalisation of Islam.

More and more, middle-class women's dress in public is subjected to strict Islamic requirements as well as fashion and experimentation. An example of such an authorised version of Islamic understanding involves legislation to enforce religious conformity passed by some state religious councils in Malaysia. For instance, in 1987 the states of Selangor and Pahang introduced 'legislation for prosecuting Muslim women caught wearing revealing clothes in public' (Ackerman and Lee 1997: 136). At the same time, there has been a

> ... greatly stepped-up activity on the part of the increasingly high-profile Islamic Center (Pusat Islam), which is based in Kuala Lumpur and has as one of its key mandates the reduction of vice among Muslims and the upgrading of Muslim morality generally. (Peletz 2002: 266)

I argue that regimes may be modes of self-discipline that are not un-contested or stable, but moulded by individual and social group understandings and practices concentrated in performances. Examining the body politic from an anthropological optic highlights the interlocking of official and state articulations and that of the private sphere to capture 'two discourses that are in practice a single rhetoric of community, family, even body, and both of which are therefore intensely entailed in each other' (Herzfeld 1997: 171).

In a discussion of the body and reproductive technology in Malaysia, the central argument is that to Malays as social actors the body is made up of a biological, social-cultural and moral body, each with a number of sub-components (Shamsul 1998c: 11–14). These conceptualisations of the body evolved through interaction between local conditions and historical as well as global influences (ibid.: 11). The author sets out to explain how the concurrent existence of distinctive bodies bears reference to quite different cultural and historical understandings. He argues that the notion of the Western consuming body appeared and developed 'in the context of crass materialism' characteristic of Western imperialist modernity and concludes that 'the expressions of the consumerist-social body are often contemporary, capitalistic and, surprisingly, existentialist in nature, with few "moral-theological" concerns' (ibid.: 13). Conversely, the moral body is strictly a 'moral-theological' or religious one, which is responsible for certain kinds of private and public behaviour such as dressing patterns etc.

(ibid.). After listing these different notions of the body, the question of the body in connection with material status and the Islamically inspired dress worn by the majority of Malay women, the long loose robe in Arab style (*baju kurung*) and headscarf (*mini telekung*) is adressed.

Apparently, there is no actual tension between these two domains as they relatively unproblematically pertain to the different notions of the body. The dress and practices of Malay women refer to divergent 'meanings and relations to different parts of the body concept' in the self-understanding of women (ibid.: 14). Analytically, one may be able to separate these bodily spheres in detail, but in the everyday lives of social actors, as will be evident in regard to Malays in TTDI, these divisions are not that smooth and functional.

This type of analytical distinction may instead blind us to the social ambivalences and contradictions existing between the various notions of bodies. The body is always evoked in performances that endeavour to strategically contain the above ambivalences. In this type of conceptualisation, bodies are shaped by consumption and religion as seemingly independent spheres. Against this compartmentalisation, I suggest that religious and consuming bodies in the Malay middle class are inseparable both in terms of analysis and to the social actors themselves.

Clothing and bodies occupy a central place. This discussion of the body is predominantly focused on women's bodies, as it is women who most forcefully have been subjected to intensified Islamic requirements in the wake of the nationalisation of Islam and halalisation. It is, nevertheless, mostly men who have articulated these Islamic requirements. Once again, the realm of the family in the home is the site where these ideas and practices are negotiated. In spite of male dominance, my female informants possessed a strategic knowledge of dressing as a particular form of Islamic consumption, situated between public display of class and covering the body. Moreover, this strategising has everything to do with performing in the spaces of the front and back regions, respectively. However, halalisation in its most basic form is most forcefully present in the case of food – in bodies – and it is to that aspect I will turn first.

EATING HALAL

This object domain has traditionally been subject to the inscription of Islamic understandings of halal and haram, and from this starting-point these ideas have deepened and widened in Malaysia to be inscribed into a large number of other object domains. Historically, the halal/haram distinctions in Malaysia gained momentum in the wake of *dakwah*, but have been diversified and individualised as understanding and practice in everyday life.

Jeti declared that Islam and consumption could not be differentiated or thought of as separate entities or practices. Islam performs a dual function in consumption. Firstly, it works as a symbolic guide demarcating the boundary between moderation and excess. To Jeti, as to many other informants, Islam provides this limit: 'We're thought not to be too excessive and only buy what one needs. It's best to be in the middle. Islam guides how excessive my buying could be.' Secondly, there is the whole complex of Islamic commodities that in the Malaysian context was initiated by groups such as Arqam and their mass-production of halal commodities. These new forms of Islamic capitalist enterprises are often co-ops, and an informant like Jeti finds that these alternative sources in halalisation are more authentic expressions of not only halalisation embodied in products and services, but also action and engagement.

Capitalism, however, is adjusting to the recent requirements of a growing number of Muslims in Malaysia and the Islamic market is expanding rapidly. Jeti explained that previously it was very difficult to go to a restaurant and ask if products were halal or not because there were no 'signs' or 'logos'. Now, even many Chinese shops have started putting up signs and sell JAKIM certified products, and they are thus recognised as 'halalised'. In other words, these Chinese shops are now subjected to state controlled halalisation. In the end, it is the privilege of the state to recognise and standardise these businesses according to halal requirements, which obviously is an immensely complex endeavour inviting a wide range of more or less legitimate interests to influence this type of decision making. Another issue is that for the most dedicated among the purists, halal requirements are by no means fixed or stable, but instead elastic and expansive. For these Malays, halal products must also be produced by Muslims in order to be Islamically acceptable in the wave of halalisation.

Halalisation can contribute to the fusing of myths of the historical Islamic nation with more modern imagining. These imaginings can be enacted through rituals that are individualised to invoke different notions of the nation. More specifically, the ongoing nationalisation of Islam is discursively driven in that it encompasses constant competition for the most appropriate Islamic practices, pushing and contesting boundaries between the sacred and the profane. Simultaneously, Malay middle-class groups resisting the pressure for correct conduct and piety are subjected to forms of moral pressure.

In the group of Malays performing purism, halalisation is morally given, while pragmatic Malays either reluctantly accept the imposition of halalisation or simply reject it as a material and thus shallow display of belief – as Islamic materialism or excess. An expression of this type of resistance is Azmi's phrase that 'Islamic belief alone should be fine.' This observation is supported by Sloane's work on how Malay entrepreneurs negotiate between their newly acquired wealth and Islam. She writes that the pursuit of wealth in Islamically approved ways is central to modern Islamic identity formation. These Malays rejected the very visible and Islamic manifestations of the *dakwah* Malays:

> ... my informants carefully distinguished their demonstration of faith with that of the highly visible, highly conformist fundamentalist Malays. These ideas about the visibility of faith, and moreover, how to demonstrate faith, became the modest terms of their contestation. True faith, people told me, could not be seen by anyone but Allah. (Sloane 1999: 71)

The practice of veiling was described by these informants as 'merely a costume' that did not necessarily reflect the true faith of a person. Likewise, praying in the mosque was seen as a visible ritual act, which, nevertheless, did not indicate that men who did not pray in the mosque neglected their prayers (ibid.). The faith of the modern Malay individual was personalised in ways that only Allah could comprehend. Sloane's account, however, may be too fixed on the way in which these public representations are literally producing and produced by Islamic discourses. Conversely, attention should be paid to pragmatic Malays' perception of the material piety of the other register as merely a public performance in the front region, often to be matched by material and quite un-Islamic excesses in intimacy. Moreover, the element of class as a powerful conditioner in Malay middle-class identities is left unexamined in Sloane's analysis. Finally, the question of food in halalisation is far more subtle, confused and private compared to that of public demonstrations of faith and fashion. Paradoxically, food, compared to dress, is far more subjected to halalisation in the form of a wide range of legislative measures.

In the eyes of Azmi and Henny, Islamic business was tolerable as long as it was not 'extremist'. Extremism in this context can signify two points of scepticism: firstly, radical groups such as Arqam promoting overly alternative ideas through the marketing of Islamic products; secondly, the apotheosis of the state involved in the certification, legitimisation, and, ultimately, inscription of commodities with sacred or profane qualities. In most cases, pragmatic informants would argue according to the logic that 'Buying things is totally personal, but Islam forbids overspending.' This flexible standard image is entirely open to interpretation and practice. Consequently, purist informants critiqued it for being elusive and pragmatic. Another point of criticism materialises in the case of Siti, who felt that the whole idea about Islam in consumption, for example Islamic banking, was insufficiently argued and altogether unconvincing. Islam as an everyday guide to consumption was to her a question of halal food and clothes that would cover the body in an acceptable yet fashionable manner.

Conversely, to Yasir, for example, halalisation is not a recent trend but a compulsory and authoritative moral invocation of the roots of Islam: 'It's something that is required. And something Muslims must support, actually.' This is a mythical return to the era of the Prophet and the ideal community. Irfan and Murni provide perhaps the most accurate account of the force of consumption in Islam. They stress that it is mandatory for Muslims to be aware of halal and haram and that this knowledge cannot be externally imposed, as was the case with the Taliban in Afghanistan – it must start from within. Therefore, it is the moral obligation of individuals to buy into Islamic consumption and return to the master plan of the Prophet that will provide modern consumers with Islamic enlightenment.

In conjunction with halalisation, which can be seen as modes of purification taking various forms, it is noteworthy that urban Malays are often worried and afraid of being poisoned or sorcerised: 'These fears and anxieties attest to heightened concerns with bodily vigilance, the integrity of the Malay social body, and the stability of the Malaysian body politic' (Peletz 2002: 237). These fears can easily target food and drink that formally are halal certified, but suspected of being haram and thus impure. Food is probably the most essential object domain of all, where a multitude of social, religious, and material transformations intersect.

Taste in food,[1] the context of buying it, and the transformation of the kitchen (*dapur*) where it is being prepared are now the centre of attention. Statistically and through participant observation, it was evident that house culture is being transformed since the kitchen in the typical Malay middle-class house has been radically modernised and industrialised with the import of a multitude of kitchen appliances. In the survey I learned that besides a refrigerator and oven, the vast majority of families regardless of class grouping, ethnicity and religion owned a toaster, blender/mixer, microwave oven, baking machine, rice cooker (over 98 per cent!), juice maker, electric kettle, and a number of other appliances.

These transformations of the inner domain mirror wider societal changes, most notably in the form of increased affluence, material status, and the fact that a large number of Malay middle-class women worked outside the home while still being in charge of buying groceries and preparing food.

The feast as culturally contested between *dakwah* and ordinary Malays highlights a whole range of Islamic distinctions that add another layer of signification to Bourdieu's categories. For ordinary Malays, the attacks by resurgent Malays are commonly seen as aimed at the 'sanctified elements of their basic values and cultural identities' (ibid.: 227). Especially, the realm of feasting (*kenduri*) is subject to these points of criticism of sinful wastefulness and the incorporation of pagan animistic and Hindu–Buddhist beliefs. Feasting can be seen as a concentration of excessive presentation, handling and context. These controversies are all the more apparent when it is taken into account that the hosting of feasts in connection with all kinds of celebrations is one of many routes to status and prestige.

Food consumption and its religious, social and cultural context may be the closest one can come to a core symbol in the everyday lives of Malay families. I was invited to celebrations in the homes of informants on numerous occasions. A typical dish served in these homes was beef cooked in rich coconut gravy (*rendang daging*). In addition to Peletz' insightful comments above, there are other dimensions to food consumption, namely the context in which it is bought.

My survey shows that 28 per cent of Malay respondents as their first priority bought groceries in a supermarket, often the nearby Jaya Jusco (Figure 11) in One Utama, 22 per cent in the wet market, 18 per cent in a mini-market, most likely Pasar Raya (Figure 12), 16 per cent in a hypermarket (Figures 13 and 14, overleaf), 14 per cent in a local grocery store, and 2 per cent elsewhere. The majority of respondents, 51 per cent, listed that they commonly bought their groceries in two different shops, 27 per cent in one shop, and 18 per cent in three shops, whereas only a minority went to more than three shops. Finally, the vast number of choices with respect to buying groceries indicates that strategies involved in food consumption have increased in the wake of the pluralisation of the food market.

Figure 11: Jaya Jusco supermarket in One Utama.

Figure 12: Pasar Raya, a mini-market. Outside, Islamic books, pamphlets and cassettes/CDs are on sale. This is also where the PAS newspaper Harakah is sold.

Figure 13: Entrance to the Carrefour hypermarket in Mid Valley Megamall, KL.

Figure 14: Inside Carrefour.

When discussing the significance of halal certification in the lives of modern Malay families, an official in the Ministry of Domestic Trade and Consumer Affairs pointed out that the Malays, and Malay families in particular, are becoming extremely particular about halal requirements, and state certification of these commodities: 'Beef at the supermarket, if it doesn't have that logo, halal–haram logo, it will be a very big issue. We Muslims believe that what we eat contributes to what we are.' (Interview 1 March 2002) (Figure 15).

Figure 15: The halal logo issued by Jabatan Kemajuan Islam Malaysia (JAKIM, Islamic Development Department of Malaysia).

The halal/haram dichotomy is not only about maintaining the separateness of these two binaries, but simultaneously also about protecting the status of the sacred against the impurity of the profane. An example of this could be separation of halal and haram food products in supermarkets such as *Jaya Jusco*. The non-halal products are for the most part stored in a small, secluded room away from the main shopping area. Hence, sacred or profane effects are to a large extent generated in objects by inscription, classification and context. Of course, the way in which these effects are presented is of crucial importance.

In *Masyarakat TTDI* No. 2, September 1996, the Message from the Chairman on the front page read:

Much has been said about our buoyant economy, affluent life-style, high-rise apartments, new housing estates, expressways and now the multi-media super corridor. There should be no doubt in the mind of any Malaysian that we will achieve Vision 2020 under the able leadership of our Prime Minister and his Cabinet colleagues. However, amidst all the signs of prosperity and good living, it is timely that we consider tackling the problem of proliferation of hawker stalls which we encounter along most of the city streets today. Many of these decrepit 'premises' are operated by aliens and are breeding ground for flies and rodents. The social costs behind their relatively cheap fare are apparent in the attendant litter, clogged drains, stuck traffic and their insidious hazards to health and public safety. [...] As our country prepares for the Commonwealth Games in 1998, we would urge the Kuala Lumpur City Hall to spruce up the streets by relocating these hawkers in properly constructed hawker centres [...]. This will no doubt enhance our country's image as an emerging Newly Industrialised Country.

The central argument is that hawker stalls are anachronisms blocking the passage to the order of urban and suburban modernity. Removing the overt impurity of these food stalls will pave the way for the Commonwealth Games as a platform for the global display of national progress and development.

Furthermore, the mass availability of imported food can increase anxieties about contamination while this food may also be a sign of re-fined and exotic taste. This is symptomatic of and corresponds to the commercialisation of the kitchen within each Malay middle-class home as described above. In short, food consumption is a crucial component in the market for identities.

Three different types of approaches to the field of proper Malay food consumption emerged. Firstly, the approach seen in the cases of Azmi and Henny. Azmi and Henny would go to either the Pasar Raya or the wet market in TTDI, or one of the hypermarkets, but never to Jaya Jusco in One Utama, where Azmi found that 'The prices are quite stiff so we prefer the hypermarket.' Having guests for a meal, Azmi would prefer that the family served food that was oriented towards simplicity and was appetizing and economical, whereas 'original and exotic' was openly rejected. In Azmi's view, there was an element of familiarity present in going to local shops, but it was not a determining factor in the everyday life of the family. Most important were price consciousness and thrift as determinants for food consumption. In relation to the tension between feast and meal, Azmi and Henny often attacked the excess feasting and celebrations of wealthier groups as excessive displays whose sole function was the performance of luxury.

Necessity is the driving logic in this type of reasoning, signified by price consciousness and thrift. An effect of necessity in the everyday choices of the family produced a radical critique of the luxury and excess of the affluent.

This criticism was expressed in much more political terms, however, than in the purist group. Consequently, there was no stress on halalisation in itself, but rather narratives that would call for a more equal distribution of resources against state nationalism as materialism benefiting the rich.

The second approach is extreme variation as personified by Izura and Yusof. Izura would go to every kind of shop for various reasons. The grocery store 'to buy certain things, easy parking and long opening hours.' The mini-market 'for conveniences, parking, because they also sell wet foods, vegetables and fish. When I have run out of fresh food and I just need a little bit, I go there.' The supermarket 'for certain products that are not available in the mini-market, especially imported products like cheese.' Hypermarket 'when I want to buy something in bulk that is cheaper. I don't go there every day.' Wet market

> … when I need fresh foods and normally I go there once a week. It's quite fair. Not to say the price in the wet market is cheaper than the mini-market. We never know because we can't see the weight. We just believe what they say. The mini-market is cleaner.

The buying of food appears to be a highly ritualised practice that involves careful planning and organisation. Its ritualistic features emerge as reiterated and temporally structuring practices that require certain skills and knowledge for optimal performance. Izura was extremely conscious of the particular audience, or guests. She declared that she would serve almost anything depending on the particular audience of her performances. If there were 'special' guests such as foreigners she would serve something 'ethnic' or

> If I know that this particular person loves Western food, then I present Western food. If I have my *kampung* friends here, I cannot serve spaghetti. They won't eat it. So, I have to serve them rice, curry and a proper meal. And if I have a minister coming to have a dinner in my house, which I do sometimes, then I'll have a very good presentation, it could be mixed fruit. Whereas appetizing and economical – that is a daily affair. Original, of course, I do that because I was a home science teacher once.

This clear example of performance signifies how food works to constitute class as a performative category through proper knowledge of legitimate taste.

Izura: 'Traditional Malay food of course we serve friends or foreigners or … not really foreigners, but Chinese or Indian friends.' In the accounts of the remaining informants, sharing food and socialising with the other ethnic groups was, at best, limited to yearly open house arrangements. Secondly, Izura prefers to serve Chinese and Indians authentically rich national food as if to compensate for their lack of nationness and re-embodiment of the national. The category 'delicate and exquisite', in Bourdieu typical of 'upper class', Izura associated with French cuisine: 'I don't really serve French food because it is so little food, they might think I'm stingy.'

In this instance, the performance aspect depends on the proper audience and its ability to recognise legitimate taste. Izura was not quite convinced that these skills were always present in her guests. Altogether, she was extremely conscious and accommodating in terms of food, and also in her own family:

> Today, I am cooking a black pepper steak for my daughter because she doesn't like to eat rice. She prefers Western food, so I have to accommodate her taste whereas my eldest son loves rice and grilled food, an American barbecue kind of thing.

Sharing of food in the family, which may be seen as one of the basic rituals of family life, is transforming into a performance of accommodating the diverse taste preferences of the younger and far more globally oriented generation. On other occasions Izura complained that materialism was most clearly embodied in the spoiled yuppie culture imported from the West, where for the most part her own children had received their education. Izura and Yusof were the most consistent buyers of organic food. Organic food in Malaysia can be seen as a novel form of purity in food available to the most affluent groups. This attests to a very expressive form of food culture in which elaborate ideas and knowledge of superior taste are prominent. They bought their organic products in a supermarket or a small store specialising in organic products that had opened in TTDI. On the occasions I visited the home of Izura and Yusof, a soft drink or tea together with biscuits were served. In the eyes of both Azmi/Henny and Izura/Yusof the question of halal preferences was presupposed but not carefully elaborated to the extent that will become evident below.

Yasir most strongly embodied the power of halalisation involved in consumer preferences in everyday life. He minutely divided Malays into segments according to their adherence to extremely elaborate ideas about what was considered Islamically acceptable and what was not. These distinctions produced and maintained purity versus impurity, and, in

Figure 16: Azlinah.

the end, legitimate Islamic taste. There was an expression of halalisation as the support of Malays vis-à-vis the Chinese through consumption. Consequently, he maintained that his favourite shop was the small Malay-owned Azlinah (Figure 16) right next to the condominium where he lives. Going to this local shop was also in accordance with his principle of buying a minimum of ten per cent of the family's goods in *bumiputera* shops. He also shopped at Pasar Raya, owned by Malays, because they had a good range of things at a fair price, and to support Muslim businesses. Nevertheless, the family would regularly go to Jaya Jusco in the One Utama mall to buy fresh food that they could not buy in the small shop even though this store presumably was owned by Chinese. Yasir was equally attracted to serving food that was 'simple and well presented', 'delicate and exquisite', 'appetising and economical', 'original and exotic' and 'traditional Malaysian cuisine'.

Purist Malays work hard to stretch food halalisation to involve proper preferences, taste, handling, presentation and context. Thus, the whole complex of food has been subjected to processes of ritualisation in a world of consumer choices. However,

> ... food is not likely to be polluting at all unless the external boundaries of the social system are under pressure. [...] Before being admitted to the

body some clear symbolic break is needed to express food's separation from necessary but impure contacts. The cooking process, entrusted to pure hands, provides this ritual break. (Douglas 2004: 157)

The uncertainty involved in food consumption seems to incite this new form of stringency within the logics of halalisation. The halalness of a product is not directly verifiable through smell or appearance so, as in the case of organic products, it is mainly a question of trust in its certification. Ideally, this certification will remove or mend malevolence in the commodity. Instead of delivering what I would call a stable ontology of Malay consumption, halalisation appears to cause confusion and social fragmentation.

In terms of the social context of eating, the preferences of most informants were preconditioned by who the guests were. Other informants reflecting comparable ideas would be Binsar, Jeti and Irfan/Murni. The purist register, interestingly, does not consistently reject establishments that are associated with materialism or Chinese capitalist dominance. Most of all, everyday choices based on convenience and thrift seem to be determining for their decisions. Another point is that comparatively there was no discursive difference between the two groups concerning the modernisation of the kitchen in the form of the import of kitchen appliances into the house. From survey material and participant observation I learned that the only visible difference was one of quality and design in these appliances and that point could for the most part be explained on the basis of class fraction above anything else. There is, however, a tendency to see that the local, patriotic, moderate, ethnic and Islamic element is discursively more present with the purist Malays compared to the other register. Most significantly, these concerns for the purist register do not work through the practice of abstention, but rather as careful organisation, weighing and juxtaposition of the clearly acceptable against that which is more problematic.

In sum, informants reflected a general adherence to halal principles in terms of food. All informants conveyed that this was the single most significant principle. Comparatively, the aspect of moderation and excess involved in the object domain of food seemed to be far more informed by ideas and practices of class than by Islamic preferences. Hence, performing moderation becomes more and more difficult, and even insignificant, as one moves up the social ladder. Yasir, for one, had no problem with idealising food normally associated with the taste of excess and exoticism as long as it was halalised. Performance appears to be of particular relevance here as it highlights what each single informant wants to signal through food in the light of classing on the one hand and halalisation on the other. In this struggle, food as a crucial class conditioner is unmatchable. In fractions of the middle class, there is a high level of reflexivity involved in presenting and representing taste to a specific target group. That is, informants are not only aware of what type of food they personally would serve, but also of what other individuals or groups, audiences, would expect from them.

Most urban Malays consider alcohol and its consumption haram. Nevertheless, the consumption of alcohol was embedded in a number of strategies. Only Hazan admitted to consuming alcohol even though he was aware that a Malay drinking alcohol was 'always considered sinful. You really have to know the group, the crowd itself. I know Malay Muslims who are drinking alcohol here, but they are always careful whom they address.' On one occasion, I was with Hazan and a few of his colleagues in Bangsar, one of Kuala Lumpur's entertainment districts plastered with bars, discos and restaurants. There he drank beer in public while his colleagues from University Malaya did not. Hazan's admission of drinking was in accordance with his more general critique of Islam as the suppressive moral system he knew so well from his childhood in Terengganu and the moralistic *dakwah* student groups at University Malaya. The question of where alcohol is consumed, in public or privately, is of central significance to the pragmatic group, who would emphasise that alcohol consumption is a personal choice and clearly forbidden in public. There is a stark contrast between the discursive haramness of alcohol consumption following the whole *dakwah* intensification about the proper conduct and piety of the body, and the question of personal freedom in the private and covert domain of the home.

Against this image of drinking, Malays performing purism considered alcohol consumption completely forbidden. Evoking the powerful literalness of scriptural argumentation, Irfan explained that the prohibition against alcohol in this lifespan of maybe seventy years was bearable as 'In the next life, God will give you a river of wine. The prohibition is actually just a test because the knowledge of the religious is not there.' Murni further explained that the Prophet clearly forbids alcohol on the ground that 'We humans do not know how to control ourselves. But I promise you everything in the next life if you can only control it now. A lot of people don't know that.'

DISPLAYING CLASS AND COVERING THE BODY

The middle classes have 'a degree of anxiety about external appearances, both sartorial and cosmetic, at least outside and at work' (Bourdieu 1984: 201). The project for the Malay middle class, and especially for women, is displaying the classing and fashioning of the body in material terms while performing piety. Thus, the *tudung* has taken on meaning as an essential commodity in everyday life. In women's magazines in Malaysia, the proper wearing and handling of the *tudung* was a frequent issue. Younger girls in particular are subjected to a plethora of advice seemingly intended to instil standards for correct appropriation against experimental personalisation.

Hence, Islamic meaning is inscribed into the attire in a way that retains modesty and control while simultaneously signalling experimentation – halalisation on the body. The company Sri Munawwarah located in TTDI has specialised in clothing aimed at a Muslim audience, initially produced especially for haj and *umrah* (a pilgrimage to Mecca that can be undertaken at any time of the year). Among my informants, this clothing was considered Islamically fashionable as an expression of legitimate taste by those who could afford it and excessive and unattainable by those who could not. The company is run by a Malay family, where the mother is a designer and head of production and the daughter is in charge of marketing and PR. When I met the PR representative in the shop, she argued that the marked interest in this type of clothing is taking place because 'It appeals to human nature. I think lots of people are trying to get in touch with their inner self rather than being materialistic.' Similarly, dress is 'a means of symbolic display, a way of giving external form to narratives of self-identity' (Giddens 1991: 62). The question then is how dress materialises in the narratives of taste and dress among my informants, how dress as a specific form of commodity is personalised and appropriated as a class conditioner in Islam.

In an interview with a representative from the feminist Islamic organisation Sisters in Islam (18 January 2002), the discussion was mainly focused on debates over the wearing of the *tudung*, which she personally had abandoned. She argued that the culture around the mandatory status of wearing the *tudung* in many cases started in conservative universities such as University Malaya: 'I don't feel comfortable going to that university because if you're not wearing *tudung* they will look at you.' Moderate students told her that they often felt pressurised and controlled by the *dakwah* students there. Her own family were unaware of her decision to abandon the *tudung*, which she had formerly worn because of family and peer pressure, she explained. When she started working, the *tudung* was taken off because 'I feel that it's not me. I don't want to be pretentious. Normally, I will just put on a simple headscarf if I go to see my family, but they are very particular.' She described how she knew other women who did not wear the *tudung* before they got married, but 'Once they get married, the husband will pressure the woman to wear *tudung*.'[2]

In general, Bourdieu's data show that, in terms of clothes, 'suit my personality' as well as 'chic and stylish' are the preferences in the New Petite Bourgeoisie and the middle-class groups (Bourdieu 1984: 534–5). In comparison, moving from working class to upper class, the category 'classically cut and good value for money' becomes less prominent.[3] I am aware that dress probably more than anything else embodies divergences according to gender, generation, class and one's own interpretation of Islam. A crucial characteristic of dress is that it both physically covers the body while revealing personality regarding fashion, class and Islam. The two groups of Malays that emerge from their religious and material divergences throughout this monograph are actually self-constituted with regard to dress. By that I mean that there is a high level of reflexivity involved in clothing preferences as appropriate communication. To me, the way informants dressed was a first indication of their place in social and religious space.

The public performance of the purist group was correct and respectable. Binsar, for example, preferred clothing that was 'comfortable' and also 'classically cut and good value for money'. This taste preference reflected the thriftiness of lower middle-class taste and moderation so central to understandings of the proper Islamic way. Normally, Binsar would buy most of his clothes in a chain store and often at Sri Munawwarah. He modestly explained that 'The quality is good, but I just buy one or two things because it's expensive. I wear it for teaching.' Teaching as a particular part performed with specific properties seemed to legitimise what could be seen as excessive in shopping at Sri Munawwarah within his class grouping. Typically, Binsar would be dressed in e.g. grey trousers with knife-edge creases, a light blue silk shirt and a black skull cap, and he grew a beard. However, I once met him in One Utama where he was dressed quite differently, for a quite different part, it seemed; he was wearing none of the clothes mentioned above, but rather plain casual dress for strolling in the mall. Binsar's wife covered the body in a plain grey robe when working in their Islamic school.

To Yasir, preferences were multidirectional. He strongly opposed the extremes of 'sober and correct' and 'daring and out of ordinary', and instead preferred 'comfortable' and 'chic and stylish', which are quintessential markers of middle-classness in Bourdieu. Normally, he bought his clothes at Sri Munawwarah or from a chain store. Yasir had worked in the fashion industry, advancing from sales executive to supervisor to manager for Cerrutti 1881, which he described as an

> International brand. High fashion. One suit costs RM3–4,000. I do the buying in Paris or London. I was also involved with another brand, *Replay*, Italian brand, predominantly jeans theme. The regional office in Hong Kong. I travelled to Hong Kong frequently and was in charge of boutique outlets in Singapore.

The times I met with Yasir he was dressed in a light short-sleeved shirt, black trousers, and a white *kopiah*. I could not help wonder about the nature of the rites of passage in Yasir's life that might signify these bodily discontinuities.

Irfan straight away would select the 'comfortable' category whereas Murni was far more flexible and felt that all categories appealed to her. Irfan would be wearing a white *kopiah* and a white traditional outfit for men consisting of shirt and trousers (*baju Melayu*), and grow a beard, and Murni a light green silk long-sleeved loose fitting long blouse (*baju kurung*) and a colourful *tudung*. Jokingly, she remarked to me when I asked permission to take their picture: 'So this will be your typical Muslim couple posing!' Murni referred to proper dress and covering the body as a core point in Islam that Malays choosing pragmatism neglected or misunderstood. In the eyes of Murni, this type of negligence was socially constitutive of the pragmatic group. Dress style precisely signified the hybrid of fashionable experimentation within Malay middle-class Islam. The imprint of Islamically correct attire strongly shapes the following accounts of informants.

Maslina preferred clothes that were comfortable, but strongly rejected the category 'daring and out of the ordinary':

> That one is out of my mind. Because we as Muslims cannot dress in something that is so daring and makes other people stare at us. So, we have to avoid that. Sometimes, anyway. Muslims in Malaysia are different from other Muslims, they tend to follow the Western style. They want something new and turn fashion into Muslim fashion. Even though they're wearing *tudung*, they also wear what those who are not wearing *tudung* wear.

This statement is expressive of how the body in Malaysia is constantly ambiguously signified as an object of discursive conflict between Islam and fashion for the puristically orientated, and Islam as fashion for the pragmatic Malays. Maslina's background in a reputable Islamic school in Penang is significant. Most importantly, perhaps, her current status as a student may financially and morally restrict this kind of experimentation. Both Jomono and Maslina primarily bought their clothes in chain stores in one of Kuala Lumpur's shopping malls. After graduation, Maslina would favour high quality branded clothes to go with her then acquired middle-class status. The times I met Jomono and Maslina, they were both dressed in moderate clothing and Maslina was wearing her *tudung*. Economic necessity coupled with belonging to the age group most strongly subjected to Islamic claims of piety, morality and virtue was a strong influence in Maslina's life. Interestingly, middle classing acquired after graduation in the case of Maslina signified a passage from moral and economic necessity to affluent respectability and experimentation. In effect, this was a passage from being 'lower class' as a student to becoming 'middle class' the year after graduation.

To Azmi and Henny, economic necessity had transformed their preferences in clothes. Azmi explained that over the years he had lost interest in brands such as Calvin Klein: 'As you grow older there's actually no living to that.' Regardless of this narrative, the family still bought most of their clothes in a factory outlet for affordable designer brands, which would suit Azmi's ideal of something 'comfortable'. This strategy is all about maximising the display of status at minimal cost. Conversely, Henny would prefer more traditional and homemade clothes such as a *baju kurung*. Normally, Henny would be dressed in for example a white T-shirt with a Planet Hollywood print on the front, black and white striped trousers and no *tudung*, and Azmi in a grey T-shirt with an East India Company print on the front and white trousers. Considering the couple's blunt opinions regarding American cultural power and the current state of politics in Malaysia, this can be said to be an interesting choice in everyday clothing. Moreover, these preferences may reflect a relaxed or indifferent attitude towards the body in Islam. In each of their preferences in dress there is an element of attempted resistance towards commercial and Islamic legitimate taste in the form of buying brands in a factory outlet and toying with tailoring Islamically acceptable dress according to personal preferences. In the accounts of Sardi and Ahmad, there were similar narratives structured around modesty, thrift, comfort and contentment, and their style of dress fitted these relaxed notions. In the eyes of both informants, buying branded clothes (Ahmad) and Islamic clothes in Sri Munawwarah (Sardi) were seen as excessive and unnecessary displays.

Jeti's preference would be 'comfortable' and 'suit my personality', supposedly exemplary of middle-class taste. She would 'Just wear what's my move for the day.' Conversely 'daring and out of ordinary' seemed both alluring and frightening: 'I know when I wear certain things ... not what most girls with *tudung* will wear. But I won't consider it daring and out of ordinary.' Most often when I met Jeti she would be wearing jeans, a loose-fitting white blouse and sneakers with her white *tudung*. On one occasion, however, when I was invited to the house of her family, she was not wearing the *tudung*. 'Sober and correct' were absolutely not keywords that appealed to her. As a child, Jeti's clothes were made by her mother, who had a small tailoring business. Now, Jeti bought most of her clothes in chain stores around Kuala Lumpur. These ideas comprise another example of how Islamic preferences are inseparable from wider ideas about class affiliation. Jeti declared that she was 'at least middle class'. This obviously legitimated a level of experimentation that was not seen in other female informants. Jeti's strong preoccupation with Islam was not directed towards a fixed moralistic codex of conduct, but was rather a religious framework for discussing modern living. At the same time, she was more engaged in critiquing the government than in defining ideal faith and practice of Malays.

Izura and Yusof most clearly of all represent high economic and cultural capital. Izura explained that her preference in clothes was 'classically cut and good value for money' and 'comfortable' and explained that 'we don't really follow the fashion now because we are old. We did in our younger days.' Yusof commented that 'We follow fashion in relation to our religion.' Izura was very detailed about the variety of places in which she went shopping for clothes: 'I do like a tailor to make my dress like this.' She was wearing a brown *baju kurung* and a brown *tudung*. Likewise, Yusof was dressed in brown and dark colours.

On another occasion when I visited Izura and Yusof in their mansion-like house, both were wearing T-shirts, Izura's with a reprint of Picasso's *Guernica* on the front. Izura explained that she bought her clothes wherever she found what she liked. The performance of simplicity is hard to miss as Izura explained:

When I was young and middle-aged I was very westernised, dressed up to what is going on around me. But as I grow older, I'm more subdued so I go more for a simple dress style. Not really to follow fashion; wear something that I'm comfortable with. It doesn't matter people say it's an old-fashioned thing. Basically, I prefer to use fabric, either silk or cotton. I don't go for artificial fibre because it's too hot.

Discussing clothes and taste was a favourite topic among my informants and not only the women. Male informants were surprisingly explicit about appearance and preferences. I contend that fashion, experimentation and resistance are involved in shaping the taste preferences of the female informants in particular. In suburbia, the elements of respectability and modesty infuse the practice of dress. Neighbours will often be an audience of strangers to whom you want to show a perfect façade. Thus, in terms of appropriate dress and practice, the ideal woman 'acts properly in social life, highly attuned to her relative position in all interactions. There is also a spillover into general comportment, which should conform to the behaviour appropriate to modesty' (Abu-Lughod 1999: 108).

To sum up, this exploration of dress shows that despite the nationalisation of Islam and influences from *dakwah*, the practice of dress is both split between the public and the private and linking these two spheres. Many of my female informants would wear the *tudung ad hoc* in the home, while it would be respectably worn in public to be taken off when the door was again closed. In this sense, the body is subjected to very different forms of control and opportunities in private and public. Informants were not particularly articulate about Islam in their discussion of taste preferences. They would rather as their starting point take the fusing of Islam and consumption as having created a whole new range of meanings and possibilities in the market for identities. Among the more puristically inclined Malays, the complexity involved in signifying status, fashion and piety had been made easier in the wake of halalisation, as I have shown in the local context with Sri Munawwarah. Here fashion, comfort, respectability and Islam fuse in perfectly balanced halalisation, which is simultaneously supportive of the local community. In a way one could argue that Bourdieu's functionalist and aesthetic extremes in this instance tend to meet as he asserts that the keyword for middle class in terms of fashion and dress is a 'fashionable and original garment' (1984: 247). Conversely, I have shown that due to the influences outlined above, the favourite keyword of informants was 'comfortable', which Bourdieu quite differently links to middle-class ideal perceptions of the interior of the home. This twist may signal that most informants strategically or reflexively confer the comfortableness of the safe home to their dress, which quite differently transfixes the public/private boundaries. A whole range of choices and preferences in dressing the body has taken effect. For the purist register, excessive revealing of the body is immoral. Conversely, the other group often see *dakwah* attire as excessive and material without being a sign or proof of inner dedication. Both groups find the ways of the other regressive, unfamiliar and excessive.

Female informants in particular were aware of how far they could take fashion and status within a framework of acceptable and respectable Islamic dress. In general, there was deep knowledge of performing legitimate taste in different contexts. Bodily techniques are used to fuse personal and class material status on the one hand, and the requirements of piety in wider social systems on the other. While halalisation has worked as disciplining middle-class Malay bodies, it has also encouraged the availability of a new range of Islamically legitimate tastes and fashions.

In this chapter I have discussed how the mass availability of commodities in contemporary Malaysia has effected a Malaysian ontology of consumption that is split between individual consumer desires (material status and social mobility), social anxieties and halalisation. The extension of consumer goods markets has helped to shape an aesthetic community that increasingly is being subjected to expansive forms of halalisation – especially with regard to food in the body and dress on the body. The ever-increasing influx of foreign goods into Malaysia has necessitated state halal certification and these processes are a driving force behind halalisation – a particular form of Malaysianising foreign brands in a national setting. Simultaneously, the markets for a plethora of Islamic goods have increased due to the mass production of religious commodities.

The two modern Malay registers of consumption legitimated and performed proper Islamic consumption in distinctive ways. Particular processes of socialisation in families were central to these ways. It was overwhelmingly in cultural intimacy that the binary of halal/sacred/pure and haram/profane/impure was negotiated. The respectability and virtues of the suburban context apparently reinforced these trends. A whole range of choices and preferences in feeding and dressing the body has taken effect and these imperatives and preferences are inseparable from halalisation, shopping for the state, the nationalisation of Islam and expanding markets.

NOTES

1   Inspired by Bourdieu (1984: 514), I tested the keywords below to set off discussions of food and taste. The questions were: when you have guests for a meal, what kind of meals do you prefer to serve? Simple, but well-presented (*ringkas, tetapi cara hidangannya istimewa*); delicate and exquisite (*halus dan sunguh istimewa*); plentiful and good (*banyak dan bagus*); pot-luck (*pot-luck*); appetising and economical (*membuka selera dan menjimatkan wang*); original and exotic (*asli dan eksotik*); traditional Malaysian cuisine (*masakan tradisional Malaysia*) (in Bourdieu's text, French cuisine) or other (specify).

2   My male Malay research assistant felt offended by these statements when transcribing the interview with the Sisters in Islam representative. He told me that she was exaggerating the level of the pressure on women to wear the *tudung* and argued that wearing the *tudung* was mostly a personal choice for the majority of women.

3   Following Bourdieu (1984), I tested the following keywords to map informants' taste in clothes: classically cut and good value for money (*potongan klasik dan nilai yang baik atas wangnya*); reflect fashion and suit your personality (*menggambarkan feshen yang baru dan sesuai dengan citarasa*); sober and correct (*sederhana dan berpatutan*); daring and out of the ordinary (*berani dan luar biasa*); comfortable (*selesa*); chic and stylish (*cantik dan bergaya*); other (specify). I am well aware that some of these keywords, e.g. 'daring and out of the ordinary' may be understood quite differently in contemporary Malaysia compared to their original application within French class distinctions (for example, see the informant Maslina's comments below). However, in Malay middle-class families these keywords inspired many lively discussions of taste and morality in contemporary Malaysia.

4

Housing Suburban Halalisation

Consumption is most often inscribed in discussions of individuals versus institutions, ideologies or regimes of power. Against this image of duality, I argue that relations between individuals and institutions are almost always filtered through the processes of socialisation in families. Following Miller (1998) I argue that shopping has more to do with love, devotion, sacrificial rituals and devotional rites than the sheer individualism of the shopper. Shopping may be directed at two forms of 'otherness':

> The first of these expresses a relationship between the shopper and a particular other individual such as a child or partner, either present in the household, desired or imagined. The second of these is a relationship to a more general goal which transcends any immediate utility and is best understood as cosmological in that it takes the form of neither subject nor object but the values to which people wish to dedicate themselves. (Ibid.: 12)

Sacrifice is explored as that which transforms expenditure or consumption 'into a primary means by which the transcendent is affirmed. The true act of sacrifice seems to be one directed as a devotional act to a divine agent' (ibid.: 78). These two aspects of consumption, the significance of particular others and the cosmological, permeate the analyses in this chapter.

Clearly, shopping as a daily activity is ritualised to exorcise the non-certified or haram, contributing to the performance of Malay identity. As we have seen, food consumption is very much charged with symbolic representations of purification and it is in the domain of food that halalisation was first developed to expand to more and more types of products. Nevertheless, it is at home, in the family, that restrictions and permissions are settled. Halalisation can be seen as distinct sets of invocations of haram or taboo. Taboo can protect distinctive categories of the universe, consensus, and certainty about the organisation of the cosmos, and reduce intellectual and social disorder (Douglas 2004: xi). However, certainty and order easily mirror feelings of uncertainty and disorder. These doubts mostly surface in everyday confusion about how to go about practising ever intensifying demands for the Islamically proper in consumption.

In this respect, the purist register is often seen by the more pragmatically inclined Malays to urge a constant deepening and widening of these moral requirements. Douglas argues that taboo works as coding practices that produce and maintain spatial limits in precarious relations. The fear of contamination can extend dangers of broken taboos to the surrounding community (ibid.: xiii). The inherent danger threatening transgressors works as 'danger-beliefs' that 'one man uses to coerce another as dangers which he himself fears to incur by his own lapses from righteousness. They are a strong language of mutual exhortation' (ibid.: 3). These anxieties cast and recast distinctions between the two registers of modern Malay middle-class consumption. These processes are strikingly similar to Douglas's point that pollution powers most of all 'inhere in the structure of ideas itself' and that these ideas are all about punishing 'a symbolic breaking of that which should be joined or joining of that which should be separate' (ibid.: 140). As I shall show, the middle-class home in suburbia with its quest for moral virtues and respectability is a universe that is subjected to a wide range of ideas of pollution. These ideas help shape the home as a moral and social sanctuary.

In this chapter I discuss how the homes of middle-class Malays work as a semi-domain into which a wide range of ideas and commodities are imported, understood and contested. This discussion entails a focus on cleanliness as a crucial aspect of everyday life in Malay middle-class families. Subsequently, suburban migration narratives of informants are explored in greater detail. This discussion involves a close look at essential aspects of suburban everyday life – the aesthetic of security, how the ethnic other is given shape through proper Islamic consumption and the way in which cars figure prominently in suburban narratives of physical and social mobility.

I will now briefly discuss a few examples of the way in which everyday Malay Muslim consumption is reflected in a number of commodities. The essential commodity in the lives of Malay middle-class families is their house. The house is the pre-eminent stage for the performance of middle-class identities. The bourgeoisie craved land for their visions of ideal middle-class homes (Fishman 1987: 13). Hence, each single middle-class house regardless of its modesty represents a collective assertion of the wealth and privilege of class (ibid.: 10) and constitutes the core of middle-class society. Large portions of a home are intended to be presented to visitors as well as performed for those living in the house itself. The house, thus, functions as a stage for every aspect of family life including as a link between the semi-public and the semi-private. Spending or consumption in public and the visibility of these practices urge speculation about the actual level of prosperity in the intimacy of the home and the family. This notion is very similar to IKEA's slogan launched in a campaign in the Malaysian media in 2002:

> Prosperity Begins at Home. When you're prosperous it shows. From plush sofas to practical cabinets, colourful rugs to little knick-knacks, there is so much to choose from *IKEA*'s gorgeous array of home furnishings. To flourish in comfortable style, trot over to *IKEA* for Chinese New Year with a Swedish touch. (*NST* 18 January 2002)

The nationalisation of Islam and halalisation are intimately tied to the way in which Islam has become domesticated in Malaysia today. Moreover, these houses functioned as the dominant stage in my study in terms of interviewing and participant observation.

A global trend in recent years is a thriving business in Islamic goods. Everything from stickers, rugs, holiday cards and plaques with Islamic calligraphy, to special types of holidays aimed at a Muslim audience,[1] watches displaying prayer (*salat*) times and other features, logos and ringing tones on mobile phones and clothes touch upon and Islamicise virtually every aspect of life (D'Alisera 2001: 97). Especially in the case of the interior of homes, one often finds an abundance of Islamic paraphernalia, which work as effects of wider structural transformations of state and market. At the same time, there has been a marked change from craft production to mass production of religious commodities (Starrett 1995).

In fact, mobile phones and their widely marketed Islamic paraphernalia provide a classic example of the way in which a commodity in modern Islamic consumption may work as what I would call a benevolently charged fetish. At the time of fieldwork, the latest development in this field was a mobile phone manufactured by a Dubai company, Ilkone Mobile Telecommunications. Besides sending an SMS (Short Message Service) at prayer times, it can point to the exact location of Mecca from anywhere on the globe. On the one hand, the mobile phone in itself is a quintessential example of a commodity that has been introduced fairly recently into the Malaysian market. At the same time, it is a relatively expensive commodity that is often seen as a trendy and technologically advanced piece of Westernisation or globalisation. On the other hand, it is a social piece of equipment through which large middle-class families can communicate in a rushed everyday life where both parents and children are away from the home. In halalisation, this type of modern fetish is re-signified and thus transmuted from mass produced commodity into something that may be partly commodity and partly 'authentic' artefact or non-commodity. In spite of the 'Islamic' mobile phone claiming false relation to origin so typical of fetishes in Siegel's understanding, it may be capable of working as a personal everyday reminder to the wearers of their relationship to God. The Islamic ringing tones, the SMS and the logo can all be seen as attempts to bring out the benevolence and authenticity in the ambiguous fetish.

My informant Mascud, a wealthy Malay businessman, in order to teach his seven children moderation rationed the use of mobile phones given to them by him through a monthly donation of prepaid phone cards. This effort to control the use of mobile phones draws attention to the above dilemma. When both parents in many cases are busy working outside the home, the children are often left to themselves after returning from school. Therefore, material goods, as in the form of mobile phones, or the money to buy these commodities, are given to the children as a form of compensation. Hence, these commodities, and the malls in which they are most often purchased, simultaneously take on morally and socially subversive powers in the eyes of parents. As everyday fetish, the mobile phone signifies the modern craving for uninterrupted 'hooking up' to two forms of otherness – family and the cosmological or transcendental.

In the Malaysian context, a multitude of commodities such as candy, credit cards or mobile phones consumed and discussed by informants are often, and especially by the purist group, seen to embody ideological and hidden (Western) residues (alcohol, gelatine, toxics/additives, excess, exploitative capitalism) of malevolent forces. The influx of more and more foreign produced commodities into Malaysia has deepened and expanded anxieties about potentially haram substances in everyday consumption.

The most visible manifestation of the domestication of Islam in Malaysia is the import of Islamic paraphernalia into Malay middle-class houses. The effect of this import of Islamic paraphernalia is to singularise the house and thus transform it from being a mere commodity into a home (Dovey 1985: 53). This ambivalence between the profane nature of the house as structure and the emotionality of the home is evident in a suburban context such as TTDI. In suburbia, the homogeneity of the house types accentuates the fact that these houses are mass-produced commodities planned and constructed by state and entrepreneurial capitalism catering for the emerging Malay middle class especially.

A plaque with Islamic calligraphy may serve a number of purposes, firstly, of course, as an Islamic symbol or emblem protecting the house and its inhabitants. It was my impression that this type of knick-knack was mostly bought in malls such as One Utama. My observations are supported by a similar study acknowledging that 'What are most often seen in the living rooms of the new Malay middle-class homes are Islamic calligraphy, pictures of the Ka'abah in the Mecca mosque, pictures taken with dignitaries, and sometimes a few pictures from the family album' (Embong 2002: 105).

Azmi and Henny expressed strong sympathies with the whole notion of political Islamic revivalism and its critique of the government, especially Mahathir's assumed involvement with the trial of former Deputy Prime Minister Anwar Ibrahim (as I shall come back to in greater detail in Chapter 7). The couple felt threatened by government persecution and censorship in respect of their opposition loyalties and work. Azmi, who was educated as an engineer and at the time unemployed, refused to try to influence government officials and 'cronies' within the construction business in order to get a job. These circumstances generated a certain type of oppositional Islamic performance, especially when the family itself experienced economic constraints. The couple primarily attended the 'independent' mosque in TTDI. Consumption in the family was heavily oriented towards rejection of what was seen as state encouraged excessive consumption giving in to Western consumer culture, materialism and teenage loitering. Due to financial constraints, the interior decoration of the family's home was very simple and basic. This fact seemed to support the idea that the state with its fascination with mega projects and consumption in general encouraged a particular type of Malaysian excess inaccessible to this family.

Yasir, an outspoken representative of the purist group, explicitly criticised the hanging of a plaque like the one referred to above. He expressed doubts that the inhabitants would possess any relevant knowledge of its true Islamic meaning. The plaque reads 'In the Name of God the Most Gracious the Most Merciful'. According to Yasir, it is to remind the occupants to always remember Allah when entering the house, and at the same time let outsiders know that it is a Muslim house. He explained that 'to be honest, there are a lot of Muslims doing it for the sake of decoration only. You do not become more Muslim by erecting the plaque and neither will you be less of a Muslim if you don't hang it up.'

This is an example of the way in which Malay consumption and taste is constantly subjected to critique and distinctions that are equally political, religious and social in orientation. More importantly maybe, this example points to the significance of context, appearance and handling rather than the existence of intrinsic properties in commodities. In spite of the plaque's obvious claim to origin and authenticity, Yasir was unable to translate these seemingly intrinsic properties into a meaningful decoding without deeper knowledge of the people inhabiting the house. In itself, the plaque was mainly open to a materialistic and excessive reading.

As more and more Islamic products appear in the market and are certified by the state, the range of legitimate and proper Islamic alternatives expands. These processes produce halalisation as the legitimate in taste that can rub off on, modify or balance other types of excessive consumer practices. Commodities, thus, are embedded in three spheres of signification: firstly, their inner composition in terms of Islamic or un-Islamic surpluses; secondly, the proper/improper context of consumption vis-à-vis other modifying commodities that can work as either polluting or purifying; and third, the performance context in which commodities are employed as fronts.

Material goods and their appropriation can work as building blocks of life-worlds and constituents of self and other. An example of othering is Mahathir's articulation of Western excesses, as we shall see. Zizek writes:

> The national Cause is ultimately nothing but the way subjects of a given community organize their enjoyment through national myths. What is therefore at stake in ethnic tensions is always the possession of the national Thing. We always impute to the 'other' an excessive enjoyment: he wants to steal our enjoyment (by ruining our way of life) and/or he has access to some secret, perverse enjoyment. (Zizek 1993: 202–3)

Imbuing westerners with material excess is an endeavour to construct a unique and balanced Malaysianness. Moreover, a similar function in halalisation is the promotion of requirements that only Muslims can produce halal products. This form of Malaysianising or ethnicising consumption is all about coming to terms with compelling commodities in a rapidly expanding national market. At the same time, the other is right next door. In the suburban world of seclusion, the front region is mirrored by the secretive back region, in which excesses are seen to be hidden.

Halalisation in Malaysia constantly targets and exorcises that which is considered impure in order to ritually cleanse commodities so that they are transmuted into things or artefacts. Unevenly, the two registers of consumption promote the idea of transforming or re-signifying commodities. Translating these ideas and ideals into practice is, of course, much more complex.

Malay middle-class homes work as structures that frame the new national family. There seems to be a striking resemblance to the way in which the English suburban middle class pictured the house as a shrine or altar taking on religious meaning (Gillis 1996: 112). The feeling of the house as the naturalised emotional core in living was further strengthened as work and education left the house and pushed adults and children in different directions. Accordingly, the symbolism of home took on even stronger forms such as synchronicity in imagination:

> Just as new family times coordinated the disparate schedules, providing family members with a common sense of anticipation as well as a store of collective memories, the symbols of home provided a domestic mecca that, wherever family members might be physically, brought them together in a shared mental terrain. (Ibid.: 122)

This is of special importance in suburban middle-class families where the spheres of work and domestic life are strictly separate. Gillis stretches this point even further and demonstrates that the national became the sum of a hierarchy of households – a 'mythic democracy of homes, sharing common characteristics by virtue of being rooted in the same territory' (ibid.: 113). In this sense, homes within a national territory had more in common with one another than with homes elsewhere:

> *Home* and *Homeland* were now paired in the spatial imagination in such a way that one was inconceivable without the other. Home functioned as a symbol promoting the unity of the family in the same way that homeland promoted the unity of the nation. Every nation began to imagine itself as more home-centered than the next. It was not enough for people to be housed; now they had to have homes of their own for the good of the homeland. (Ibid.: 113)

The home thus became a miniature imagined community comparable to that of the homeland. This idealisation of the moral bonds meeting in the home is clearly reinforced in the commercialisation of the home as an object of consumer culture and advertisement, as well as Islamic discourses. In actual fact, however, the household is far from a stable, uncomplicated unity. It is a social site in which a wide range of conflicts and interests intersect. The household should not be seen as a stable social system, but rather as a locus of difference, social change and class politics in the form of individual narratives with transformative effects (Gibson and Graham 1997: 68).

With reference to Claude Lévi-Strauss, it has been shown that the house as a social institution combines a number of opposing principles or social forms, thus reuniting and transcending incomparable principles adding to an appearance of unity (Carsten and Hugh-Jones 1997: 8). The house 'transfixes' an unstable union, becoming 'the objectification of a relation: the unstable relation of alliance which, as an institution, the house functions to solidify, if only in an illusory form' (ibid.: 24).

It occurred to me that while my informants' lives had been shaped by countless events and celebrations, the house basically remained the same. The house is the material cornerstone of stability and socialisation, 'our corner of the world' (Bachelard 1994: 4). Houses work as a body of images that offer an illusion of stability, a vertical and concentrated entity that appeals to our consciousness of centrality (ibid.: 17), and takes on the protective qualities of a redoubt (ibid.: 46).

The movement of goods and people between the inside and the outside of the house is a movement sometimes represented as those of the orifices vital to sustaining the body (Bourdieu 1990: 277). Similarly, the movement of goods from both inside to outside and the reverse is itself vital for the way Malay families perceive material status through public performances. Distinctions between public and private are closely tied to the binaries of individual/society and civilised/natural (Davidoff and Hall 1987: xv). Especially, concealment as a dimension of the private relates to the binaries of inside/outside and open/closed, highlighting the dimension of public and private in the use of space. Hence, families mediate between the semi-private and the semi-public, and thus connect domesticity to the market (ibid.: 32).

111

DECORATING DOMESTICITY

Bourdieu[2] (1984: 247) writes that while the working classes are preoccupied with 'essential' goods and virtues such as cleanness and practicality, middle-class preferences are aimed at warm, 'cosy', comfortable or neat interiors. The keywords listed below were presented to informants to set off discussions of taste in interior decoration. Out of the large number of informants interviewed, four significant homes represent divergent taste preferences. For Udzir and Nur 'comfortable' and 'cosy' took prominence. Secondly, 'classical' was a preference whereas 'studied' and 'harmonious' appeared to be restrictive and normative, as Udzir explained: 'We like something where we can feel free to do anything.' Nur added: 'Don't have to follow rules too much.' This tendency was strongly reflected in their ideal preferences in furniture, which were 'mixed'. Modern decoration IKEA style was rejected. Udzir found that modern or classical styles were confining and more suitable for an office. Their decoration reflected choices stressing personalised style rather than conventions. Dominating in their living room was a large beige leather sofa with a similar one next to it. In terms of art, only one painting of flowers decorated their walls. Their dining room furniture and cupboards was a mix of classical and country style. Interestingly, 'country living' became a focus of real estate development in Malaysia in the 1990s (Bunnell 2003: 121). Neither in terms of decoration or paraphernalia was there any indication of Islamic influences.

The children's playroom was fitted up so that young children could play and make a mess of things. The couple reasoned that this room was the domain of the children and thus it should not be subjected to strict requirements of adults. This relatively liberal attitude towards cleanliness and order matched this couple's ideas of not being restricted by conventions in terms of Islam or interior decoration. Apparently, this family embodied a more relaxed and personalised attitude towards making the home available and flexible in terms of the different needs of family members. This relaxed and somewhat easy-going attitude was confirmed when I visited the family for a celebration to which friends and relatives had been invited. This family in their one-storey terraced house, together with the next informant, represented the most individualistic among informants. Cleanliness or order was never articulated as desirable.

Siti preferred the categories of 'clean and tidy', 'comfortable' and 'easy to maintain'. Most of all, though, cosiness was significant. The 'sober and discreet' category had no place in her home, as she preferred Chinese antiques: 'When people look at my home they say it's very Chinese. In fact, somebody asked me, are you a Chinese convert? They came to my home when I was sitting at the table eating these noodles with chopsticks. No, I'm Malay!'

The Chinese influence was obvious in Siti's home, especially in terms of furniture. The feeling in her house was a bit like that of an exhibition – classical and presentable, with large and small mirrors covering the walls, marble floors, and glass cupboards with representations of China. The home was very 'full' in the sense of the number of pieces of furniture and their ornamented appearance. There was no indication in the condominium flat in the form of Islamic paraphernalia that Siti was Muslim.

In the home of Azmi and Henny, it was Azmi who mostly articulated preferences in terms of taste. He would prefer 'clean and tidy', 'comfortable', 'warm' and 'easy to maintain'. The family lived with Henny's mother and had little direct influence on the decoration of the house. This fact generated a whole range of ideas as to how their own future home should look. Azmi: 'Anything. Not to say antiques all over. Some people, they go to the furniture shop, they start filling their house from A to Z. We don't have the finances.' Henny explained that classical was what came closest to her preferences. Concerning the furniture in Henny's mother's house where they were now living, Azmi complained that it was unfashionable 1980s rattan furniture that had to be replaced. Their primary preference in furniture would be Bali style furniture. Azmi explained: 'It's very cooling. If you go to MPH bookstores, to one section in a book under interior décor and flip through, you can feel the environment there.' The rattan furniture and a discreet rug constituted the scarce decoration in the living room of the one-storey terraced house that the family hoped they would be able to leave as soon as they found a place of their own. There was no discernible Islamic paraphernalia in the house – only the plaque with Islamic calligraphy above the doorway on the outside. These accounts, together with the decoration of this home, gave the impression that necessity most of all determined the present choices of the family.

Sardi found that 'clean and tidy', 'easy to maintain' and 'comfortable' were acceptable. He explained that they had no modern furniture in the house, which was quite true. The furniture was old and he and his wife were satisfied with not having any antiques or luxury. If their financial situation were different, Sardi would invest in antiques for his home. At the core of Sardi's taste preferences were modesty, unpretentiousness, contentment and even indifference towards 'taste'. In the house, there were several plaques with Islamic calligraphy and other types of Islamic paraphernalia.

Sardi's house could not be more different from that of Izura and Yusof. Even though Izura agreed to most of the keywords, 'classical' was her favourite whereas 'sober and discreet' were rejected. The furniture in their enormous house was a mixture of many different tastes and styles: antique, modern and country style:

> Basically, my hall is a European kind of setting. You find my Chesterfield there. In this room it's more Asian, a Balinese surrounding, the concept of water, the natural. On my floor a pool with fish. I call this Asian, not only Balinese. People want to be associated with Bali because it's a very well-known area.

Izura then pointed to a house next to hers and explained that it was supposed to be Balinese design: 'They try to import a lot of things from Bali like pictures, carvings in wood and brick, rock, but I don't have these kinds of things because in Islam you're not supposed to have images, idols and souvenirs.' Consequently, Islamically acceptable plants, flowers, and a fishpond compensated. In Izura and Yusof's home, their high cultural, social and economic capital enabled them to realise virtually any taste preference of luxury. In terms of paraphernalia, there was a number of large plaques with Islamic calligraphy in the house.

Comparing the pragmatic and purist registers of proper Malay consumption, the latter was far more protective of the intimacy of their private domains. This is not in any way to say that this group was not helpful or accommodating during the fieldwork, far from it, but rather that they did not seem to place emphasis on formal or informal invitation and thus open up the intimacy of the home. Maybe they felt uncertain about the researcher's intentions, or perhaps unwilling to reveal the back region where preparations for more public performances took place. Finally, there could be an effect from 9/11 with all the suspicion, confusion and mistrust these events caused. In spite of purist Malays' hesitation, I have a clear idea about their preferences in the back region.

On my numerous visits to Binsar's house, in which he ran his Islamic school, we normally talked outside on a small terrace adjoining the house with its large windows facing the street. Through these windows, it was obvious to see that the interior in no way differed from that of the pragmatic register of Sardi or Azmi/Henny. The decoration did not in any way reflect or signal particular modesty, frugality or piety. In other words, the furnishings and decoration altogether were comparable to what you would see in other homes, and more than one item had been purchased at IKEA. Consequently, the interior of this home did not reflect any uniquely Islamic taste or style. In the little classroom used for the Islamic school, pupils were seated on ordinary chairs at their desks and Binsar used a whiteboard in his teaching – pupils were not taught sitting on the floor. Qualitatively, all this substantiates that in Binsar's house there was no inclination towards the piety through abstention that we have seen in groups such as Arqam, but rather an individualised and personalised expression of moderation through consumption. Moreover, informants performing purism do not in any way seem to embody the collectiveness or communal spirit of Arqam where followers reportedly sat on the floor in a circle eating from one large metal dish. The informants in the purist register of consumption lived in nuclear families in either a single storey terraced house like Binsar, a two-storey terraced house house (Irfan/Murni) or a condominium (Yasir). As we shall see, these Malays' attempt to perform private and public piety is rather unconvincing in the eyes of the other register.

From detailed survey data and in discussions of this data with the purist group, it was clear that no single object domain reflected significant divergences that could be ascribed solely to their piety. In this way, this register did not significantly reject certain kinds of media products, furniture, electronics or kitchen appliances. Thus, the image of these homes as the concentration of asceticism can be dismissed. Relatively, these Malays were more interested in the preference 'studied' compared to other informants. Most significantly, however, these purist Malays comparatively stressed 'simple' as the most accurate keyword to describe their taste in interior decoration. Yasir, like Binsar, explained that IKEA was his favourite: 'I like the design and the price is also quite reasonable. A lot of simplicity in the design. It's just something that we like; both me and my wife share that. And IKEA is just around the corner in One Utama.' In respect of purchasing simplicity in style, Yasir chose to disregard the fact that he was fundamentally against the immorality of malls. The same tendencies were present in the case of other informants in this register.

In sum, a number of keywords such as 'clean and tidy' and 'easy to maintain', which in Bourdieu are all time favourites with manual workers, craftsmen, and small shopkeepers, recur throughout the interviews. There is no apparent evidence from survey data and participant observation in the homes above that there exists a marked difference in taste preferences between what I consider the more individualised versus the purist group. What really matters is that as the level of cultural, educational and economic capital rises, the articulation of reflexive taste judgements in the form of juxtaposition and aesthetic composition increases. It is, nevertheless, significant to note that preferences for 'studied' or 'harmonious' do not exclude preferences for 'clean and tidy' and 'easy to maintain'.

Interestingly, according to informants, it is in the privacy of the home that material status is secretly crafted. These divisions strongly evoke the distinction between the front and back regions giving shape to performances (Goffman 1971). Interior decoration is obviously an object domain that simultaneously is extremely significant in terms of taste and lifestyle and kept out of the public gaze in the suburban context. An example of this logic is Azmi's idea that it is in the intimacy of the private sphere that status is situated. Publicly, Malays mask their class affiliation:

> We can't really differentiate. People go to the same supermarket, mosque, but you cannot differentiate within the low income, middle class and the upper class. But when you go to their houses then you see, they show their true colours. When you go to the bungalows and ring the bell, they don't respond. So, the only place where you can go to find out is to their houses.

The status generated in cultural intimacy is entirely dependent on the consumption of these objects in the front region and their import into the house. One last point is that male informants seemed very interested in interior decoration. Maybe this could be explained by the fact that men, as well as women, presumed that it was within this private domain that status and respectability were crafted. Consequently, knowledge of legitimate taste in the home was essential. The quintessential back region nature of the fortified middle-class home spurs endless speculation about the 'real secret' of the interior. This fortified secret works as 'an invention that comes out of the public secret, a limit-case, a supposition, a great "as if", without which the public secret would evaporate' (Taussig 1999: 7).

Magazines are major vehicles for advice on interior decoration as well as a pedagogy of the modern national family in Malaysia. I shall end my discussion on interior decoration and taste with a few examples of how these aspects are handled in Malaysian women's magazines.

In the women's magazine *Wanita* (lit. 'woman') (June 1971), the article 'Petunjok untuk menghias rumah' (Guidelines to decorate a home) guides the housewife in her decoration of the home. The most important furniture such as cupboards and sofas must be given first place before you decide where to situate the remaining furniture in order to achieve a harmonious interior. Colour is of importance so you should choose wall colour to match the furniture. Moreover, the context of purchasing goods for interior decoration must be taken into consideration. Firstly, goods should always be bought at the same store to avoid being cheated. The inference here is that the unskilled Malay consumer should be cautious about the cunning Chinese dealer. In the early 1970s, it was still unusual to find that ethnic groups other than the Chinese would sell commodities such as furniture. Secondly, the article urges that both husband and wife must be satisfied with the furniture. Here, as well as in other similar articles, gendering is about making men more interested in and attached to the home and domestic affairs. Finally, the consumer is advised to buy only if sufficient funds are available to avoid credit. Saving up will enable one to buy good quality, which is always expensive.

In another *Wanita* issue from May 1992, the heading reads 'Cara menyusun perabot yang baik' (Ways of arranging furniture nicely). If you organise and balance your furniture in the right way, it will make your house seem larger. Similarly, an article in the *Ibu* ('mother') magazine (May 1993) 'Paduan rekabentuk tradisional dan moden' (Guidelines to traditional and modern design) reports from the house of a famous composer in whose home everything is mixed yet convincingly balanced. There is ratoon furniture vital to Malay taste and identity, and simultaneously modern design.

In yet another issue of the same magazine (October 1994), an article entitled 'Lambang kemanusiaan dan kedamaian' (Symbol of humanity and peace) stresses that the correct decoration and arrangement of the furniture, plants, and trees symbolise peace and humanity. Moreover, the advice is to mix furniture from different periods. Much the same topic on harmony is present in the articles 'Harmoni warnai kebahagiaan rumah tangga' (Harmony paints happiness in household) (December 1994), and 'Pilihan yang sesuai lahirkan suasana harmoni' (Choosing the right colour creates a harmonious atmosphere) (February 1997).

CLEANLINESS BACK AND FRONT

The question of cleanliness follows a more general trend towards the purification and ordering of the home. This tendency is greatly influenced by popular culture in the media, especially magazines and the nature of suburbia itself. On the face of it, cleanliness was a virtue with informants and their homes were actually clean and tidy. However, it was not possible for me to establish to what extent cleanliness in these homes was an 'everyday standard' or if it rather was performed in connection with the visit of the researcher (and his son). In a wider perspective, dirt is never absolute, but subjective (Douglas 2004: 2). Most importantly maybe, 'Uncleanness or dirt is that which must not be included if a pattern is to be maintained.' (ibid.: 50). All these ideas and practices are intricately tied to domesticity against its outside: 'We are separating, placing boundaries, making visible statements about the home that we are intending to create out of the material house.' (ibid: 85)

In the suburban world, the street as inherently disorderly and boundless contrasted with the domestic virtues of order and cleanliness. The quest for order and cleanliness was matched by the external artificiality of suburbia. Consequently, the back region of the home is where control is ensured and maintained as a resource against front region anxieties. As we have seen with my informants, decoration and taste are a primary means of personalising harmonious homes.

An abundance of advice guides the housewife and mother as to how to achieve the faultless home producing the ideal site for family living. Secondly, cleanliness in a more public form is prominent in the TTDI Residents' Association's newsletter. In several issues, the theme of cleanliness materialises, for example in No. 3, September 1994: 'A more caring attitude to make things work':

> Together with the whole nation, we have just celebrated our 37th anniversary of independence from colonial rule and our existence as a sovereign nation in our own right. Well, we have lots to be proud of. Our economic growth, our standing in the international community, and the peaceful coexistence of the multiracial communities are worthy of study and emulation by most other developing and maybe some developed countries too. But let us not be too carried away as one finds there are still a lot of things not 'working' properly in our everyday life. Look at those complaints about rubbish not collected. In fact one has only to wander a bit off the main roads of the city to find our side streets and backlanes in less than pristine condition. Take a trip to the sub-urban or rural areas and the situation is even worse.

National purity is idealised, and this should be emulated in TTDI. In No. 1, March 1995 it is argued that cleanliness should be an integral part of children's socialisation to the benefit of the community in TTDI and to uphold the label of 'model township': 'teach our children that littering is wrong and morally unacceptable by being role models ourselves' and ensuring that 'our frontage and the portion of road adjacent to our gates are spotless. Please devote perhaps fifteen minutes a day to this endeavour.' In No. 2, October 1998, there is an on-the-spot report announcing 'Winners of the cleanliness & landscaping contest' held in TTDI. In the Message from the Chairman (No. 2, September 1995) the editorial reads as follows:

> Our country has been blessed with an incomparable economic growth, a stable socio-political environment and freedom from natural disasters that we take for granted our good fortune. On a micro-scopic level, Taman Tun Dr. Ismail is similarly fortunate with our clean wide roads, lush greenery and efficient services.

The following examples are from women's magazines. In *Wanita* (March 1971): 'Mengurus kebersehan rumah tangga anda' (To manage and clean your household). If the house is well maintained and clean, this will provide you with a mentally and spiritually harmonious family life. The article 'Rumah kemas hati gembira' (A tidy house makes you feel good) in *Ibu* (September 1992) argues that once your house is neat it will make you happy and, maybe even more importantly: the tidier the home, the more time the husband wants to spend there. In all this, there are elaborate ideas of the linkages between purity, control and happiness.

In an *Ibu* issue from September 1995, happiness and materiality is brought up: 'Kebahagiaan keluarga amat penting' (Family happiness is very important), but in this context, the argument is that a large bungalow does not necessarily mean happiness. Against this, the crucial question is how the home is decorated and personalised. It is in the intimate details and the knowledge of these that distinctions between the pompous and the persuasiveness of the discreetly legitimate emerge. Most importantly, the personalisation of taste is achievable only if the house is clean, tidy, and neat. The central idea in the above articles is that family harmony, well-being and happiness are intricately linked to material distinctions, organisation, and dispositions.

The things of the house carry a family biography or narrative of the people who inhabit this space. I contend that 'It is the material culture within our home that appears as both our appropriation of the larger world and often as the representation of that world within our private domain' (Miller 2001b: 1). Moreover, the house and the things of the house work 'as both the source and the setting of mobility and change' (ibid.: 4). At the same time, the longevity of the house and things of the house can generate a feeling that agency resides within (Miller 2001c: 119). It seems that magazines contribute to the creativity of schemes of legitimation among my informants, e.g. the idealisation of 'balance' and 'harmony', which is not necessarily translated into actual practices of consumption.

KAMPUNG, CITY AND THE SUBURBANISATION
OF THE MALAY MIDDLE CLASS

In July 1979, the article entitled 'Penghijrahan dari kampung ke kota' (Migration from the village to the city) in *Wanita* discussed what at the time was a fairly recent trend towards Malay mass migration. The article is an interesting historical example of the way in which migration and urbanisation were understood in a period of major social upheaval. Simultaneously, it shows how popularised sociology started to be concerned with the question of migration in the new national Malay family.

The article establishes that migration from the *kampung* to the city, especially in the last part of the 1970s, had increased greatly and posed a number of serious economic, social and political problems for the government. Because of the traditionalist worldview and poverty in the *kampung*, migrants were pulled towards the dynamic city full of education, industrialisation, employment, and economic opportunities – the city was the place to improve one's livelihood. The problem, however, was that the values of the Malays were basically still rural and backward because of laziness, and existential and religious fatalism.

Against these images of the rural Malay, the New Malay is different in every respect. In this section, I will look at my informants' trajectories of migration. The quintessential cycle of Malay middle-class migration is from *kampung* to city and then after graduation and/or an improved job situation, to a suburb such as TTDI.

One specific narrative permeates my informants' accounts of migration to TTDI. On the one hand, moving to TTDI signifies social mobility, as this suburb is known around Kuala Lumpur as a model residential area. The darker side of planning, orderliness and affluence, however, is sterility, excess, arrogance and social isolation. Mascud and his wife, for example, moved first to a low-cost settlement in Kuala Lumpur from a *kampung*, and in both places 'People were more friendly, more caring, take care of children. In TTDI it's quite different, everybody is busy.' Most informants supported these ideas. Ahmad mentioned that residents in TTDI kept to themselves in their bungalows and did not want to mix with lower middle-class people such as himself: 'Compared to my *kampung*, it's very different. Sometimes you don't even know the people next door.' Azmi and Henny both found that the individualism and arrogance of the privileged in their bungalows were unbearable and they were disillusioned with the promise of social life surrounding the mosque. According to Azmi, these Malays were 'Government super skilled, corporate figures, well-to-do businessmen, among that circle. So, we meet them during the prayer, but then in the mosque you are not allowed to talk, you're just praying and going back.' Informants mostly contrasted suburban respectability and social distance with the imagined or real 'community space' of their (backward) *kampung* or (noisy/polluted) low-cost urban settlement. In other words, social mobility, status, and respectability acquired in suburbia had displaced the feeling of community in the *kampung* and the city.

Some informants explicitly articulated criticism of the suburban world. Yasir, for one, said he was planning to move to an exclusive newly established *kampung* area, which he felt would be more natural and green: 'There's a stream. And my dream is always to have a house and home where I can retire with a stream nearby.' In much the same way, Irfan and Murni expressed that Islamic revivalism was initiating a process of reversed urbanisation, meaning increased consciousness of the immorality of urban/suburban life. In opposition to these ideas, other informants (Siti and Udzir/Nur) were pleased with suburban living. In all these ideas, families completely take centre stage in everyday life. Ironically, the family of the other was often seen to subtract energy or surplus from sharing in 'community space' – when families turn in on themselves, they turn away from community. The *kampung*, so central to informants' accounts, strongly mirrors such ambiguous positions. For many informants there is a marked difference between the two worlds. The boundary is demarcated by the material excess of the city versus the spiritual excess of the *kampung*. In this image, there is an obvious element of charging the *kampung* with romantic ideas of national authenticity.

One example of this is Yasir's idea that the excesses of Kuala Lumpur contrast with the moderation of village people (*orang kampung*). Of special significance in this type of understanding is the fact that the *kampung* is a strangely anachronistic yet piously primordial pocket of self-sufficiency and subsistence economy independent of external capitalism and excess.

Yasir explained that *kampung* people inhabit a *bumiputera* haven so that 'the food is just behind their backyard'. In a way, the *kampung* materialises as the prophetic visionary model as in Irfan's account. In the *kampung*, 'They realise slowly that town people are going back to nature.' Conversely, the *kampung* is simultaneously regressive in terms of job opportunities and low income. This view reflects a tension between the romanticised and authentic *kampung* and the *kampung* as peripheral in terms of more pragmatic and everyday concerns. The *kampung* works as the natural core of the Malaysian nation linked to Malay ethnic religious identity, which will once again prevail when authenticity returns as a response to depraved urban modernity. Most importantly, the *kampung* in terms of consumption retains an intact form of indigenous pride and piety that is lost in the city. From a class distinction perspective, the *kampung* of tradition and necessity mirrors the city of shallowness and excess.

Against this vision of the *kampung*, the majority of the more pragmatic Malays, e.g. Siti, would argue that *kampung* people were conservative, lazy, detached and reserved. Siti: 'If you don't mind, most of them are just loitering around.' Coming from a *kampung* himself, Hazan saw the difference in terms of overly tight social relations in the *kampung* versus the freedom of individualised choice in Kuala Lumpur: 'In the *kampung* we know each other, the busybody type, I know everything about you and keep asking about it. Here you don't really care about your neighbours.' In terms of consumption, the interior of the house in a *kampung* is crucial as this is where you meet friends, neighbours and relatives.

Jeti said that '[t]he buying of gold is still compulsory for any girl and they're willing to go all the way to buy it even though they're poor. To me, that shows you want to be materialistic.' This tendency, Jeti explained, is a cultural effect in a rural place such as Terengganu. Conversely, Kuala Lumpur was populated with 'A lot of middle-class people and we don't really care what we do.' Central to more pragmatic notions of city and suburb is that these spatialities do not embody or produce radically different identities. *Kampung* people are no more simple or pious compared to the city, but rather materially backward without the ability or ingenuity to advance.

Looking at the modern suburb of today, the tendency is to see that these new spatialities contain specialised functions such as industry, shopping malls, hospitals, universities, cultural centres and parks. Diversity has come to represent the suburban landscape and this is evident in the case of TTDI. The geographical location exposes TTDI to a number of often contradictory spatial and temporal influences: the *kampung* as a concurrently idealised community, the subject of a romantic voyage back and historical signifier of backwardness; the expanding city of Kuala Lumpur; religious fanaticism in Arqam; enforcement of state and entrepreneurial planning versus the organicness of the *kampung*; TTDI as a point of intersection between the world of urban material excesses contrasted with the moderation of the *kampung*; progressivist visions and dreams of social mobility in TTDI injecting the city and urban lifestyle into Sungai Pencala; sediments of the exploitative colonial rubber economy in the *kampung* versus suburbia embodying the modern nation; the backwardness of the state-protected *kampung* Malay stuck in his reservation versus the New Malay in TTDI, inherently socially and spatially mobile.

Historically, plantation estates established in the period between 1890 and 1920 surround Sungai Pencala. Sungai Pencala borders on a small indigenous people (*orang asli*) reserve beyond the Damansara-Kepong road to the west, and village land of Segambut Dalam to the east. Extensive estates lay both north and south – where TTDI is situated today. Large blocks of land under rubber cultivation extended down to the tin mining areas in the Klang Valley to the south. Sungai Pencala holding the status of Malay reserve was an island among rubber estates by 1920 and continued to be so until the 1970s (Brookfield et al. 1991: 50). The Structure Plan of 1982 envisioned Sungai Pencala as one of the three sites for commercial subcentres in the metropolitan area.

To sum up, the fence between TTDI and Sungai Pencala is a symbolic division between the reserve and middle-class suburbia to the south. The division in itself works as a demarcation of TTDI. The boundary also highlights the fact that Sungai Pencala contrary to TTDI is excluded from the domain of effective planning by authorities or private enterprise (ibid.: 86). Despite the clear physical separation of the two areas, residents in Sungai Pencala are highly dependent on the shopping and job opportunities in the city. From the terrace in the condominium on the boundary between Sungai Pencala and TTDI, I could frequently see Malays from Sungai Pencala cross over to the shopping area in TTDI, as there were only a few small grocery stores left in Sungai Pencala. Often the Arqam people on mopeds wearing turbans, long white robes, and rifles on their backs would cross over as well. Regarding the continuation of more traditional values and ways of life in Sungai Pencala, Brookfield et al. conclude: 'When the city comes to the village, as it is doing at an alarming pace around Kuala Lumpur, no rural way of life can survive' (ibid.: 171). Regardless of the production of new identities in Sungai Pencala, the *kampung* form is still there in the shape of house styles and blurred boundaries with one's neighbour.

The existence of an intimate relationship between *kampung*, city, and suburb is central. A suburb such as TTDI functions as a powerful yet ambivalent symbol: on the one hand, it is a parameter of achievement, affluence, status, respectability, and state privileges. On the other hand, there is an obvious element of moral ambivalence, tension between material consumption and Islamic piety, social isolation, and desire for community.

When outsiders see families turn away from community, a strangely 'materialistic familism' arises. At the core of such materialistic familism there is an enjoyment of privatised forms of consumption that prevent any social investments in the common good. Consequently, any kind of public consumption or shopping are seen to signify performances that may give public audiences an idea about what is actually imported into the home of the other. In all this, cultural intimacy stands out as a meaningful approach to capturing the overspills between the parallel semi-domains of front and back. And a suburb such as TTDI is the perfect stage for performing class and ethnic distinctions according to certain internalised moral, social and religious scripts subjected to careful preparation in privacy. In suburbia, residents are physically close, and yet separated only by thin walls. In this design there is an intrinsic vision or potential for community and nationness.

The linking and thus distinction between different spatialities (rural, urban and suburban) are prominent in family narratives. A typical cycle in these Malay middle-class migration narratives is moving from a *kampung* or provincial town (backward, rural, intimate, remote, traditional, modest, familial, harmonious, poor, pre-colonial) to a modest habitat in Kuala Lumpur (modern, monumental, spectacular, noisy, polluted, immoral, bustling, chaotic, colonial), often in connection with studies, and finally to one of the affluent middle-class suburbs (clean, planned, orderly, respectable, family friendly, impersonal, excessive, tranquil, affluent, post-colonial) after graduation and newly won social mobility. Informants clearly distinguished between the characteristics of these divergent spaces and the way they were 'practised' (de Certeau 1984: 117).

THE AESTHETIC OF SUBURBAN SECURITY

Suburbia materialised as an archetypal middle-class invention and a new way of considering the relationship between residence and the city (Fishman 1987: 3). The history of suburban design is not so much the product of professional architects as a collective creation of the bourgeois in the late eighteenth century outskirts of London (ibid.: 9). The element of planning so evident in my fieldwork site of TTDI is closely linked to the forms and styles the suburbs took when exported and proliferated through British conquest and colonisation. Still, ethnographic specificity is required to illuminate the representation and responses of the local. This insight links the influence of colonialism and the particularity of space: 'through attending to the local, by taking the local seriously, it is possible to see how the grand ideas of empire become unstable technologies of power which reach across time and space' (Jacobs 1996: 158).

The encroachment of Kuala Lumpur on agricultural land, primarily former rubber estates and forest encircling the existing city, follows a distinct pattern of expansion and developmental optimism. The suburban idea is built on the transformation of cheap agricultural land into highly profitable building plots. The process of encroachment signifies a commodification and consumption of both rural land and the suburban house as objects of middle-class family fantasies of 'the good life'. These imaginaries and desires then feed the real estate housing industry in its attempts to construct a modern nation in contradistinction to the surrounding environment of the city and the *kampung*.

The division between the rural, urban and suburban has its root in the suburban world of exclusion – work excluded from the family house, segregation between middle and working class housing, and suburbia's greenery contrasting the annoyances of the city (Fishman 1987: 4). In terms of social distinctions, these were preconditioned on physical segregation between social groups, their behaviour and personal cleanliness (ibid.: 32). The positive ideal of family life of the middle class in union with nature exists in interplay with their fears of life in an inhumane and immoral metropolis (ibid.: 27). The city was not only seen as 'crowded, dirty and unhealthy, it was immoral' (ibid.: 38). The immorality is most clearly visible in terms of the excess of consumption, enjoyment and pleasure threatening religion and the integrity of the family. Furthermore, the fear of crime in contemporary urban and suburban Malaysia seems to stress the immorality and depravation so central to the creation of the historical suburb: in the government-censored newspapers and the electronic media, crime in every form has a most prominent place in the everyday coverage. Crime mostly materialises in the form of offences against property, prostitution, rape and drug addiction. Offences against property in particular are a concern among residents in TTDI. The house form and the styles of the terraced and semi-detached houses, bungalows and condominiums seem to emphasise the house as an arena of everyday tension, the house as a 'public' and 'political' space, especially when the outside world is perceived as divisive and threatening (Carsten 1997: 282–3).

In 'fortified enclaves' in Brazil, these new residential forms emerge in response to what is seen by the affluent classes as outside crime and evil. A whole new model of aesthetic security is shaped by the expansion of condominiums especially, and thus transforms newer forms of housing and the prestige invested in and signified through these (Caldeira 2000: 257). In Malaysia, the condominium concept was introduced late in the 1970s and 'endorsed by the government in the Fourth Malaysia Plan as a means of optimizing land usage' (Goh Beng Lan 1999: 180).

In TTDI, the author, Yasir and Siti all lived in such fortified enclaves in the shape of condominiums. Interestingly, Yasir and Siti represent two quite contradictory ways of performing condominium living. Unsurprisingly, Yasir, who in many ways embodies the more puristically inclined ethos, stressed the social isolation and limited interaction in his family's condominium. As we shall see below, Yasir would idealise living next to a stream in a rural area as a far more balanced way of living. Conversely, Siti, who lived in a condominium next to Yasir, was far more pragmatic and content about life with her family in the condominium. Comparatively, Siti enjoyed the kind of social interaction that was actually taking place, e.g. having friends over for dinner in the family's condominium flat. This is a clear example of the way in which suburban living is comparable between the two registers of suburban Malays families while the legitimation of this lifestyle differs significantly.

Demarcation through physical barriers and distancing, most importantly perhaps, 'is complemented by a symbolic elaboration that transforms enclosure, isolation, restriction, and surveillance into status symbols' (Caldeira 2000: 259). The home occupies an almost universal place as the conditioner of symbolic systems that shape individual sensibilities. Five fundamental elements (security, seclusion, social homogeneity, amenities and services) figure prominently in advertising the suburban lifestyle (ibid.:

264). All these features are clearly detectable in TTDI as the quintessential frontier suburb squeezed in between and demarcated by the Darul Arqam commune inside Sungai Pencala and Kuala Lumpur. This type of urban environment is intensely advertised by the real estate industry playing on the high safety standard in protection of the family and its property.

Residents outside the condominiums, in their terraced and semi-detached houses and bungalows, often have an even deeper need for control by fortressing their houses against external fears in the form of undesirable social interaction and crime (ibid.: 283). Consequently, house living in comparison to serviced and guarded life in the condominiums stresses an individualised form of inner, self-maintained aesthetic of security so that living behind walls and fences constitutes 'a language through which people of every class express not only fear and the need for protection but also social mobility, distinction, and taste' (ibid.: 291). This is most visible in the field of the aesthetic of security. In TTDI, fences, walls and bars become elements of decoration and the expression of personality and invention in the constitution of social class. This aesthetics of individual security is clearly expressed in the article 'Beautifully different' in *Masyarakat TTDI* No. 2 October 1992:

> Many foreign visitors to Malaysia, and even those who have travelled extensively overseas, have at one time or other commented on the dreary monotony of the houses (especially link houses) in our housing estates, all looking the same. Taman Tun is no exception. For this article, our roving cameraman went round the neighbourhood to see how some link house owners have added their personal touch to their gates and fences.

Outside houses, space itself is ordered so that streets are built for cars, making pedestrian circulation difficult. In effect, desolate streets evoke suspicion, isolation and anxiety. There is a striking resemblance between Caldeira's fieldwork experiences and those of the author in TTDI. For several months I walked the streets of TTDI in order to hand out questionnaires to respondents and contact prospective informants. It was somewhat strange to be the object of the surveillance the deserted suburban streets invited (Figure 17, overleaf).

Before a breakthrough with my informants, what I noticed in these suspiciously empty streets were the echoes of the domesticated life of families inside their houses and occasionally the expressed curiosity towards the outside in the form of a curtain discreetly lifted. In my own

Figure 17: The streets of TTDI.

condominium, daily life was deeply structured by the constant supervision by armed guards in their guardhouses. When I visited my informants and friends living in other condominiums, it usually proved difficult to pass their security check, and the same was the case when visitors came to my condominium. In addition, the condominium as a fortified enclave embodies an unnoticed and much darker social side. In my condominium, there were constant rumours of the guards being in collusion with criminals, subverting any feeling of security and instead causing anxiety about being *trapped with outside evil on the inside*. This rumouring climaxed when individual or groups of guards occasionally were replaced: residents

Figure 18: Guarding the fortified enclave.

felt sure that this was proof of some conspiracy either unravelled or in the making (Figure 18).

Below, I shall provide a few examples of the security hype presented and advertised in the national and local media. The heading of an article in the women's magazine *Wanita* (November 1992) was 'Tinjau dulu bila pintu diketuk' (Check the situation when there is a knock on the door). In this infomercial it is argued that most crimes in the home are caused by residents' carelessness. Steps to take are to carefully watch the appearance of strangers before letting them into the house. To that end, a 'doorscope' is a new instrument introduced on the market to ensure a private kaleidoscopic view of the outside from the inside. Consequently, fighting crime is a question of being properly equipped in the market for security.

In the local *Masyarakat TTDI* newsletter, security was a recurring issue. A few headings are: 'Burglaries in the neighbourhood' (No. 2 October 1992). Residents are advised to check if they are being followed when returning to their homes at night; 'Cooperate to fight crime in your neighbourhood' (No. 3 December 1992). In the article it is stated that 'One of the thieves has been apprehended and he is a local, not a foreign worker type, as widely speculated'. The somewhat vague signifier 'local' brings crime even closer to the neighbourhood. In another issue (No. 2 July 1993) residents are encouraged to ensure that 'their houses are properly secured and locked when they leave their homes and reporting to the Police any suspicious movements in their neighbourhood'. Finally, this theme is replayed in the No. 1 August 1997 issue under the heading 'Help maintain security in your home'. This type of crime 'from within' is, of course, much harder for citizens and authorities to contain, classify and thus address.

The tendency here is to portray crime as a city symptom that infects and pollutes suburbia. The cure, therefore, lies in correct security precautions for the home. Building up boundaries is of vital importance to protect family and possessions. In media representations in urban Indonesia, the criminal is always on the edge of society and that fact makes him available for political discourse (Siegel 1998: 3), and this is obviously also the case in Malaysia. Criminals are those who 'show the absolute necessity of the law because, once making themselves felt, and appearing the way ghosts appear, the law is bound to show up'. As a consequence, criminals form the basis of legality because through their actions they summon the law and cause it to appear (ibid: 88). The effect of media hypes surrounding crime is that it calls upon the state, its spectacles, rituals and actions.

As you would expect, the fear of crime figured in diverse ways in the lives of informants. In general, however, all informants in their different forms of suburban housing accepted and acknowledged what was discussed above as a particular aesthetic of security in the fortified enclave. Fences, gates (often remote-controlled), walls and locks are standard 'items of progress' as it were in a suburb such as TTDI. At the same time, this aesthetic of security evokes a kind of routinisation or disciplining in suburban everyday life. For inhabitants in condominiums this involves the investment of trust in the tedious control by guards in everyday life. Conversely, inhabitants in houses and bungalows perform a more individualised form of aesthetic of security.

THE ETHNIC OTHER OF CONSUMPTION

During fieldwork in TTDI, some Malays, who had been living in the area since it was constructed in the 1970s, speculated that Indian and especially Chinese paraphernalia were brought out onto the façades or front gardens as a response to the nationalisation of Islam, and a feeling among Chinese and Indians that Islam was encroaching on their lives. This encroachment materialised in terms of the ethnicisation of the state to become a signifier of Malayness and an unambiguous Malay identity. These sorts of

Figure 19: The spirit of the home: a Chinese house in TTDI.

paraphernalia can take on an ethnic labelling or distinction effect on the façade of houses that without paraphernalia are virtually homogeneous (Figures 19 above and 20, overleaf).

At one point Mahathir was asked about which problems gave him the biggest headache. He answered that

> The biggest headache comes from trying to balance the development of the indigenous people with the non-indigenous Chinese and Indians. The Chinese are used to urban living, and to wealth. So they are able to deal with prosperity. But the Malays are rural people, very poor people and suddenly they have moved to the towns. In the urban area the life style is different. And they have more money. They cannot handle these changes in a way that is productive. (Mahathir 2002: 124)

In the eyes of Mahathir, widespread social ills among the Malays are a feature of urbanisation. Moreover, broader anxieties over economic development, urbanisation and globalisation are prominent in both state nationalist and challenging Islamic discourses in contemporary Malaysia. The integrity of the family unit in particular is seen as threatened by the above forces (Eighth Malaysia Plan 2001–5: 18).

131

Figure 20: Holy cows at the gate in a middle-class suburb.

Historically, cities such as Singapore, Malacca, and Penang were mostly dominated by Chinese. The tendency is for in-migration from rural areas to increase the number of Malay urban dwellers and thereby modify the configuration of Kuala Lumpur in an ethnic perspective. In the vernacular literature of the 1920s 'the town was sometimes portrayed as a place of opportunity for those clever enough to thrive in its economically competitive life but almost always as a source of moral peril and cultural alienation for good Malays and Muslims' (Roff 1994: 253). Not until the 1970s did Malays account for a substantial part of the in-migration to Kuala Lumpur. Mixed Chinese–Malay areas are mainly found in the middle and upper class residential areas in which the quality and location of the dwellings are the important factors of residential selection (Lee 1976: 45–7). This is a clear tendency in the fieldwork. TTDI is ethnically mixed in terms of Malays, Chinese and, to a lesser extent, Indians. After the Second World War the urban axis of Kuala Lumpur began to transform in accordance with rapid development, and Petaling Jaya, in which TTDI is situated, was designed according to the concepts of the British new town movement of that time, complete with residential, commercial and industrial components (Brookfield et al. 1991: 11). Simultaneously, Petaling Jaya was constructed as a model of an ethnically mixed town pursuing heterogeneous occupations

Figure 21: The market for ethnicities: a furniture store in Kuala Lumpur.

attractive to middle and upper class groups (ibid.: 12). So these new residential estates catered for new segments that became significant as national and socially progressive subjects.

Diverse object domains are mobilised as conditioners of ethnic self-identity and distinctions especially in the light of the halalisation so central to the nationalisation of Islam. Moreover, the market for ethnicities assumes special significance in a plural society such as Malaysia (Siegel 1997: 56) (Figure 21). It follows that consumption is tightly linked to specific practices of self and other that are strategically charged and recharged.

Before exploring how the ethnic other arises in the everyday lives of middle-class Malays, I will briefly discuss the British colonial identity politics of race. The ethnic categories of 'Malay', 'Indian' and 'Chinese' were to a large extent colonial constructs that have survived and filtered into both the discourse of the modern post-colonial state in Malaysia and been formative of stable, naturalised and perfectly workable everyday categories as we shall see subsequently. Indeed state discourses of 'race' qualify as a 'language of stateness' (Hansen and Stepputat 2001). In other words, the colonial power codified, fixed or 'immobilised' already existing distinctions between the British, Malays, Chinese and Indians.

133

What took place in the latter part of the nineteenth century was a popularisation of a 'scientific' theory of racial difference (Hirschman 1987: 568). Similarly, in a colonial perspective, anthropology was an integral part of the administrative science of the colonial state and formative of the colonial imagination and its knowledge about the 'natives' of Malaysia. Moreover, the colonial construction of the categorisation of Malays and Malayness arose through the educational system and literature (Shamsul 2000). In the course of the colonial period, racial census categories became ever more stable, visible and naturalised, displacing classification according to e.g. religion. At the same time, relatively intact racial categories, which materialised on the background of local ideas of ethnic distinction, were transferred to the post-colonial state in the shape of the three major categories in existence in contemporary Malaysia – 'Malays', 'Chinese' and 'Indians'. I was acutely aware of the way in which 'race' and 'ethnicity' as 'meaningful' identity categories were constantly negotiated between the authority-defined and everyday-defined in the lives of my informants. I will now discuss how modern forms of ethnicity can be explored in the context of performing Malay consumption.

The pragmatic grouping of Malays maintains that ethnic distinctions and interaction mainly materialise in this market for ethnicities in a quite unproblematic manner. The idea is simply to be sufficiently cautious of halal and haram – when going to a Chinese shop especially. Siti's ideas were indicative of this trend. She explained that religion more than race determined the shopping behaviour of Malays – if a Chinese shop was selling halal food she was perfectly content. Even though the Chinese in the restaurant or shop were not Muslims, Siti felt that it was acceptable according to her individualised standard of halal requirements (which was forcefully rejected by the purists). Going to a Chinese shop was mostly motivated by convenience. Hazan reinforced this notion. The urban multitude of choices and preferences is in stark contrast to the small Chinese shop in the *kampung* like the one Hazan is from in the state of Terengganu:

> Normally, the Chinese shop offers a variety of items, which are not in the Malay shop. In my Malay *kampung*, all the groceries are Chinese. So, you don't really support the Malays, you just go where the best bargain is, Muslim or non-Muslim. In my *kampung*, on Friday mornings, there's a morning market with religious speeches and at the same time they do business. Many people go there because normally they can get cheap stuff so it's religious in a way.

Contrary to the Chinese business *kampung* dominance, the selection in Kuala Lumpur now made it possible to find alternatives on a much larger scale than Hazan's Friday market. Izura started to attend a Chinese health and fitness club practising *Qigong*, a traditional form of Chinese medicine involving breathing patterns, movements and postures. Her Chinese neighbours in similar bungalows socialise from time to time on the occasion of celebrations. Typically, the higher the economic capital, the more unproblematic and relaxed was interaction between the ethnic groups. This point has been empirically substantiated in a recent sociological study of Kuala Lumpur and Petaling Jaya: 'One's presence in a multi-ethnic surrounding [...] does not automatically induce one to establish meaningful relationships with people from other ethnic groups. On the contrary, it may make one feel a greater need to stay within ethnic boundaries' (Embong 2002: 145).

The next set of ideas materialises as an effect of much more fixed divergences between ethnic groups. When discussing the implications of going to a shop owned by one's own ethnic group, Azmi explained that this tendency was most clearly detectable when the Chinese in particular wanted to buy certain non-halal items. Normally, they would only go to one particular place. Chinese loyalty to the owner of one single shop over time was affirmed by many Malay informants. This loyalty signified the texture of Chinese networks,[3] and maybe even gave rise to suspicions of the existence of traditional Chinese fraternities always working in the back region of intimacy and secrecy. Chinese herbal medicines and mysticism fuelled ideas of Chinese excess, fortifying the secrecy and taboo for Malays. Azmi:

> The Chinese go to their own medical shop, *sen-se*. Islam doesn't allow us Muslims to go there because they have all these insects. They boil the things and drink it. If you have asthma they will advise you to swallow small rats. The Chinese they eat anything under the sun, so we're not allowed to go. And the Indians, they also have certain items so that we can't go, special items for prayers.

In the light of halalisation, the omnivorous character of Chinese consumption and vulgar Indian ritual remedies are both symbolically excessive and repulsive. However, Azmi and Henny themselves visit a local traditional healer (*bomoh*). The *bomoh* embodies living folk religion, *adat*, a form of customary law, invoked when, as Henny put it,

The children can't sleep at night and are disturbed by spirits. So we consult the *bomoh* for a cure. But in Islam we're not allowed to believe in *bomoh*, we can only believe in one God because sometimes people worship the *bomoh*.

Chinese herbal medicines and the *bomoh* tradition share similar challenging alternative and supplementary functions for Azmi. Referring to his Chinese neighbour, Azmi explained his moderation:

Even though it's Chinese New Year, I don't think they change their furniture. In terms of economics, they're more stingy compared to us. We tend to earn 1,000, we spend 2,000, and we need to address this unnecessary spending. We buy the things we don't need. Changing this TV or sofa is something like a yearly fair. When it comes to *Hari Raya*, we have to change the furniture.

Material excess and greed of the Malays against the entrepreneurial yet moderate Chinese capitalists are the most significant parts in Malay ideas of ethnicity. The disturbing Chinese embodiment of seemingly incompatible qualities is powerful in Malay middle-class imaginations. In both national histories replayed in state nationalist versions as well as in informants' accounts, there is bewilderment about the impact of Chinese immigration and its impact on *bumiputera* culture. The character of the Chinese other emerges as partly entrepreneurial and partly excessive and hedonistic in a strangely un-Asian manner. In effect, the Chinese other ironically seems to share the character of the westerner in Occidentalism. In Malay national myths, Chinese material enjoyment is often fuelled by doubts about Chinese possession of national devotion because of more powerful ethnic loyalties. Rather, Chinese are seen to possess an 'ethnic surplus'. Yasir made clear to me that

Chinese are permanently immigrants. They come from mainland China, a very difficult place. Moved to different places. So, they know how difficult life is when they arrive in Malaysia. They started with nothing so they know they have to save, to work hard, to be committed and dedicated, to sacrifice a lot of things. When success is a theme, you don't simply throw it away like that. Whereas Malays they have not been in these kind of difficulties. There's no such thing in Malaysia where people don't eat like in mainland China. Mainland China once upon a time was like the desert. Millions of people died because there was not enough food. In Malaysia, food is in abundance. There are not many difficulties for the Malays here. So, they take things easily.

In spite of Yasir's government antipathies, his statements are a replay of Mahathir's ideas in *The Malay Dilemma* (1970: 21):

The lush tropical plains with their plentiful sources of food were able to support the relatively small number of inhabitants of early Malaya. No great exertion or ingenuity was required to obtain food. There was plenty for everyone throughout the year. Hunger and starvation, a common feature in countries like China, were unknown in Malaya. Under these conditions everyone survived. Even the weakest and least diligent were able to live in comparative comfort, to marry and procreate. The observation that only the fittest would survive did not apply, for the abundance of food supported the existence of even the weakest.

In his brilliant discussion of Mahathir's classic text *The Malay Dilemma* Yao states that 'Malay frailty has to be seen against the strength of the Chinese who came from a tough environment which truly tested the fit and stout-hearted, weeding out the weak and turning them into "hardened and resourceful" people' (Yao 2000: 73–4). The significance of ethnicity and ethnic identities in Malaysia is especially prominent in the urban context, where widely different patterns and logics of migration between the ethnic groups have produced ethnically mixed residential areas such as TTDI. In the stereotyping of Chinese resilience, the Chinese emerge as perfectly equipped to practise their natural urban and suburban habitat contrary to the somewhat naïve *kampung* Malay. Ethnic tension runs all the way through modern Malaysian history.

Unsurprisingly, in the eyes of some Malays, Chinese may be omnivorous while Malays, in line with halalisation, are particular and sensitive about food. Logically, the halalised food domain must be protected from the 'pollution of indifference'. Malays can only actively challenge the entrepreneurial and networking skills of the Chinese through ethnically conscious consumption in Malay shops. Yasir:

I will tell my wife to include at least ten per cent of the things that we buy daily or monthly to be a product that is made by *bumiputera*. Because we find that if the Malays don't support the *bumiputera* manufacturers or businesses, who else is going to support them? Their networking is not strong and their goods not present in the supermarket because they are controlled by the Chinese. They refuse to take in Malay products.

Yasir strategised that the most obvious way for *bumiputera* to market their products vis-à-vis the Chinese was through what he called multi-level marketing or direct selling. This is the strategy employed by major American companies such as Avon and Amway and supposedly a number of *bumiputera* have managed to successfully promote their products this way. Therefore, ethnic loyalties are effects of daily practices of consumption. Malays have a moral obligation to support Muslim businesses, as the Chinese have always supported their own consumers through complex networks of loyalty, questionable moral business standards, and a concealed system of credit given only to Chinese.

Lastly, Jeti's ideas are expressive in exemplifying the bewilderment of what I call Chinese thrift as excess. Jeti did not believe that the Chinese were extravagant in the interior design of their houses. In terms of ethnicity, her ideas play on the stereotypisation of the Chinese as socially outward-looking and overly conscious of public material status. Another aspect of this perception of the Chinese in Malaysia that informants draw on is that the Chinese remain in a modest house even if they have acquired a substantial amount of wealth because this house brought them good luck. The effect of this in the urban context is that it is even harder to measure the actual social position of the Chinese due to the strategic charging of excess to the inside/outside domains. There is a strong resonance here of Mahathir's contention that 'The Chinese give less priority to immediate needs. They think over the long term. And so they are willing to make sacrifices in order to gain later. That is why the Chinese have thrived and prospered wherever they are' (Mahathir 2002: 93).

Nevertheless, Jeti felt that regarding goods such as cars the Chinese were extravagant: 'My neighbours prefer the car and the house is empty.' Another issue Jeti brought up was Chinese investment expertise that enabled them to spend extravagantly on 'Food, cars and gambling. They will spend a lot because it's part of their culture.' In another discussion with Jeti, she articulated a quite different view: 'Chinese also like to fill up their house with extravagant furniture.' These ideas fit an analysis of the everyday conceptualisation of fixed and uncontested Chinese economic success (Yao 2002: 3–4). Thus, the hard-working, economically successful Chinese 'comes alive in the twilight zone between reality, ideological construction and social imagination' (ibid.: 4).

In this sense public and private domains are constantly charged and recharged with ideas of purity and excess. Everyday life experiences and practices fuel these conceptualisations of the consumption of the Chinese. Jeti concluded that:

I think Malays are even worse shoppers, don't really know the reason why. They shop more, the amount of things, look at the sales, the first ones to rush there are Malays. We don't know why, maybe it's just the culture.

Jeti linked the question of Malay excess vis-à-vis the Chinese to the emergence of the New Malay: 'Malays are trying to catch up for lost time.' Her feeling was that even this point did not justify Malay excesses in houses, designer goods, antiques or cars, whereas the increased concern with children's education was seen as crucial to the emergence of the New Malay in the first place. The frequently celebrated religious festivals in multicultural Malaysia, to Jeti, kick off the Malay shopping craze: 'Raya festival, Chinese festival, *Deepavali*, we shop like mad. I think we get it too easily, more buying power and high debt. I always fear that's happening. And all this because of state support of the Malays.' Consequently, the festivals are understood as quintessential occasions of excess, which especially the Malays seem to seize. This is a direct critique of state sponsored consumerism.

A Jamaat member from TTDI argued that the increased influence of Islam together with the emergence of an open-minded middle-class identity is improving both community and ethnic interaction:

Professional people tend to be close to the mosque, to learn more on religion. That means they're already affluent and at the same time they learn religious things. This combination is very good. A multi-ethnic community is not a problem to me. Because I do attend weddings of my neighbours who are not Muslim. They also attend my parties. We're fortunate because we belong to the middle-class group with education. They understand. And Malaysia, being Muslim, Islam is the national religion, they already understand that.

Ethnic interaction is premised on the full acceptance of Islam as the national religion – the nationalisation of Islam. Then well-educated middle-class groups representing social mobility and open-mindedness can socialise freely. The statement demonstrates the power of social group constitution, but also the conditionality imposed by wider structural patterns such as Islam as a national hegemonic influence. Interestingly, in the quote ethnic interaction is associated with functions such as parties and weddings, which constitute obvious stages for performing status.

These ethnic tensions may be latent in the majority of the middle-class segments, excluding the upper strata that stage and perform shared codes of status and consumption instead. Another contributing factor to this division is the nature of suburbia itself; the seclusion of the house style and form and, more generally, the planning and development behind the perimeter city seem to stress the significance of the nuclear family as the primary source of personal and group identification rather than a broader imagined and existing multiethnic community. Moreover, the nationalisation of Islam and halalisation impact more on object domains, which are central to Malay ethnic identities than it is the case with Chinese and Indians.

To sum up, we can say that in the eyes of informants, proper Islamic consumption was a quite naturalised and wholesome part of national development. Both groupings of proper Islamic consumption, for diverse reasons, agreed that consumption properly handled, displayed and contextualised was quite unproblematic. This is an expression of the emergence of a new ontology of consumption. In this ontology, a range of others figure prominently. Previously, I discussed how consumption may be contested in terms of class (front region). In this section it was demonstrated how 'national' others outside of conventional class distinctions help informants map a spectrum of desired/undesired consumer practices and then plot themselves in. Obviously, there are elements of protest and hostility involved in these preferences. As a consequence, the psychology of shopping hostility between cultures was explored because people easily recognise 'what they do not want' – 'standardized hates' (Douglas 1996: 83). As we have already seen the discursive struggle in Malaysia between state nationalism and challenging Islamic discourses has essentialised an image of the excessive westerner. In spite of the latency of this image in state nationalist and Islamic discourses, interestingly informants were not really articulate about the excesses of the West. Instead, they were far more concerned with 'getting consumption right' in relation to the prominent others figuring in their everyday lives. In the above discussion we often witnessed the confluence of political and popular discourses in cultural intimacy. In the eyes of middle-class Malays, divergent forms of consumption may give rise to ethnic distinctions. Most importantly, perhaps, ethnicity is overwhelmingly conditioned by particular practices and performances rather than essentialisations of 'race'. Most informants, for example, would frequent a Chinese shop or restaurant as long as the products were halal certified. This point testifies to the fluidity and malleability of contemporary ethnic relations in Malaysia.

Figure 22: Proper food for Muslims (makanan Islam).

What I found in TTDI was that ethnically mixed estates with an increased emphasis on class affiliation through consumption are becoming more and more significant in terms of Malay self-perception and boundary construction of individuals and groups. Moreover, ethnic distinctions are fuelled by halalisation. In TTDI, for example, many Malay or Indian restaurants advertise their food as halal certified on their façades, i.e. as proper food for Muslims (*makanan Islam*) (Figure 22). These establishments are often neighbours to Chinese restaurants selling non-halal food, alcohol, and pork served to customers with more individualised and challenging dress codes.

EXTERIOR AND INTERIOR CONVERTIBLES:
OF PROTON, MERCEDES AND MPV

I suggested that there was no absolute division between the interconnected spheres of the so-called semi-public and semi-private. In the suburban context, cars work as the most prominent examples of overt commodities that are seen to straddle and weave in and out of these semi-territories. Consequently, the overtness of cars evokes speculation about the nature of the linkages between the above spheres on the one hand, and the make-up

141

of the covert middle-class home on the other. In other words, cars shape ideas and performances of status, boundaries and (social) mobility.

In the history of the suburb we see that in the US from the 1920s and onwards, due to 'interrelated technology of decentralization' (Fishman 1987: 16), e.g. cars as a means of private transportation, urban institutions spread out over the landscape to form a more complex outer city with both jobs and residences located outside the city centre. The explosion of the city into the rural areas is a revolution in transport varying according to one's financial resources and social group.

Cars imply much more than personal ownership, namely 'externalities', that is 'aggregate effects, landscapes of roadways, patterns of work and patterns of pleasure' (Miller 2001a: 15). In the context of the fieldwork, sample data showed that about 60 per cent of respondents owned one car, 30 per cent two, 6 per cent three, and a small percentage more than three cars. The Malaysian-produced Proton was the most popular brand by far. Other popular brands were Honda, Toyota, Nissan, Mercedes, Ford, Volvo and BMW in that order.

In both Kuala Lumpur and TTDI, the number of expensive and highly taxed luxury cars produced by BMW, Mercedes, and Volvo is impressive. In suburbia, where there is limited direct visual access to the intimacy inside the various kinds of fortified enclaves, the front region of the house and cars inevitably become signs of what life could be like in the back region. Not surprisingly, cars were a favourite topic with male informants in particular. Some informants spread rumours about the way in which access to the state was an obvious avenue for acquiring expensive and foreign cars in spite of a relatively moderate income. Yasir, for one, explained to me that

> The government allows Malaysian students overseas to bring in one tax-free car. So, a lot of used car dealers use the students to bring in cars. The government and car dealers target students. The student gets paid about RM500 or RM1,000. Students just have to give their name and sign a few documents, and the cars come in. You can get a Mercedes for the price of a new Proton. So, no big deal.

Obviously, informants such as Yasir were aware not only of these avenues for acquiring cars, but also the value and status that might be ascribed to this commodity. Yasir confided that a car is what people tend to judge your status by: 'If you drive a Mercedes, even though it's not yours, they will look at you.' This may be the quintessential performance – employing, 'taking on' or handling a specific kind of expressive equipment to convey social messages to a large audience in public.

In Trinidad, the car signifies a form of dualism, and embodies distinct values formative of images of person and nationhood (Miller 1994). This dualism is what I refer to as the convertibility of cars as 'convertibles'. Cars are capable of incorporating and expressing 'the concept of the individual' (ibid.: 237), and the most valuable insight in all this is that while a public audience notice performers' 'aestheticisation' of cars, this is surely not always the case with the money and time invested in the interior of the house (ibid.: 239). Thus, covering the upholstery with plastic, for example, suggests links to home furnishing and may evoke interiorisation (ibid.: 243). Consequently, cars may be expressive of

> ... a contradiction, a replication of the aesthetic of the interior which then has the potential for protecting the values of transcendence by maintaining them in the 'outside' world. Equally, the car provides an ideal objectification of individualism and mobility, to be used in opposition to any association with the home. (Ibid.: 244)

These points reflect the domestication and individualisation of Islam, meaning the import of Islamic paraphernalia, ideas and practices into middle-class homes. While these trends in suburbia are mostly aimed at a family audience, the car is much more publicly expressive and convertible. In Kuala Lumpur and TTDI it was common to see Islamic and other religious paraphernalia used as 'labels' or 'tags' on cars – in all cases smaller and inexpensive cars (Figure 23).

Figure 23: Islam in the rear window.

I could not help hypothesising that this type of branding in and on cars that generally were considered low in status effected some form of compensation or fulfilled a lack in their owners. Another point reflecting the dualism of the car is the way in which suburban houses are all designed to protect, fence in and encompass cars no matter how limited the space that might be available. The tendency is that as one moves upwards class-wise (one-storey; two-storey; semi-detached; condominiums; bungalows), the security of cars becomes more and more urgent, elaborate and organised as a natural part of architectural design and aestheticisation (Figures 24, 25 and 26).

A major focus in the fieldwork in TTDI was informants' ideas about status acquisition. It was in these discussions with informants that it became apparent that cars were expressive of not only ideas of status, but also dualism, confusion and a spillover between the semi-domains and the way in which these were constantly charged and recharged with excess and frugality. Symptomatically of most informants, Udzir pinpointed the everyday difficulty in assessing the material or social status of others by judging from their interior decoration. Cars would supposedly, or rather hopefully, replicate this interior, the everyday spending power of the household as well as this household's strategies of display or concealment:

Figure 24. Securing cars in a one-storey terraced house

Figure 25. Securing cars in a semi-detached house.

Figure 26. Securing cars in a bungalow.

145

You cannot see their items – it's more or less inside the house. But an expensive car means it's more expensive to maintain, high road tax, spare parts are expensive, the petrol it consumes. You don't know about status inside the house. We can't really see.

The car is much more overt and thus has the capability of inscribing the interior of the house with certain imaginary qualities in the eyes of outsiders. Interestingly, it is not so much the cost price of cars that inscribes it with value, but rather the everyday maintenance and costs, e.g. expensive spare parts. Udzir and Nur drove both a Peugeot they liked for its design and a Proton that was far more economical to both purchase and maintain.

Mascud owned eight cars, a Volvo for himself and one car for each of his seven children. In Mascud's eyes, the car was a public measure of one's success that people actively play on: 'Some have very moderate houses, but then a very big car.' He added that 'The car you can move everywhere whereas people have to come to your house.' So the overtness and mobility of cars make them perfectly suited for display when the suburban audience generally is unsure about the position of the other's residence. Irfan and Murni concurred. Irfan: 'What you can show to people is a car. Second is the house, because people don't visit it that often.' Murni commented that the tendency is that when one sees somebody driving a Mercedes one reasons this person must be well off: 'So, when you have this car he's probably staying in a big house. When he comes out you do another assessment according to dressing. He's got a Rolex. Stuff like that.' Cars, dress and brands have clearly replaced the role of the *kampung* residence as a traditional marker of identity, taste and distinction. Irfan and Murni drove a Proton, and were quite aware of the piety involved in this specific choice. They emphasised that even though they could easily afford a more luxurious car, it was a conscious decision on their part to drive a Proton.

Ahmad, who similarly owned a modest Proton, reasoned: 'If you want to show your friends that you are rich, a prestige car follows your financial situation and chandelier lights and wallpaper in the house.' Besides this explicit concord between car and interior, to Ahmad the car assumed special significance in a Malaysian ethnic context: 'The car shows I'm rich. Good car, Mercedes. My purse. The car is number one. Especially for Chinese because Chinese they buy Mercedes, but they live in a squat.' Ahmad's statements here replay what I have discussed above as a commonly held idea among Malays about the Chinese in Malaysia – they tend to live in a modest house even if they have acquired a substantial amount of wealth.

According to this perception, Chinese superstition prevents them from leaving even a modest house in which they acquired wealth. Moreover, for a bachelor such as Ahmad, there is another interest in the status of your car: 'Even girls are looking for guys who are driving Mercedes and not looking for me because my type is a cheap Proton. This is the Asian attitude – wanting a big, expensive car, big house. Beautiful wife. Married to a model!' Unlike Irfan and Murni, Ahmad desired a Mercedes or BMW.

One last example stands out in this discussion of cars. Binsar had purchased an expensive Nissan MPV (Multi Purpose Vehicle). When we were discussing the advantages of this vehicle, Binsar was much more talkative and elaborate than usual, and seemed eager to legitimise the purchase of it. This is his explanation:

> First of all, it's practical and functional. We need a Multi Purpose Vehicle because sometimes we bring the children for a trip during the weekend, and also it's useful if we arrange activities like sports day and other activities. It's easy to bring all the things and equipment. Last time we had to rent or borrow someone's van to bring all the things or equipment. In terms of design, I think it's okay. The price is not cheap and not too expensive. It's good value for money. I like the engine because I think it's better than a normal one. The difference between a Multi Purpose Vehicle and a van is that the van engine is under the front seats. So, in time, the seat will get hot. But for this MPV, the engine is in front like a normal car.

In Binsar's eyes, everyday considerations regarding design, functionality, family and the work in his Islamic school explained why he chose this particular car. This preference ultimately seemed to signify balanced consumption. The MPV thus worked very satisfactorily as a piece of expressive equipment that helped shape a performance of perfectly moderate consumption for the sake of family, Islam and education. It has to be mentioned that among the more purist middle-class Malays Binsar was the owner of the most luxurious car, and this might help explain his somewhat defensive attitude towards this particular and public type of consumption.

In conclusion, we can say that cars as convertibles may be the principal signifier or modifier expressive of status in the semi-domains. Classifying the car consumption of others gives rise to charging and recharging these domains with pretence and frugality. In most cases, my informants did not regularly access the interior of the homes of members of their own or other class group. Exterior thrift in cars can signify concealment of excessive and irreverent practices behind closed doors. Conversely, what may appear as materialistic and extravagant in public can signify a moderate lifestyle in the home. Mostly, however, middle-class Malays believe that cars replicate the interior of the house they are a part of and that protects them. The car as the ultimate suburban status symbol personalises the otherwise indistinguishable house so hard to classify for the outsider or neighbour. Moreover, expensive European cars were seen as quintessentially excessive and inscribed with masculine status. Such imported cars may be 'un-patriotic' compared to the locally produced Proton, but were essential 'positional' commodities with respect to showing-off in public – either in terms of wealth or access to state privileges. Miller makes the case that 'More than any other item of mass consumption the car has become that classic instrument of modernity: the means of enabling contradiction without anxiety' (Miller 1994: 245).

I have shown how proper Malay middle-class consumption (of houses, mobile phones, Islamic paraphernalia, interior decoration and cars, for example) and legitimate taste is subjected to critique and distinctions that are equally political, religious and social in orientation. At the same time, status generated in cultural intimacy depends on the consumption of these objects in the front region and their import into the house. The back region nature of fortified enclaves in suburbia evokes endless speculation about the 'real secret' of the interior. Seemingly, the way Islam has been domesticated in suburban Malaysia is shaping novel forms of cultural intimacy that transforms commodities imported into the house into non-commodities. I shall discuss this in detail in Chapter 6.

Among the informants, migration narratives are essential in linking and distinguishing between rural, urban and suburban spatialities. The aesthetics of security and cleanliness work as markers of status, purity, order and respectability and were obvious keywords in magazines as well as in the lives of informants. The suburban form invites a particular form of aesthetic of security that becomes a normative standard as 'items of progress' in everyday suburban life in condominiums and houses. In an ethnically mixed estate such as TTDI class affiliation through diverse forms of consumption is gaining momentum with respect to Malay self-perception and boundary construction of individuals and groups.

In the wider perspective, ethnic distinctions seem to be fuelled by the nationalisation of Islam and halalisation. An Indian man who lived in a one-storey house in TTDI with his family confided that the 'race issue' in

Malaysia was the country's biggest problem. The *bumiputeras* were 'overfed' and Islam was encroaching on non-Muslims nationally as well as locally. Fifteen years ago in TTDI, the man explained, Malays, Indians and Chinese could still share a meal on their dinner tables and the three ethnic groups would recognise the other's preference for pork and beef. Apparently, the nationalisation of Islam and halalisation have changed that. There cannot be a more marked contrast to Mahathir's comment on the success of multiculturalism in Malaysia, reflected in the powerful symbolism of food sharing:

> The Muslim Malays abhor pork which the Chinese love, while the Indians do not eat the beef which the Malays love. But somehow we manage to sit at the same table to eat, each sensitive to the sensitivities of the others. Muslim leadership achieved this. (Mahathir 2001: 38)

Most of all, perhaps, the ownership of expensive cars signified a particular performance of status that was both private and public and at the same time somehow linked to certain groups' accessibility to the ethnicised state.

NOTES

1   In an advertisement (*The Star* 2 May 2002) the reader is ensured 'meals prepared by a local Muslim chef. Flight Muslim meals [...] sightseeing, shopping, shops, and sights of Muslim interest in addition to other popular attractions'. As with halal requirements in connection with ethnicity, it is interesting that halalisation in the context of the nationalisation of Islam has deepened this aspect to cover a craving for food prepared by Muslims as outlined in the ad. The ad shows two young Muslim women in London. We see a distorted, unfocused, and twisted image of Tower Bridge in the background adding to the impression that the Occidental setting is disturbing, to say the least. This eerie feeling calls for the comfort of stabilising Muslim-friendly services and activities on the trip.

2   In his questionnaire, Bourdieu (1984: 513) asked the following three questions: Firstly, which of the following keywords best describe the type of decoration/interior you would like to live in? Clean and tidy (*bersih dan kemas*), easy to maintain (*senang untuk di jaga*), practical (*praktikal*), cosy (*nyaman dan selesa*), comfortable (*selesa*), warm (*mesra*), harmonious (*harmoni*), imaginative (*imaginatif*) and studied (*belajar or mengkaji*). Secondly, is your furniture modern (*moden*), antique (*antik*), country-style (*gaya atau feshen desa*)? Lastly, if you had the choice which style of furniture would you rather buy: modern, antique or country-style?

3   Networks in everyday imagination are circular in nature: 'Once it is conceptualised as having tightly patrolled boundaries and bearing benefits only for those inside, then a business network – or a social network generally – becomes real and operates exactly as so defined.' (Yao 2002: 143)

149

5

Consumption, Moral Panic and the National Family

I shall show how the national family works as the primary model of social and moral identification in the lives of middle-class Malays. Rather than community or other models of identification, there is an inherent 'moralistic familism' to modern middle-class living in Southeast Asia (Kessler 2001: 42–3). The field of tension within many families is that while individualism is a binding force, e.g. in expressive, materialistic or excessive consumption, 'middle-classness' is viewed as a form of cultural formation based on implied togetherness and domesticity (Davidoff and Hall 1987: xxxii). Middle-class Victorians turned families into objects of worshipful contemplation. Worship of God was practised through these families as a kind of sacrament through which archetypes were brought down to earth in a turn away from cosmos and community for families to live by. In effect, this was the creation and sustaining of their personal symbolic universe, which, in turn, meant that families could no longer be taken for granted, but were in need of constant attention. This transformation

> ... opened up vast new possibilities for individuals to construct identities, marriages, and family worlds to their own specifications, but it also placed huge burdens on marriage and family to produce those models of behavior – that had previously been found only in a divine original or communal exemplar, never in the family itself. (Gillis 1996: 71)

These points are strikingly similar to the idealisation of the New Malay national family. Domesticity in Malay middle-class families is important in at least three respects. Firstly, the home is the primary domain for the valorisation of proper Islamic consumption, e.g. smaller children's and teenagers' desires to import novel and/or costly commodities sold in malls into the home. It is important, secondly, in connection with the breakdown of traditionally more authoritarian models or religious identification. Lastly, middle-class families have become subjected to a number of moral calls and requirements from the Malaysian state and a number of Islamic discourses all competing to impose morally correct models of understanding and practice on families. One such call is that of 'Asian values'.

The majority of commodities imported into Malay middle-class houses are purchased in malls, and, more generally, malls have become dominant, and contested, domains in the everyday lives of suburban Malays. I shall explore political as well as everyday discourses and debates over malls in contemporary Malaysia. I also examine the private sphere as a site for manufacturing new modes of material gendering together with kinship/generation. These dimensions of gender and generation in Malay middle-class families diversify and deconstruct the understanding of the families as homogeneous social entities.

RECOGNISING THE NATIONAL FAMILY

Much has been written about the Asian values debate and this topic does not occupy a central position in this monograph. In the Malaysian context, I regard this debate as embedded in the staging of state spectacles. Nevertheless, the debate over Asian values is rather similar to discussions in Indonesia about the cultural construction of the family as the domain where national politics and identity are most forcefully contested (Shiraishi 1997: 166). In Malaysia, middle-class homes are significant semi-domains of cultural intimacy. Ironically, it is in the private sphere of the family and in the household that the potential for articulating challenging views comes into existence. The inseparability of family and nation is a crucial component in state nationalist discourses. Mahathir (2001: 69) writes that

> First of all, Asian values are community- and family-oriented. We place greater value on the family and on the needs and interest of the community than on the individual and his or her rights to absolute personal freedom. Fulfilling your responsibility towards your family and your community comes before your right to claim individual privileges. [...] Asian values also include respect for authority. Authority is seen to guarantee stability for the entire society; without authority and stability there can be no civility.

During my fieldwork, examples of newspaper articles on the need to construct and maintain bonds between family and nation were particularly numerous. For example, 'Ministry seeks policy to strengthen family unit'

151

(*The Star* 27 October 2001); 'Help achieve target, youth urged. Don't sell yourself short, says Dollah' (*The Star* 30 October 2001). Deputy Prime Minister Datuk Seri Abdullah Ahmad Badawi

> ... has made a plea to youth to direct their energy towards helping Malaysia achieve Vision 2020. He said it was disheartening to note that many were squandering their time indulging in crime and activities that were detrimental to their health. Youth would only be an asset to nation-building if they become good and healthy citizens, he added. [...] They get involved in drugs, they join activities which could lead them to contract HIV/AIDS, they get involved in black metal cult. [I shall return to the issue of the black metal cult below.] Juvenile crime is becoming a big problem.

Other examples of the family–nation edifice are: 'Broken ties'. The article states that the family unit faces 'degradation and disintegration' (*The Star* 5 November 2001); 'Good parenting key to reducing unwed mums' (*The Star* 8 January 2002); 'Teen anger can kill!' (*NST* 9 January 2002); 'First roadshow in campaign for promoting family ties. Fathers urged to participate' (*NST* 18 January 2002); 'Praise for concerned youth. PM: "They must temper idealism and impatience with pragmatism"' (*NST* 7 March 2002). Mahathir explained that '[i]t is, therefore, important that we temper idealism and impatience with pragmatism and a willingness to learn from the mistakes and the successes of the past so as to ensure that the mistakes are avoided and the successes are repeated.'

'Dr M: Younger generation can help realise vision 2020' (*NST* 7 March 2002); 'Datuk Seri Dr Mahathir Mohamad said the younger generation must do their bit to help achieve Vision 2020 as it was not easy to achieve this goal.'; 'The making of wholesome families' (*The Sun* 30 March 2002) and 'Working towards wholesome families' (*NST* 1 April 2002). A 'Wholesome family' gathering was held to stress the importance of wholesome families as integral to the sustenance of a dynamic and progressive nation.

The moral concern for the well-being of the national family is evoked through perils and moral panic. Moral panics can signify threats to the established way of life (Thompson 1998: 1). An example of state stagings of such moral panic appeared in newspapers in April 2002. It was suggested that incest and rape were symptomatic of a depraved Malay mentality in particular, e.g. a heading such as 'Prevention better than cure'. 'Dr M: Instil good values to avoid incest' (*The Star* 15 April). This type of staging of the moral imperfection of Malays by Mahathir is only one example among others. Apparently, these calls seek to incite a continuous feeling of moral panic or inferiority. Moral panics or calls can be seen as forms of forcing the other into 'good citizenship' through a distinction between moral values and 'dangerous contagion' (Douglas 2004: 4). The effect of staging moral panics in the media seems to be the invocation of a protective state that legitimately can produce and uphold authoritarian power. While this may be true, another, and unintended, effect is that Malay middle-class families retreat into a defensive and intimate familism in the refuges of fortified enclaves.

In 2001 a satanic Black Metal Cult was exposed in the Malaysian and international media. The BBC on 13 August 2001 (http://news.bbc.co.uk/1/hi/world/asia-pacific/1489407.stm), under the heading 'Herbal cure for Malaysian metal fans. Prime Minister Mahathir wants to curb foreign music', reported that in the state of Kedah '150 teenage rock fans accused of belonging to a Satanic cult' were to be given herbal medicine. An official told Reuters that 'This herb is to stimulate the brain so that students can concentrate on their studies.' In the future, foreign groups had to submit videotapes of their concerts to the government before being allowed to play publicly. Mahathir 'criticised both rap and heavy metal music for corrupting the morals of Malaysia's population'. In effect, the state radio was ordered to play less heavy metal music. The official explained that Black Metal members recruited new ones through heavy metal and were 'accused of sacrificing animals, drinking blood, smoking cannabis and desecrating religious texts, such as the Koran'. Besides rehabilitation, the herbal medicine was developed by a private company to treat drug addicts and was 'found to be effective in stimulating their thinking'. This staging most of all draws on the elements of folk religion, with its reference to herbal remedies applied to exorcise evil spirits. It nevertheless signified a wider concern with the hedonism and moral excess of Western popular music. My informants seemed to have internalised these anxieties and on several occasions they demonised heavy metal and the black metal cult.

More broadly, there was no pronounced disagreement between the two registers performing proper Islamic consumption concerning their taste in music. Not surprisingly, generational differences were far more determining for the informants' preferences. The tendency was that informants such as Yasir would select mainstream Western pop music of his generation. This said, he would point out that he regularly listened to Islamic radio stations broadcasting 'Islamic messages and entertainment. Not really quiz shows, but more Islamic song (*nasyid*) and melodies allowed by Islam.' For favourite music artists, Yasir mentioned the local Islamic singer, Raihan, Sting, Boyz To Men and Babyface. Consequently, performance here works as a form of juxtaposition of legitimate Islamic taste and that which is seen as less acceptable. The worst genre of music would be metal music as 'it worships the devil in the way they sing, in concerts and images. It's not right.' Quite a number of informants followed the moral panic over heavy metal, rap and hip-hop, which could be seen as support of the harsh government line on foreign music.

In the local context of TTDI, the monthly *Masyarakat TTDI* (No. 1 March 2001) reported that a parenting seminar was scheduled. This type of education of parents should be seen as a localised response to the emergence of a national pedagogy. The seminar stressed the difficulties of modern parenting and how to address these:

> It will cause you to reflect on your influence over your children and whether you are the role-model for them to learn values and life skills from. Your children will be the leaders of the next decade. Will they be effective, productive citizens of the next generation?

In a subsequent issue (No. 2 June 2001), the topics of the seminar were outlined:

> ... parenting is teamwork; fathering is not just limited to bringing home the pay-packet and abdicating all other duties to the mothers. Children learn by imitating adults, so parents setting a good role model is so important. More time spent working on the job means less time for the family. Eating together at dinner time at the same table is crucial for family bonding, while weekend evenings for the family to do fun things can further strengthen this bond.

The dinner table seemingly holds it all together as the major symbolic object of family life. Historically in the American and British middle class, the newly invented dining room table allowed families to turn in on themselves. The heavy dark wood of the dining table suggests solidity and continuity, setting the scene for eating as a carefully arranged sequence, sharing more than just food (Gillis 1996: 93).

Informants in TTDI generally found that this type of seminar was necessary in order to strengthening the skills of modern parenting. On a multitude of levels, the effect of this grand naturalisation of the cultural linkages between Asia, nation, authority, community, family and individuals presents families with unattainable ideals of values and practice. As a consequence, strategic 'moralistic familism' instead becomes the order of the day. Novel styles of domestic life have created modern types of inner-directed and self-reliant personalities that have transformed the middle-class home into a 'Haven in a Heartless World' (Lasch 1979: 4) or a fortified enclave. In the seclusion of the home families can find 'ideological support and justification in the conception of domestic life as an emotional refuge in a cold competitive society' (ibid.: 6). The safety of this type of haven ensures that imports are emotionally accommodated. Money earned outside as it passes through the house is transformed from divisive, commercial, and competitive associations with the way it is earned (Carsten 1997: 155). Instead, it becomes imbued with the values of kinship and unity associated with the house, and above all with the *dapur*. The hearth, which was previously the natural centre of many Malay houses and kitchens has now been replaced by an abundance of kitchen appliances.

I now move to a discussion based on my reading of magazines. From the reading of these magazines it was obvious that over the past three decades the Malay family has been subjected to ever more calls for the production of a new 'familial–national' ontology. This type of idealisation involves the family as a forceful and resistant urban/suburban social unit that lives up to national responsibilities as patriotic Malays. The main focus below is on the way in which these magazines have been vehicles of a number of broader debates and imaginings of current interest in Malaysia. The construction of and concern for the integrity of the national family is a theme that is present throughout these discussions.

The TTDI survey shows that magazines are a major source of everyday information in terms of proper Islamic lifestyle, home and consumption. These were major themes that motivated the everyday reading of magazines for both respondents and informants. 28 per cent of all Malay respondents listed that as their primary preference they would regularly read entertainment magazines, 23 per cent religious magazines, 9 per cent family magazines, and 14 per cent finance/business magazines. 9 per cent read other types of magazines, and only 5 per cent did not read magazines. Chinese respondents differed significantly. 41 per cent of Chinese respondents listed that they did not read magazines at all. Religious magazines in particular did not interest Chinese respondents, and only 4 per cent listed that they would read these on a regular basis. Comparatively, Malays were clearly most interested in reading magazines with special emphasis on entertainment, religion and family. Thus, in the object domain of magazines, the whole issue of family domesticity in Islamic consumption seemed to come together. Consequently, I extensively read a number of the most popular family and women's magazines going back about thirty years.

Entertainment in magazines was approached from two contradictory perspectives. Firstly, as exemplified in the magazine *Female*. This magazine focuses on fashion and lifestyling without any moral or religious implications in terms of consumption. Excess in this type of magazine is idealised rather than demonised. A telling example of the way in which excess can be displayed is an article in *Female* (March 2002) entitled 'Confessions of a shopaholic'. In the article, a young Malay girl, Yani, with her hair uncovered, shops like mad, and 'the most when she's feeling down. And for some women (or perhaps all), the fastest and easiest way to perk up from feeling down in the dumps is to simply shop. Yani swears that retail therapy works for her.' In the article one is defined as a shopaholic if

> Shopping is your primary activity of choice; you have hidden or lied about your purchases; you have felt nervous and guilty about telling others about the frequency of your spending sprees; you can't differentiate between needing and wanting something; you spend quickly and freely without being fully aware of where the money goes. It just seems to disappear! Your shopping has left you in debt.

These few lines concentrate the entire complex of excessive consumption: overt display of material status; individualism; over-enjoyment; gender and generational conflicts.

Secondly, in the magazine *Muslimah* on July 1997 in the article with the heading 'Budaya berhibur. Suatu kemestian kini?' (The entertainment culture. Is it a must today?). The article discusses various scholarly approaches to the morality of entertainment. In essence, however, the article brilliantly signifies halalisation as a particular mode of conceptualisation and practice. In spite of these scholars' diverse points, e.g. that the material world is not everything, in their discussion of entertainment as excessive, one common argument runs through the article. Entertainment *per se* is not morally problematic as long as it is properly Islamic. The task is to creatively set up Islamic entertainment outlets such as sports centres and picnic areas. At the same time, it should be acknowledged that entertainment is not everything and that it must be balanced with Koranic teachings in order to counter typical Western entertainment. In sum, Islam does not oppose entertainment, but solely forms that are un-Islamic and excessive. Islamically proper entertainment could actually compel the creation of good individuals. To purist Malays, entertainment represented moral ambivalence particularly with respect to the location of entertainment. None of these informants rejected the thought or practice of reading entertainment magazines or watching entertainment programmes on television. Improper and excessive public entertainment to them was the primary object of critique.

Practical and moral aspects of child rearing were a prominent theme in many magazines. Even younger male informants such as Jomono said that he would like to learn more about how to educate children, and that magazines provided constructive guidelines on everyday life in families. Izura appreciated 'light' and 'generalised topics' in magazines, which could be educational for teaching children to understand the basics of issues pertaining to the practice of Islam, e.g. fasting and the Islamic calendar. Another area where Izura felt that magazines offered valuable advice was in terms of commendable or non-mandatory acts. The everyday performance of these acts, e.g. certain types of prayers, is explicated in articles and problem pages in magazines. Izura commented that 'If you want to perform these, we get extra points.'

The following articles in *Wanita* all testify to the emergence of the Malay national family with respect to the morally correct raising of children. The heading of this article (April 1983) was 'Keburukan tabiat anak-anak terletak di tangan ibu bapa' (Children's bad habits are in the hands of the parents). The proper socialisation of children is preconditioned on parental responsibilities in raising children. On the one hand, parents must be able to communicate their support, love and a caring attitude so that the children become responsible for both themselves and community. On the other hand, punishment should be firm because if parents are weak the children will disobey. Children should be raised to be independent; if not, they will solely depend on others in their lives. Parents have to work hard, and never let the children control the situation. The father and mother should cooperate when raising children so that when one of the parents scolds a child the other should support this, or the child will hate the scolding parent. Only through continuous work on gender and generation conflicts can the family assume its proper role as a truly national family. Thus, the social integrity of this family is not given, but emerges as an ongoing social project.

Under the heading 'Mengatasi masalah anak-anak yang mencuri'(To find a solution to children who steal) (June 1983), the argument is put forward that parents have to balance firmness and respect for children when guiding them on the correct way to spend and save money in order to prevent the children from stealing. These pieces of advice should be seen in the context of an emergent social consumer ontology gaining impetus in the 1980s. At the same time, novel sets of values have to be instilled, e.g. the value of money and balanced spending in order to become a skilled consumer. Otherwise, the child will resort to moral corruption and stealing.

Yet another article (July 1983) addresses the issue of praise in upbringing: 'Memuji anak-anak pencapaiannya atau peribadinya' (Praising children for their achievements or personalities). It is a myth that praising children will give them self-confidence and a feeling of safety; in reality it exerts pressure and provokes negative feelings in the child. Unjustified praise will distort the self-image of the child and distrust towards the parents. Praising is emotional and should be based on ability, achievement and effort, not on personal values or attitude. These ideas echo the wider need for Malay introspection persistently articulated by Mahathir. Thus, the family metaphor fits state nationalist visions of the New Malay.

The following article (December 1989) 'Orang kaya anak tak ramai, manusia tidak normal?' (Rich people do not have many children, are they normal people?) addresses the relationship between wealth and fertility, arguing that the decline in births in urban areas is due to higher levels of education, the social and physical environment and excessive lifestyles. Against this tendency, it is argued that the number of children in families is an indicator of positive family values reflecting the wider values of nation and society. Psychologically, children bring happiness, pride and satisfaction. Clearly, material excess is seen to displace traditionally rural and healthy patterns of family living in which the large family was a resource invested in survival.

The subsequent article (January 1991) 'Anak diupah supaya berkelakuan baik' (Children are paid to behave) questions the tendency to buy off children with e.g. desserts as this causes more problems than solutions. Parents should be careful and skilled in rewarding their children. In the article 'Anak-anak lemah tidak dapat mencapai tahap hidup yang damai' (Weak children cannot achieve a peaceful life) (January 1992), knowledge of religion and piety is essential to a peaceful and happy life. You have to follow the right way according to the concept of faith (*iman*). This theme is developed further in another article (March 1992) in which modernity itself is questioned: 'Membesarkan anak-anak di zaman moden membingungkan ibu bapa' (To raise children in the modern era can be confusing for parents). On the one hand, some parents' idealisation of raising polite and obedient children in an increasingly complex modern era compels them to overemphasise discipline without love and care, which are essential to upbringing. On the other hand, parenting skills have deteriorated in contemporary Malaysia because of work and busy lifestyles, so that parents grant their children excessive freedom while forgetting that one universal rule applies: children always emulate their parents.

In the magazine *Ibu*, similar themes are replayed. The article (January 1995) 'Bentuk nilai keluarga dalam rumah tangga bawa kebahagiaan '(The shaping of family values in a household brings happiness) argues that respect for gender equality, closeness, encouraging children to achieve according to the best of their ability, and individuality are essential to the happiness of modern families. A similar message is put forward in another article (February 1996) 'Ibu bapa yang jadi impian anak' (Becoming the ideal parents for children). Parents must advise their children as a friend would in order to help solve problems.

A number of issues arise from reading the above magazines. Firstly, that the family is subjected to a plethora of specialist advice ranging from psychology through economy to religion. The import of these expert ideas of the happy family posits a number of ideal models to be emulated in everyday life. The therapeutic aspect of family life is prominent in the articles discussed. More broadly, the articles take up central questions of contention in the modern urban lifeworld of which Malays are part: the rightful place of work, family, material excess, urbanisation and religion in the production of patriotic citizens in Malaysian nation-building. All these transformations are intricately tied to the production of the new middle-class Malay in a suburban setting.

Reading these magazines from 30 years ago attested to the fact that Malay families increasingly are subjected to moral national ideas and imaginings. In these discourses, the modern nuclear family is not given, but rather an ongoing social and moral project in need of constant attention from the state, religious and educational experts, and, most importantly, family members themselves. Moreover, the rise of a Malay ontology of Islamic consumption has re-signified the ideal of the modern urban Malay family. When the nationalisation of Islam intensified in the 1980s, such magazines truly came into their own. An abundance of advice attempted to identify and standardise the proper Islamic way. An example of this was advice to women about proper dress. Persistently, the urgency of maintaining family integrity is articulated. This construction parallels the state nationalist insistence on the urgency of nation-building. More specifically, the metaphor of the affluent urban Malay family comes to symbolise the whole construction of the Malay middle class produced by, and thus indebted to, the state. In all this, family bodies are constantly subjected to moral calls concerning caring, discipline and reward.

Above, moral panic in newspapers was discussed. In the Islamic women's magazine *Muslimah*, which was introduced in 1984, moral panic is a recurring theme, for example, in the article (May 1988) with the heading 'Gejala keruntuhan moral. siapa patut dipersalahkan?' (The collapse of morality. Who is to blame?). The majority of Muslims have a questionable moral attitude and it is the responsibility of parents to address this problem and not only through providing proper education, but by acting as role models. Another article (April 1995) in this magazine is 'Fenomena kaburnya konsep kemajuan Islam' (The phenomenon that the Islamic development concept is fading). For the few past decades of nation building people have put position and materialism before spiritualism, rejecting the existence of God as it has happened in the West. This is a critique of state nationalism and its desire for materially excessive development in e.g. Vision 2020. The argument is that material excess has polluted the ongoing progress towards authentic Islamic development.

In this section I explored the significant dialectic between powerful discourses and everyday life – popularised forms of moral panic and concerns in Malay middle-class families. This type of moral panic is clearly present in debates over malls in suburban Malaysia.

MALL IMPORTATION: HALAL, HARAM OR WHAT?

The TTDI survey showed that malls in 77 per cent of cases were the primary place for purchasing non-food products. Merely 14 per cent would go to local smaller shops, 7 per cent to markets and 2 per cent elsewhere. Thus, a wide range of commodities is imported from malls into middle-class houses. In other words, malls are particular forms of public space and their statements about décor, taste and class are imported into the privacy of everyday life (Miller 1997: 300). Malls have become dominant domains in the everyday lives of middle-class families in terms of consuming non-food, food and entertainment. Stivens writes that 'the behaviour of teenagers has become a site for the negotiation of anxieties about possible ills of modernity, the embodiment of parental and societal failures to produce the right kind of Asian family values and Islamic modernity' (1998a.: 70). In a sense, the ability of teenagers to explore the city and malls is a mark of maturity that may evoke concern in the eyes of parents (Chin 2001: 110). Concern and fascination with malls often evoked mentally elaborate explanations.

Yasir may be seen as the embodiment of *dakwah* purism in that he holds a position as Head of Business Development in an IT company that promotes Islamic values and 'content development'. At the same time, he is a leading member of a local NGO in TTDI that seeks to 'propagate Islam and to make sure of the delivery of Islamic information effectively over different platforms'. Yasir explained that his wife was the 'minister of the kitchen' and decided what food to buy, whereas 'Necessities such as mobile phones, VCR, normally I make the decision.' The purchase of these necessities is normally done in one of Kuala Lumpur's numerous malls. But the Prophet had warned against spending unnecessary time in the market 1,400 years ago 'when the market was just a market'. Yasir elaborated:

> Our religion advises us that when we go to a market we do what we have to do and go back quickly. Because the market is not a very good place. Things that you cannot see are there. There's a lot of Satan there. You should spend more time in places like the mosque, but not the market. (See Figure 27, overleaf)

Interestingly, the Devil, a.k.a. Iblis or diavolos within Islamic theology, retains a certain ambivalent relationship to God, his creator. The Devil is not absolutely anti-divine, but rather acts as an instrument of God (Schimmel 1992: 84).

Today, the market is a much more dense and complex environment that is also a social meeting place. Yasir's main concern with the malls, shared with many other Malays in Kuala Lumpur, is that everything is under one roof. The market itself, education centres, cinemas and restaurants are all there. He felt that adjustment was in its place as 'Islam always encourages you to use adjustment.' We discussed how PAS had addressed the construction of malls, especially in the PAS-controlled state of Terengganu. Yasir declared that PAS did not seem to be against malls *per se* and the consequent social illnesses because they had taken no action against malls or mall construction so far.

Figure 27: The Devil in the mall: MacDonald's Hell.

Shopping in malls is a constructive example of how proper Islamic consumption can be ritualised. Ritualisation can work as sets of practices that should ideally support the benevolence of the fetish against its malevolent sides. These rituals are attempts at transforming what could be seen as excessive consumption into meaningful and acceptable practices. When asked about shopping behaviour in everyday life and his feelings about going to the malls to shop, Yasir pointed out that malls were clearly haram, i.e. in malls all sorts of temptations and sins lurked. Most frightening, however, was the mixing of halal and haram; halal in the form of supermarkets and food courts selling strictly halal certified food ensured by government certification, bookstores and playgrounds for children; haram being primarily the selling of alcohol, but also cinemas showing mostly American movies that both men and women can watch together. If you want to go there, 'you should go about your business and hurry home afterwards instead of loitering around seeing things that are not permitted by Islam'. Yasir added that 'To have malls is not wrong, but mixing it with other things is wrong. These things should not be easily accessible.' Alternatively, the things prohibited by Islam could be located in a particular district after the European model, as has been done to a certain extent in Kuala Lumpur's entertainment district, Bangsar, in which a large number of bars, discos and restaurants are located.

This type of spatial differentiation would clearly be a demarcation of halal and haram spaces. He explained that when his family visit the malls, the primary purpose was to go to a bookstore with their young son. This by Yasir was regarded as Islamically acceptable entertainment. The moral contradiction inherent in going to the devilish mall seemed to be mended through the performance of a ritual that seeks to establish a distinction between immorality, excess and chaos (haram) on the one hand, and knowledge and constructive activities directed at the family as a social unit (halal) on the other. Thus, daily rituals create coherence in unconnected links of meaning. To Yasir, the mall is signified as a morally acceptable place through the ability of ritual and '"ritualization" to draw attention to the way in which certain social actions strategically distinguish themselves in relation to other actions' (Bell 1992: 74).

Performing shopping in the mall for knowledge related to social and moral education may legitimise the practice of crossing the threshold to a mall that is seen as fundamentally malevolent and excessive. Ritualisation in the form of selectivity and legitimacy produces a distinction between the materialistic or haram space of the mall and halal pockets within. Thus, these ritualisations order what is seen as indeterminable.

The theoretisations and ethnographies exploring ritual, its meanings and functions tend to be oriented towards religious or sacred ritual.[1] Ritualisation constitutes a way of acting that distinguishes and privileges practice against the quotidian – most often as sacred and profane. As we saw in the case of Yasir and his family above, ritual and ritualisation become significant through their interplay and contrast with other strategic and value-laden distinctions (ibid.: 90). Once again, the sacred can emerge only against the antithetically profane. This dialectic is mainly produced through ritualising and performing the morally accepted in opposition to the demonised and profane. In effect, handling most of all determines the social use of objects.

Binsar would go to both local smaller shops and malls. When going to a mall, 'First, I will buy what I need and then walk around for half an hour before going back.' Even though Binsar on several occasions mentioned that he always made a detailed plan for what to buy beforehand, 'Sometimes I buy other things than what I planned to buy.' The problem with malls, Binsar explained, in particular in the case of teenagers, would only increase when One Utama was expanded.

They will have an even bigger place to waste their time. Families and authorities should cooperate to prevent this, especially in this area where parents normally are busy with work. To spend less time with children will indirectly encourage this kind of activity.

This critical attitude towards malls did not, however, prevent Binsar from going to malls on his own or with his family. To those Malays performing purism, malls were excessive because of their plurality of choices, mix of Western and Chinese capitalism, and immoral mingling of men and women in restaurants and cinemas. In this section it is argued that family rituals can alleviate these concerns.

When I discussed the moral aspects and panic associated with malls with the President of the Islamic Youth Movement of Malaysia (ABIM) (interview 24 January 2002), he stressed the significance of materialism in propagating Islam. His argument, somewhat surprisingly, was to embrace materialism: 'People are coming back after going into extreme materialism. It is not a problem becoming very rich, but do not forget your social and religious obligation.' This is where the mall as ambiguous symbol enters in:

> We have all the best cuisine, boutiques and malls in the world, but you can see that the Islamic culture and identity is still around. We want to be the role model, the catalyst that promotes this model. The Muslim world has always been tainted with violence and mediocrity, but people look at us as a role model. I have this belief that there is no contradiction at all; we can harmonise, balance it. I like to bring my family for fast food. Just to expose them to this thing. Once in a while, we would like to go to Petronas Towers to see the best mall in the world. And of course we would like to maintain our traditional values in the *kampung*.

These malls were major attractions to informants despite the uneasiness involved in frequenting them. While Islam may have come to terms with affluence in relative terms, discussions over malls seemed to embody some of the moral panic associated with the whole way of suburban middle-class existence. These moral concerns were most pronounced in lower income families (Azmi/Henny) and among the purist Malays.

Most of all, malls expose teenagers to a realm in which they are left unobserved. Thus, teenagers' loitering clearly constitutes an excessive and unwanted social practice. No other practice in magazines and as articulated by informants is described as nearly as subversive. An example of a slightly more alternative view on this controversial topic is the following article in the magazine *Ibu* (April 1997): 'Lepak. apa pendapat remaja?' (Loitering. What is teenagers' opinion?) In the article, the teenagers interviewed complain about the boredom of staying in the home, the controlling attitude of their family, and parents who feel that, as long as they provide a material basis and education for teenagers, that is morally sufficient. This critique addresses a central theme in this entire monograph. Consumer culture is by no means limited to the excesses of teenagers even though they may be especially exposed. Rather, consumption in the form of material excess is a matter of significance for the entire 'national' family. Malay children cannot be expected to balance consumption as long as excess is deeply rooted in the practices of their parents.

Mahathir's account of Malay laziness and inferiority vis-à-vis other ethnic groups starts with loitering, expending any excess energy that should have been invested in the education of the national Malay individual:

> The number of Malay students who succeeded in getting places in universities is also not encouraging despite the vast opportunities given to them by the government. This is due to their own laziness, preferring to loiter and having a good time, as well as not giving emphasis to the acquisition of knowledge like students from other communities (Mahathir 2001: 13).

The heart of the problem lies not in the materialism or excess of consumption. Instead, loitering signifies an entirely unwanted practice that is neither nationally educating nor patriotic shopping for the state. A standard account of urban consumer culture infers that malls or shopping complexes are quintessentially commodified spaces. In Sardar's (2000: 123) vivid portrait of life in the malls of Kuala Lumpur, the commodification process is expressively spelled out as teenagers loitering:

> These are school children who loiter around looking bored out of their minds. In this jungle of brick and mortar, digital clocks and mobile phones, fast food and even faster 'rides', there is nothing real to hold on to. All experience is ephemeral; and there is no connection between what is said and done, what is believed and practised, what is sold and bought. This disenfranchising of the Malay minds from their own sense of space and time, from the folk traditions that enraptured and entertained them, is a form of self-inflicted colonialism. [...] The consumers thus become those who are actually being consumed. Despite resistance, despite the infinite adaptability thesis, the innate acumen for the subtle accommodation of multiculturalism beyond the imagination of postmodernism, the city is being eaten from inside.

Consumer culture is in Sardar's understanding materialism in its purest form: it encompasses alienation from tradition and the pollution of hitherto uncontaminated culture, producing superficiality, extreme individualism and false consciousness. The excess of consumption in the artificial environment of the mall dis-embeds the shopper in terms of space and time and inflicts a novel form of colonialism.

One specific discussion with informants highlighted moral panics associated with malls. For the puristically inclined, it was unimaginable to watch movies in a cinema in malls, where men and women mixed freely. This concern by far overshadowed that of genre or content in what was watched. From the quantitative as well as qualitative data I learned that these Malays held a rather liberal attitude towards e.g. violent content in American thrillers, and maybe even more so than in the pragmatic group that was more focused on content than spatial context. The import and viewing of these movies in the home, mostly on satellite TV or VCDs, legitimised the practice of this kind of enjoyment that in principle was clearly morally unacceptable to purist Malays. As a consequence, these informants were embarrassed to admit to the conscious consumption of a multitude of malevolent cultural residues. To sum up, family rituals of sharing in privacy purified and legitimised the understanding of otherwise doubtful practices. Going to malls was excused as either a question of pressure from children that could not be refused or of stressing that malls were also a realm of legitimate and educational culture.

GENERATIONAL AND GENDERING CONSUMPTION

The private sphere is a crucial site not only for producing middle-classness, but also the creation of a new mode of the material gendering of this middle class. The construction of class always takes a gendered form in that domesticity and households are crucial sites for producing middle-classness (Davidoff and Hall 1987). Consumption is an obvious aspect of this gendering in the middle class as it reflects specific gender practices in the division of household labour. Yet another side of the performance of middle class is that of kinship/generation. These dimensions of gender and generation in Malay middle-class families diversify and deconstruct the understanding of the family as a homogeneous social unit. In this section, it is argued that gender and generation are inseparable when examining Islamic consumption in the domestic sphere. In this respect, I am inspired by the idea that gender and kinship are mutually constructed and that these aspects 'are realized together in particular cultural, economic, and political systems' (Yanagisako and Collier: 1987: 7). In seeing Malay middle-class homes as social wholes, products of the unification of gender and kinship, I examine how divergent understandings and practices of Islamic consumption shape and are shaped by generation and gender.

Firstly, the focus is on distinctions in consumer behaviour in generational terms with special emphasis on moderation and excess. Evidently, there is divergence between younger and older informants, and this is mostly expressed in conceptualisations about individuality in consumption. Younger informants argued that individuality was the freedom of choice in the market for identities, whereas their parents' generation was seen to be guided by traditionalism. Maslina put this in the following way: 'The old generations – they tend to follow the traditional way. You follow the customs.' The cultural logic here is that culture and tradition coupled with material necessity and thrift produced a natural balance between moderation and excess.

To my informants, the almost universal logic of middle-class existence was that the previous generation was thriftier than one's own. Increased levels of income have gradually distorted any balance between necessity and luxury, which now more than ever is seen as a moral problem that splits generations. As an example of generational differences, Jeti brought up shoes: 'In shoes, my father can't see why my sister and me need so many shoes. And to me it's like different places you go to shop for different kinds of shoes. It has affected us quite a lot.' In this generational conflict, material excess has displaced piety. To the older generation, the expressiveness involved in individual choices and preferences signifies excess of and in the body. The body in consumption, then, becomes a non-verbal sign of materialism that cannot be morally justified. In terms of generational divergences, the inner moral body of the past is being transformed into an outer and shallow form of embodiment through the excesses of consumption. Contrary to the social-cultural coherence of the traditional inner body of the past, the outer body can be seen as transformative, contaminating, inconstant and destructive in the eyes of the older generation.

To younger informants, thrift as an effect of necessity is absent. Conversely, in the eyes of the younger generation, previous generations lacked a sense of class, lifestyle and taste. These ideas are mostly linked to urbanisation as we see in the case of Hazan. To him, the affluence of his generation had produced a recent culture of display, especially in terms of

167

clothing, whereas his parents' generation in their *kampung* in Terengganu were more preoccupied with furniture and decoration:

> That's what makes me different. The older people there tend to wear gold because of its value – you can take it to the pawnshop if it's necessary. But the young generations have a tendency to put money in the bank. So, my mom always said to my sister you have nothing, no gold bracelets, rings, necklaces. What do you spend your money on?

The imperishableness, authenticity, materiality and endurance of gold, and its moral and economic values fall precisely between the two generations. In contrast, the consumption of the young is seen as immaterial, transitory and subjected to ever-shifting fashion. For the older generation, gold was a kind of saving worn on the body at all times, whereas putting money in the bank may be uncertain in times of trouble and due to a more general institutional mistrust compared to the *kampung* pawnshop.

In the parents' generation, many of the above issues were of concern. Sardi drew attention to generational differences as a question of intimacy versus publicity. His generation will go for 'The personal, food and things to bring to our house. Food is always cooked at the house, to make sure it is our own taste. The younger generation they always go outside for things and fast food because they have the choice.' There is a world of difference between sustaining the body in the intimacy of the domestic sphere and the superficiality of public consumer culture. The body is subjected to a fetish-like image: it is composed of a benevolent and intimate core sustained by pure food that is threatened by external impurity.

The younger generation of individuality and luxury symbolically embody the artificiality and mass-production of the food they consume. These notions support the idea that modern bodies are signified through exposure to all that is external and pleasurable rather than authentically domestic. Another side of consumer culture among the older generation is the whole question of cultural continuities and discontinuities. Henny explained that her mother had started to like Bali style furniture because her brother introduced it to her. The situation is the same with Azmi and Henny's children: 'They will follow us in what we do, but then when they grow up I think we leave it up to them, their own taste.' This view, however, is not entirely consistent when it comes to clothing and rap culture: 'The youngsters like to dress up like rappers,' Azmi told me. Henny continued: 'I'm a bit against that, not too much of it.' This point of tension was obvious one day in the family's home when the two sons returned from Islamic school. After entering the house, they soon changed into hip-hop inspired outfits and dozed off in front of MTV.

Concerns about media influences and advertising were even more pronounced among purist Malays. Yasir explained that

> We're influenced by magazines, TV, movie stars. If they're wearing Gucci, I want to wear Gucci. If they're wearing Nike, I want to wear Nike. At the moment, it's all coming from America because they're so powerful. They have the money to spend.

Branding is the core symbol of excessive individuality and consumption in the latest wave of globalisation and American cultural imperialism. In this sense, the young generation is more exposed to consumer culture and branding effects. It is within the single individual that the struggle between secular and religious forces is taking place. Yasir asserted that 'There's no religious aspect to balance things and your lifestyle in everyday life.' In Binsar's eyes, the material and spiritual dialectic between generations was seen as the excess of pleasure: 'The young like to spend more on entertainment. We don't reject development, but at the same time we need a balance so I teach them morality and ethics. I have told them that wherever they go, they must have this balance.' Purist Malays contended that entertainment should be confined to the home, e.g. in the form of magazines or television. None of the informants within this group stated in the questionnaire that they frequented any public entertainment outlets, testifying to the fact that entertainment in itself was seen as excessive enjoyment. But when entertainment was imported into the house it was legitimated. Watching movies in the home, moreover, worked as intergenerational sharing and compensation for external 'lack' of pleasure.

Irfan used his son as the primary example of how life was changing from generation to generation. When it was his son's birthday, the son wanted what to Irfan were excessive gifts such as an expensive PlayStation. As far as I could understand, the son did get the PlayStation for his birthday. Murni had systematised the effort to instil moderation in her children: 'If they deserve it, did well in the exam, then we give them, we reward them, so we're being cooperative and flexible.' Murni elaborated, using the Internet as example. When the world changes with the Internet, the family also has to change and not just reject the Internet: 'But we control them. At the end of the day, the consumption aspect is based on values that you hold.' If not, individuality and excess will result in daring fashion and exposure of the body.

More than once, my informants explained that it was not unproblematic to reject cravings for these new and expensive commodities. Often children argued that their friends or classmates already owned such items or that the latest computer, for instance, possessed a distinct educational value. However, children are frequently excused because of their 'innocence' or ignorance in terms of proper Islamic consumption, which may be evoked to justify excessive consumer fantasies of parents. This aspect can only be fully examined in the sphere of domesticity.

In the eyes of many middle-class Malays, consuming had intensified after their children were born. Yasir, for example, complained about the wide range of things that now had to be bought. Particularly, food and 'eating exercises' proved deeply structuring for everyday life. Siti explained that 'Whenever my son comes back, several bills will go up because he is into the eating exercise. He goes for salmon, turkey. Different priority now.' There were preparations to be completed before these visits when her son came back to TTDI on a break from his college in Australia. Similarly, Izura stressed that food priorities had changed in the family in the direction of healthier food and that her daughter now was much more health conscious than she herself had ever been. Typical of the younger generation, growing middle-class awareness of health, wholesomeness, ecology and political issues filter into critical ideas of consumption. And in Irfan and Murni's family, priorities had changed drastically in several ways. Murni:

> In fact, the children dictate. Sleeping habits and even holidays we have to follow them, other sorts of travel plans. Any free weekends we used to just go. But now... oh, there's school holidays. So, actually they are the ones that decide. Even food, preparation of food, you have to plan meals that are suitable for them. I can't have too much curry or chilli.

These understandings all point to the transformation of food culture and eating exercises as a shared ritual in modern Malay families. What is seen as more traditional by parents has to give way to individualism expressed through a disjunctive multitude of preferences signifying the embodiment of excess.

In this way, children were commonly seen as embodying excess by inducing parents to import more and more commodities into the family house. In spite of parents' complaints, this import may translate ambiguous or malevolent commodities into something benevolent that can be shared and enjoyed within families. An example of this is several informants' doubt about the halalness of a candy such as fruit gum. This type of product is highly industrialised and may contain a multitude of ingredients, e.g. gelatine, that are not easily verified as halal.

Murni is here directly addressing the pragmatic Malays: 'In Malaysia there's a lot of Malays pretending to be Muslim, but they don't practise Islam in their attire, smoking, drinking, because they lack the values. When they lack values, they can't get values by learning the knowledge again.' For this group of purist Malays, the Islamic element in consumption is a crucial material marker in terms of piety and moderation. Conversely, pragmatic Malays claim that the externality of the material is only secondary to one's inner, deeper worship, dedication and commitment. In effect, the purist Malays in this instance are more preoccupied with Islam as consumption – the whole idea of excessive individuality and sexuality of the body involved in generational distinctions are explained as a series of imbalances producing a lack of spirituality and piety.

I now turn to gender aspects. I argue that gender and class at all times work together so that 'consciousness of class always takes a gendered form' (Davidoff and Hall 1987: 16). In a suburban context where virtually every father, and, more recently, a substantial number of the mothers, are absent in everyday life, this made the display of fatherhood and fathering urgent (Gillis 1996: 74). The gendered division of labour in the homes of my informants was clearly tied to divergent perceptions of the nature of commodities, their nature, use and proper context. My observations are supported by a sociological study on the Malay middle class, which concludes that 'while there is male dominance to some extent, there is some degree of balance of power within marriage in the Malay middle-class family' (Embong 2002: 86).

Not surprisingly, the dominant practice among informants embodied a gendering between 'soft' objects such as food and clothes and interior taste preferences for women, on the one hand, and 'hard' objects, such as electronics and cars, on the other, for men. Hence, the consumption that was most intimately associated with the body and its sustenance was typically the domain of women. In the case of Azmi and Henny, who lived in Henny's mother's house, there was a clear element of generational and gendering divergence present. The mother took care of everything that had to do with food. In Henny's mind, this fuelled elaborate plans of sharing household duties with her husband when they had a place of their own. Azmi, unlike the majority of male informants, was very clear in his ideas about the way their future home should be decorated Bali style.

In only two families was the otherwise strict division of labour tied to various types of goods and their appropriation unconventional. For Udzir and Nur, and Binsar and his wife, the buying of food and non-food was shared equally between them. Izura and Yusof reflected a tendency towards a re-gendering of consumption. Taking their own generation as a starting point, Izura noticed that in a gender perspective these traditional patterns were changing. The trend was that 'In Islamic societies the money is controlled by the husband.' The husband is the wage earner and it is his duty to pay for food and clothes for the children and the wife, and give them education. Izura: 'In this house my husband gives me the money to shop. I will use it in whatever way I like.' One of her daughters shared the earning and shopping equally with her husband, and Izura took this as an example of the breaking up of the traditional ways due to changed gender roles, education and the general development in Malaysia:

> My daughter and son-in-law, they go shopping together, make the decisions together. It's different from me. I will buy whatever fish or fruits I like. Of course, I will see what my husband likes to eat. So, if he likes that I will buy more of that.

What seems to be emerging is re-gendering of the object domains of decoration and food especially.

To the younger generation the world is much more fluid and open compared to their parents' generation, and even more so their grandparents' generation. Informants' concern with and desire to control hip-hop culture, fast food, the Internet, brands, mobile phones and entertainment in their children's generation reflect their own heartfelt ambiguity towards all these objects they invest in. Thus, excess in generational terms is a constant negotiation of culturally ambiguous objects that are deeply embedded in family sharing and simultaneously are seen as the root of social fragmentation and individuality. Not surprisingly, the purist Malays articulated their concern more in religious terms compared to the pragmatic register, while in the younger group Islam never really materialises.

None of the women among the purist Malays were professionally employed outside the home. Yasir, for example, explained that he preferred that his wife did not work outside the home even though she possessed the necessary qualifications. However, both Binsar's wife and Murni had each previously had a job. To my mind, this could be explained due to anxieties of exposing female bodies in the front region.

In the lives of the younger generation, gendering is clearly becoming a much more complex field. In cases where both parents are working, there often emerges an ideal of sharing of responsibilities in terms of the division of labour inside as well as outside the house. Moreover, a relatively high level of educational capital typical of the Malay middle class affords more complex patterns of domestic consumption (Davidoff and Hall 1987: 450). A frequent issue in women's and family magazines is involving men in the work and responsibilities of the home, and it may be this tendency that is being appropriated in the younger part of the Malay middle class. My impression was that in terms of intimising Islam in the home, e.g. decorating prayer rooms, preferences in and placement of paraphernalia such as Islamic effects, arranging religious class (*kelas agama*), this was mainly organised by women. Nevertheless, there was a tendency among purist Malay males to show an increased interest in translating proper Islamic ideas into the decoration and taste preferences of the home. An example of this is the quest for fashionable simplicity in decoration, which is a primary aspect of some interior decoration magazines.

The most general feature was the impact of the intensified struggle for social mobility most significantly manifest in new gender and generational middle-class identities performed through different forms of consumption. To the older generation, the expressiveness involved in individual choices and preferences signifies excess of and in the body. The body in consumption, then, becomes a non-verbal sign of materialism that cannot be morally justified. In terms of generational divergences, the inner moral body of the past is being transformed into an outer and shallow form of embodiment through the excesses of consumption. Contrary to the social–cultural coherence of the traditional inner body of the past, the outer body can be seen as transformative, contaminating, inconstant and destructive in the eyes of the older generation.

I was impressed by the number and variety of magazines my informants would read (Figure 28, overleaf). The majority of informants mix the reading of different types of magazines. In terms of generational and gender differences there were no clear tendencies. Younger informants would for example read family magazines to learn about and prepare for future family life. For example, male informants would read family as well as interior

Figure 28: The magazine section in a Kuala Lumpur mall.

design magazines. This should be seen as a tendency towards challenging the private domain as dominantly female in terms of child rearing, interior design and decoration. Moreover, in my own reading of magazines I saw a tendency for men to be encouraged to participate in and shape domestic life. In spite of this male interest in decoration of the home, it was mostly women in both registers of Malay consumers who would organise interior decoration.

A number of trends appeared from reading these magazines. First and foremost, the number of magazines in existence from the late 1960s, following a general trend of specialisation and individualisation up to today, has exploded. Today, magazines aim at certain target groups with specified consumer behaviour that supposedly is congruent with their class fraction. The segmentation, specialisation, diversification and transformation of the market are apparent in magazines. In the early 1970s, it was not uncommon to see Malay girls wearing bikinis in some of these magazines. This tendency changed dramatically later in the 1970s and early 1980s when the *tudung* became standard together with the *baju kurung* as part of *dakwah*. This proved to be a radical recasting and control of embodiment that set new standards for Islamically correct attire for women in particular.

Concurrently, expanding markets provided an increase in the availability of goods and services advertised in these magazines, including Islamic banking, savings, insurance, and increasingly more everyday products said to be halal certified. Magazines proved to be prime sites for investigating how different modes of Islamic consumption interact with new ethics of a modern Malay consumer ontology emerging and intensifying in the later part of the 1970s. In magazines, we see a concretion of the way in which Malay middle-class family living was subjected to the wider process of the nationalisation of Islam. In effect, the modern national Malay family materialised as a New Malay family. Thus, Malay families have been subjected to more and more calls for the production of a new 'familial–national' ontology. In this form of idealisation, the Malay middle-class family emerges as a forceful, loyal, progressive and patriotic social unit. Inside these families, however, the intensified struggle for social mobility as well as gender and generational transformations have all produced a type of intermediate family that experiences confusions and contradictions. Malls proved to be prime sites for the exploration of intentionality versus practice. Survey data indicated that consuming non-food, food and entertainment to a large extent took place in malls and many informants worked hard to legitimate their regular visits to these dominant and contested domains.

Divergently, generations understand and consume a wide range of culturally ambiguous objects that are deeply embedded in family sharing and simultaneously are seen as the root of social fragmentation and individuality. Not surprisingly, purist Malays articulated their concern more in religious terms compared to the more pragmatically orientated. Even though men in both political discourses as well as in magazines are encouraged to participate in and shape domestic life, it was mostly women who would organise and practise housework and child rearing.

NOTE

1   For interesting discussions on ritual in Islam see for example Bowen (2003) and Denny (1985).

6

The Excess of Possibilities

Moderation and excess are crucial to understandings and practices of consumption in Malay middle-class families. The central focus is the way in which these understandings and practices of proper Malay consumption may support, transform or contradict halalisation. Concerns with 'getting consumption right' have helped shape new forms of ethnic and religious Malay middle-class identities. Hence, halalisation and its contestation in various middle-class groups is actively reshaping modern forms of Malayness. Moderation and excess are constitutive of a discursive field into which informants plot their personal consumption.

In the eyes of informants, quotidian considerations such as thrift were prominent. Through thrift, 'spending is transformed into an act of saving' (Miller 1998: 62). This was the case with Ahmad, for one, whose personal thrift was contrasted to that of his friends, who were 'big spenders'. Hence, consumption and preferences depended exclusively on one's type and lifestyle in the spectrum of moderation and excess. In other words, the delicate balance between thrift/saving/piety and excess/investment in consumption is seen by informants as moulding divergent forms of Malayness.

The overriding significance of families in consumption is reflected in ideas of branding and branded goods. JAKIM halal certification with its state logo can also be regarded as a modern and religious form of branding in contemporary Malaysia. More specifically, Azmi avoided buying High 5 sandwich bread and preferred Gardenia bread instead because of its wheat content that arguably made it more wholesome. He explained that the family was very particular and would not feel comfortable with any other brand. Branding in food products was a question of being accustomed to

176

that brand, not a matter of 'high taste'. Interestingly, even the branding of bread follows the logics of halalisation. On Gardenia's website (www.gardenia.com.my/halal.html) it is stated that

> At Gardenia, a special Halal Committee is formed to scrutinise every aspect of Halal regulations and to ensure that all requirements are stringently adhered to. [...] All Gardenia products are certified Halal by JAKIM. Regular factory inspections are conducted by officers from JAKIM to monitor and ensure that the overall operations are following the guidelines set by them.

In milk, Henny chose Milkmaid for the family. Azmi added that products from Nestlé and Milo were of better quality than similar Malaysian products, but conversely the taste of Malaysian-produced Maggi Ketchup was superior to the international brands. Even though Azmi emphasised that they were not brand conscious, certain ideas and practices of quality and representation were clearly felt to be inscribed in different brands of products. Buying certain brands and avoiding others is an example of how consumption functions as reiterated practices in the body, which may be the ultimate purpose of the advertisement industry. Branding, furthermore, was in no way exclusively related to e.g. more expensive designer products, but commonly to everyday commodities of consumption in the household. As a consequence, any product, no matter how quotidian, can be inscribed with excess. Brands and branding have a strong imprint on the way commodities are understood and handled. Ambiguously, brands can signify material status, quality and distinctions on the one hand. On the other hand, they may contain malevolence in the form of being alien (and thus unpatriotic), and materially excessive (used for showing-off), or simply haram or indeterminable (impure, doubtful or un-Islamic).

Frequently, as in the case of Azmi and Henny, it is the smaller everyday commodities that were seen to be charged with Westernisation and excess – commodities that may not be easily classifiable and identifiable, and thus were objects of daily negotiation in everyday life in families. To Henny, Amway, probably short for the American way as she rightfully noted, is a worldwide company specialising in the sale of cleaning agents. The company has several million distributors globally and these are recruited by buying a certain number of the products from the person who recruits one. Every distributor in turn tries to recruit more distributors. Income is generated by sales of products by the distributor plus 'bonuses' from the sales of his or her recruits and their 'recruit-descendents' (http://skepdic.com/amway.html).

Clearly, Amway and similar companies symbolised US imperialism, capitalism and the values of the American way. Henny exclaimed that 'Actually, we should boycott Amway. That one is totally like the American way, but small things are so difficult to boycott.' Amway products seem to be inscribed with essential fetish properties. On the one hand, these chemical cleaning agents are effective and indispensable in order to maintain cleanliness and order. On the other hand, they are ultimately malevolent as an example of how US imperialism creeps into and pollutes Malay homes.

This discussion also evokes ideas of patriotic consumption, i.e. actively practising consumption that is seen as beneficial to state and nation. Sardi, a government civil servant for many years, and his wife clearly supported patriotic consumption. They maintained that they would always prefer local fish instead of imported meat harmful to the Malaysian economy. Two tendencies materialised through informants' ideas and practices of patriotic consumption. For food and clothes so significant for the purity of the body and its appearance, informants would ideally prefer local products first of all. Compared to imported commodities, local ones were seen as inscribed with far more national 'surplus', i.e. a form of economic and symbolic devotion to the Malaysian nation.

Moreover, informants in the purist group stressed the significance of local products in the context of government halal certification and the preference for products produced by Muslims or *bumiputera*. Consequently, the state emerges as an enormously powerful symbolic signifier of correct and non-excessive embodiment in the everyday lives of Malays. These concerns and confusions are deepening as more and more foreign-produced halal as well as non-halal commodities enter the Malaysian market. In practice, the state cannot possibly halal certify all these commodities properly. This point may especially refer to the fear of concealed and unclean haram gelatine, glycerine, emulsifiers, enzymes, flavours and flavourings in everyday consumption. A high level of technical expertise and an abundance of resources are required to perform the certification of only a fraction of commodities in which haram substances may be present. The other narrative entails object domains such as cars and electrical appliances, which are seen to be inscribed with more prestige, excess, and quality when produced abroad, even though most informants agreed that the quality of domestically produced goods was increasing. To informants, there was an element of national pride in Malaysia's capacity to match the quality of Western technologically advanced commodities. Still, Western produced cars such as BMW and Mercedes, for example, were seen to embody far more status, and thus excess, compared to local brands.

To Mascud, the covering of the body for Malays was an individualised practice, and one would not be penalised for neglecting this in Malaysia as in Saudi Arabia or Iran: 'Moderate Muslims allow their children or family to wear both Western or non-Western clothing, different styles according to your style and fashion.' Mascud's point is that the interplay between Islamic requirements in terms of fashion is flexible according to the social context in which they appear. This is precisely performance attuned to diverse situations and audiences in which the body in particular is the focus of display and covertness simultaneously. In general, Mascud was sympathetic towards and supportive of Islam in consumption to the extent this was preconditioned on individualised practices instead of mandatory requirements. Consequently, adhering to a rule would seem to violate the authenticity of individuality. Adherence to such principles would be religiously 'excessive'.

These ideas stand in contrast to those Malays performing purism. When discussing the existence of typical consumer behaviour of Malays in contemporary Malaysia, these informants invoke Islam as a discursive blueprint for valuation of requirements and prohibitions. Ritual divisions are called upon to demarcate sacred/profane ideas and practices. Yasir was the most consistent informant in this respect. While in Australia, he accidentally ate food that was not halal certified and instantly threw it away. He explained that while his family was very cautious, many Muslims were quite indifferent to these requirements. Elsewhere, Yasir drew attention to the different groups of Malays and their dedication to halal requirements, which he saw as quite incomplete and unacceptable. Yasir's ideas about particularity involved in Malay halal food preferences were elaborate, and simultaneously worked as one of the clearest examples of ethnic and religious distinctions and social boundaries emerging from the nationalisation of Islam. Yasir identified three main Malay segments in relation to halal:

> My friends go for halal food. They will only eat if they see the halal logo certified by the government and that the cook is Muslim. Top of the pyramid. Very concerned. And down the pyramid you have people who as long as they see halal, certified by government, it doesn't matter if they

don't see the cook whether he is Chinese or not, they still go and eat. Then the lower part of the pyramid. They don't care whether it's halal certified or not. As long as there's a word in Romanised halal, they go and eat even though they see that there are no Malays, it's not a Malay business.

So excess takes the form of un-Islamic, even un-patriotic, Malayness in distinction to the extreme efforts and particularity the pious Malay invests in his halal-branded food. At the same time, it is often rumoured among Malays that the Chinese, in spite of Malay requirements and sensitivity, may be using lard in food production and cooking. It is characteristic of the purist register of consumption that strict Islamic requirements become ritualistic practices that necessitate detailed planning to such an extent that these ideals are impossible to live up to in the everyday life of families. In Yasir's opinion, shopping was preconditioned on knowledge, especially in cases of rejecting certain products:

> You know that Nike is making use of child labour in Indonesia or India with high profits and paying no taxes. And violations of human rights. Genetically modified ingredients in foods. If you know, you wouldn't buy. Knowledge of this separates a bad and good shopper.

There are striking similarities between the ideas of 'green shoppers' in Europe and elsewhere and the attitude of purist Malays. Informants such as Izura and Jeti, high in economic and cultural capital, were quite aware of the introduction of organic food in Malaysia, and Izura often frequented a small shop for organic food in TTDI. Comparing organic food with halalised products, we can say that in both cases its consumption is conditioned by consumers' trust in its certification, most often by the state. In both fields, there is an apparent craving for simplicity and wholesomeness in production, promotion and consumption. While halalisation is intimately tied to the nationalisation of Islam, green shoppers seem to a larger extent to be driven by individuality and political inclinations that to varying degrees may be translated into practice. In other words, halalisation seems to be far more pervasive and elaborate claiming to be traditional in its own sense.

A recurrent narrative in the stories of informants is the vulnerability of Malays to the advertisements and material excess of consumer culture. Azmi, for one, explained that the massive influence from commercial television in the form of ads, series and movies is linked to American cultural power in particular, and this is coupled with a morally unhealthy credulity: 'Our local consumers, they're not brand conscious. They will buy anything that they see on television. Before people would buy furniture from a local Chinese shop. Now since you're in Taman Tun you go to *IKEA* to shop.' Many informants would go to IKEA situated in One Utama mall to shop for furniture and other non-food items.

These concerns with Malay defencelessness are especially pronounced with respect to the future of the integrity of Malay families in the era of uncontrolled excess and enjoyment. Mascud spoke of a radical difference between more traditional family values in Malaysia contrasted to cultural and material influences from abroad: 'We respected the old people, often the children are very restricted by parents. In fact, they scold.' These both positive and negative traditional values stand in stark contrast to the way American youth treat their parents: 'Sometimes they throw their parents out of the house. That won't happen here in Malaysia.'

The project in Malaysia today is to combine and balance these two sets of values. Binsar stressed that the influence from consumer culture and materialism can only be addressed from within families: 'We must explain why they shouldn't have or buy those things. Excessive electrical appliances, video game CDs. They want to buy more even though they already have so many.' To Irfan and Murni, Islam is most forcefully invoked as a weapon against the import of excess into families. Murni's major concern with consumer culture is that while many families now have money to spend as the country is developing, the 'Options available are much too much for our needs.' An example of this, according to Murni, is the production and marketing of mobile phones and computer models. The expanding market more and more reflected an excess of possibilities that was hard to control. This tendency was particularly pronounced as more and more Malays craved 'lowly' things. Another issue Murni raised was the question of gelatine in food, in this case sweets for her children:

> The government is allowing too many things to come in. Because I would have problems when my kids buy sweets and treats like that. I will tell them to check the ingredients because there's a lot of gelatine. They don't know. So much that we don't know what to choose.

The question of gelatine in food and other products is part of the driving logic behind halalisation. Following this logic, a shampoo can be haram if it contains gelatine made from pigs. This is what Murni reacted against; the strenuous effort persistently invested in detection of these haram substances. As halalisation intensifies, the state is seen by the purists in particular to uncritically support the import of impure and, ironically enough, un-patriotic commodities. At the same time, this group relies heavily on the state's capability to halal certify a plethora of commodities for their everyday consumption. Consequently, these Malays work hard to construct and safeguard ever more standards and requirements, as we saw in the case of ethnicity in food production and preparation. Thus, in the eyes of Murni, moderation is only attainable if Muslims acknowledge that

> The only way is going back to the right teaching. Many of us do not know what is the purpose of life. We thought life is for you to enjoy. But God sent us to this world with the purpose of correcting our faith. When we meet our Maker, we have the right faith. That will be the real life forever on the other side. Perfection of your faith in this world for seventy years will make you enjoy millions of years over there.

This literal understanding of the afterlife mirrors moderation in this life against excess in the next. Quite symptomatically for the purists, proper conduct is articulated through theologically evoked models and not as individual preferences or decisions open to negotiation. Again, the return to simplicity may be a full time occupation for a housewife such as Murni.

With respect to moderation and excess within Islam, informants would explain that ideally you should only buy what you need and never more. Jeti formulated this point in the following way:

> Islam guides how excessive my buying could be; it's a sin to be too excessive. And also a sin not to buy this or that when you have the money for that kind of thing. It's best to be in the middle. Being rational, waste is haram. Within your means and not recklessly, too extravagant, excessive. But at the same time you can still enjoy your life.

The balance between excess and shopping for the state on the one hand, and piety and moderation on the other is not easily translated into practice; there are grey areas of blurredness. Excess can be inscribed into any object and the way it is handled – from foreign cars and expensive coffee in Starbucks, to feasting on exotic dishes of barracuda or ostrich in Western restaurants.

I visited Izura and Yusof in their home on several occasions, both for interviewing, participant observation in general and for *kelas agama* arranged by Izura. In terms of economic and cultural capital, the couple are obviously more elite than middle class: they resided in a mansion-like house in a newly constructed 'fortified enclave' outside Kuala Lumpur, had three Proton cars, and elaborate ideas and practices of taste. Yusof surprisingly described the family as 'lower middle class'. Performance-wise the proper fronts were all in place. They were both wearing ragged T-shirts and more generally appeared to be laid back and unpretentious. Izura and Yusof repeatedly told me that while their younger days had been focused on material gain and career, they had now progressed into the realm of the spiritual. This particular conversation took place on their gigantic terrace in front of the house.

In many ways, the couple were the embodiment of the domestication of Islam. On another occasion, I was at their house for *kelas agama*. The religious teacher (*ustaz*) arrived at the house and the thirteen women present, who had arrived in their cars that were parked outside, were all ready for the class, each holding their copy of the Koran. The *ustaz* used a whiteboard for making notes in Arabic concerning the theme of the day – globalisation and self-realisation. The women and *ustaz* together recited passages from the Koran, questions were asked and there was a discussion before the session ended. Then the *ustaz* picked up his car keys and drove off to return two weeks later. The participants then made a few arrangements concerning their charity work and said goodbye.

In the house, Izura and Yusof had several beautiful plaques displaying Islamic calligraphy. Like quite a number of urban Malays, the couple had set up a prayer room in their house. When we discussed consumption and Islam in Malaysia, the conversation inevitably encompassed excess. Yusof: 'I spend a lot, but you cannot judge that I'm excessive or wasteful.' As an example Yusof mentioned that a prestigious car is wasteful compared to a smaller one. Some time back, the couple sold their Mercedes and now instead drove three Malaysian produced Protons and a Volkswagen. In essence, this is a performance of patriotic consumption. Concerning their house, Yusof complained that 'People say this house is big, but I say no, this house is small, it's relative.' To Yusof, excess can spur a kind of motivating envy: 'Otherwise everybody will only have a little, which is not good. You need that kind of thing.' Excess is obviously problematic in the sense of contradicting traditional piety, but supportive of state nationalist patriotic investments. Excess to Izura was most of all a question of Americanised yuppie culture embodied in establishments and brands such as Coffee Bean, TGI Friday's, Starbucks and Gloria Jeans. The family itself, however, had no problem regarding feasting in exclusive restaurants, which can be seen as a controversial and excessive activity within the purist register of consumption.

Later that same day, I went to the house of Azmi and Henny, a few minutes' walk from Izura and Yusof's previous house in TTDI. Azmi and Henny, who occupied an altogether different place in social space, would complain about the arrogance, excess and privileges of the affluent, and I could not help feeling that more different informants could hardly be found, who would, nevertheless, all claim to be middle class.

In sum, I have shown how a number of strategies are involved in working out the problematics of moderation and excess in proper Malay consumption. As a consequence, understandings and practices of consumption proved to be integral to various forms of halalisation. Diverse themes such as the excess of children; balance between thrift/saving/piety and excess/investment; brands/branding and shopping for the state versus imported goods with high status were all unevenly legitimated and practised by the two Malay registers of consumption. The more pragmatically inclined Malay register of consumption attempts to pre-empt the more puristically orientated groups' bid to standardise halalisation as legitimate taste. In spite of these distinctions, the commonly held idea that you should only buy what you need was an explanation that was not easily translated into everyday practice, but it played a significant role in the way informants try to perform a particular form of proper Islamic consumption.

I shall return to a more theoretical discussion of the concept of excess later in this chapter.

CAPITALISED HALALISATION

Islamic banking was a crucial drive in the ongoing expansion of Islamic institutions into the economic sphere in the 1980s. Islamic banking is widely advertised and marketed as the viable alternative to traditional banking. Under state supervision, Islamic banking is a cornerstone in proper Islamic consumption. The TTDI survey indicated that the majority of Malay residents here, 59 per cent, used Islamic banking while 41 per cent preferred the conventional system. Quite a number of respondents in the survey, though, listed that they used both systems simultaneously.

The modern 'recuperation' of Islamic banking is not necessarily a reflection of its scriptural or medieval contractual forms of the past (Maurer 2005: 9). In all this, interest (*riba*) is essential. Islamic banking and finance (IBF) covers a worldwide phenomenon:

> The broadest definition of IBF would include all those activities understood to be financial or economic that seek to avoid *riba* – itself a term of considerable

definitional anxiety – generally through profit-and-loss sharing, leasing, or other forms of equity- or asset-based financing. (Ibid.: 28)

As I shall try to show below, Islamic banking is often associated with a high degree of ambiguity. With reference to Indonesia, Maurer (ibid.: 148) provides evidence that while most of his informants identified Islamic banking as positive, it was simultaneously seen as 'unclear'. In support of the analysis to come, Maurer concludes that the paradoxical nature of people's relation to the state and state institutions, discourses and vocabularies is reflected in their ambiguous attitude towards Islamic banking (ibid.: 149).

Islamic banking has been a field where the state has promoted new types of businesses and institutions seemingly inculcating Islamic values into banking, insurance and pawnbroking (Anwar 1987: 3). Islamic banking must be in accordance with the teachings of Islam (Haron 1997: 1). More specifically, these principles should essentially comprise the prohibition of *riba* in all types of transactions. In addition to this requirement, a number of other principles should be adhered to the following:

(a) to engage in legitimate and lawful businesses; (b) to fulfil all obligations and responsibilities; (c) business must be based on their concepts of honesty, justice and equity; (d) overspending and wastage are prohibited; (e) wealth must be used in a proper and orderly manner; (f) to help and assist the needy; and (g) transactions must be properly executed (ibid.: 25).

Obviously, these requirements present the Malaysian and other state bureaucracies with the virtually impossible tasks of classifying, monitoring, certifying, and sanctioning 'unlawful' transactions and practices. The Islamic banks of today are the products of the Islamic resurgence and its aim is to transform capitalism in the direction of an Islamic foundation (ibid.: 2). In Islamic banks, as in conventional ones, profit is considered a crucial aspect, but Islamic banks should include social and moral aims as well.

The question is how these ideals filter down to shape the practices of consumers in everyday life. Three narratives run through informants' understandings of Islamic banking. First is the principle of exclusively using Islamic banking adhered to by purist Malays as well as Mascud, who argued that he used Islamic banking for moral and religious reasons: 'We avoid feeling guilty. Because interest is haram and God is cursing those who take the interest.' He felt that the system of Islamic banking was sufficiently certified by the government and a committee of Muslim clerics (*mullah*). Another argument for using Islamic banking was put forward by Udzir and

Nur, who normally opposed most ideas of halalisation. Not only was this type of banking in accordance with their belief, but they were also pleased with the high *Tabung Haji*[1] dividend that they received. A second narrative encompasses those who use conventional as well as Islamic banking because of loyalty to their conventional bank, habit or sheer convenience.

The third group of informants consists exclusively of pragmatic Malays who strictly used conventional banking. In their eyes, Islamic banking was a means to legitimise the politicisation of the banking system and another twist to deepen halalisation. Moreover, these Malays often quite simply found that conventional banking was a more profitable product compared to Islamic banking. In spite of this, Islamic banking has by now become the dominant banking system in the Malay middle class. There is an aspect of ambivalence in all this. The purists in general critiqued the material excesses of the state, but with respect to Islamic banking they fully and uncritically relied on the authenticity of state certification. Conversely, the other group of Malays time and again expressed concern that Islamic banking was merely an avenue for the legitimation of state authority. Islamic banking to some informants has the potential to mend malevolent capitalism while others contest these ideas and practices entirely. To these purist informants, Islamic banking is a logical necessity in halalisation. In principle, it would be altogether impossible for them to perform proper Islamic consumption with haram money from conventional banking.

A cross-cultural study of credit use and ethnicity among Malays, Chinese and Indians, respectively, showed that Malays and Indians were more inclined to use credit cards in comparison with the Chinese. The answers were found in the values, attitudes and practices of these ethnic groups (Talib 2000: 53), and obviously there was also the aspect of access to resources at play in this context. The TTDI survey showed that 69 per cent of the Malays held one credit card and 21 per cent two, whereas only a fraction held more or none. The figures for Chinese were about the same level. These figures, however, give no clear indication of the practice of credit in everyday life.

For Malay informants, however, it was naturalised knowledge that Chinese may be spending widely, but hardly ever uncontrollably or excessively. This conceptualisation of the Chinese other is embedded in two broader sets of ideas. The first is that Malay excess is intricately tied to and even encouraged by state support of indulgent Malays, who in turn are compelled to practise patriotic consumption or shopping for the state.

The question of credit is far more complex in the wake of halalisation. Only recently, the first Islamically accepted credit card appeared. Visa Card, MasterCard and Diners Club were the preferred credit cards of all respondents and informants. The Islamic alternative, the Al-Taflif credit card, was only used by two per cent of Malay respondents. On the Middle East Banker website (http://www. bankerme. com/ bme/ 2003/mar/islamic_ banking.asp) the Al-Taslif credit card was introduced under the heading 'Can a credit card ever be halal?' On the website it is argued that while at first it may appear to be a hoax introducing such a credit card, 'banks in the region are now making such seemingly impossible concepts a reality'. In avoiding *riba* and thus adhering to Islamic requirements, AmBank in Malaysia launched this type of credit card in December 2001. The logic of this credit card is that it lives up to the constant expansion and elaboration of proper and legitimate Islamic practice. This trend should be seen as merely one aspect of the way in which halalisation can only function as the subjugation of steadily more object domains that again will necessitate elaboration in terms of proper understanding, standardisation and practice.

While pragmatic informants with sufficient economic capital would unproblematically buy on credit, more disadvantaged informants were far more sceptical. In general, informants held an almost universal suspicion that credit produces excessive spending. In itself, the practice of buying on credit or 'flashing the card', meaning Malays showing-off in terms of buying power and credit in public was seen as quintessentially excessive. Conventional credit card systems would generally assume the symbolic nature of ambivalent fetishes, compelling all sorts of excess as well as providing the material base for shopping for the state in the market for class and ethnic identities. In the end, Islamic banking may be about controlling or purifying money: 'The truth of money is that it is (simply) a sign, humanly created, not ordained from on high. If it is humanly created, it can be re-created and remade into a human good' (Maurer 2005: 166).

THE EXCESS OF POSSIBILITIES, AUTHENTICITY AND THE COMPELLING FETISH

What I will do is select and discuss three recurrent key concepts – performance, body and excess – that have informed a wide range of discussions in this monograph. While performance and body mainly are discussed in relation to ethnographic details, excess together with the concepts of authenticity and fetishism are situated in a wider theoretical framework, as excess turned out to be a concept that produced more and more themes and discussions.

I have explored how the suburban Malay middle class was constituted and consolidated as an aesthetic community through a halalisation that was inseparable, on the one hand, from the nationalisation of Islam, and, on the other hand, expanding markets. As could be expected, among informants no homogeneous response to all these developments materialised. While halalisation can be said to embody new aesthetic communities, this does not entail a shared Islamic aesthetic with its own particular and normative rules to be understood by insiders as well as outsiders (Leaman 2004: 187). Indeed, the empirical evidence shows that multiple distinctions rather than a uniform type of practised Islamic aesthetic are the order of the day. This said, the legitimation of consumption in a vast number of object domains testifies to a rhetorical idealisation of moderation, simplicity and balance that was not, however, consistently translated into practice. We have seen that Malay Muslim purism and pragmatism are largely performed through proper Islamic consumption. While some middle-class Malays perform a more purist orientation towards Islam, morality, and the Islamic way of life, the more pragmatic Malays are more focused on individual consumer choices and national identity.

The *performance* of identity through proper Islamic consumption was embedded in a range of ritualistic practices. These practices strongly informed ideas of what could be considered sacred and profane as meaningful and workable everyday categories. Performance works as reflexive and strategic practices, and the force of this dramaturgical metaphor lies in its applicability along the axes of intentionality versus practice; the complexity of spatiality; and consumption of what Goffman called fronts as 'expressive equipment' that functions as the setting for performances. An essential finding gained from the fieldwork was that in the everyday understandings and practices of consumption in Malay middle-class families it was mainly the ritual and performative context in which commodities were consumed that formed individual and social identities. Moreover, performances seek to forge Malay middle-class identities by displaying proper and advanced taste that is religiously legitimate, respectable and sophisticated at one and the same time.

Performance appears to be of specific relevance, firstly, when informants, e.g. through food, signalled about classing on the one hand and halalisation on the other. Secondly, women informants in particular were acutely aware of how far they could take fashion and status within a framework of acceptable and respectable Islamic dress. In general, informants expressed extensive knowledge of performing legitimate taste with regard to different object domains and in various social contexts.

Simultaneously, performances may work under constraint with the force of prohibition and taboo shaping their production – e.g. the way in which Malay middle class women's dress in public is subjected to strict Islamic requirements as well as fashion and experimentation. Thus, bodies in performances reflect the conflict between individuality as agency and social constraint. Hence, different performances and staging apparently constitute the lifestyles of both registers of modern Malay consumption. Interestingly, in the eyes of all informants, Islam should ideally be internalised as a national–cultural consciousness or as deeply embedded beliefs manifesting themselves in a distinct lifestyle. Divergent forms of performances, e.g. in connection with food and dress, were crucial tools in the shaping of these lifestyles of middle-class Malays.

'Getting consumption right' socially in a Malay Muslim context has everything to do with the *body* of, and within, consumption. Thus, diverse understandings of proper Islamic consumption subject Malaysian middle-class bodies to new forms of order and disciplining. Bodies are always evoked in performances that endeavour to strategically contain ambivalences. Especially in the case of dress and food, bodies are disciplined by a multitude of moral sentiments. At the same time, the body of the Western, generational, gendered or ethnic other may evoke the whole connotative range of meanings of excess.

Buying certain brands (Malaysian versus foreign) and avoiding others is an example of how consumption functions as reiterated and embodied practices. Closely related to this, two tendencies emerged from informants' ideas and practices of patriotic consumption. For food and clothes so significant for the purity of the body and its appearance, informants would ideally prefer local products first of all. Compared to imported commodities, local ones were seen as inscribed with far more national 'surplus', i.e. a form of economic and symbolic devotion to the Malaysian nation – and 'national bodies'.

Moreover, informants in the group orientated towards purism stres-sed the significance of local products in the context of government halal certification and the preference for products produced by Muslims or *bumiputera*. Consequently, the state is a powerful symbolic signifier of correct and non-excessive embodiment in the everyday lives of some Malays. These concerns and confusions are deepening as more and more foreign-produced (halal) commodities enter the Malaysian market.

There is a world of difference between sustaining the body in the intimacy of the domestic sphere and the superficiality of public consumer culture. The body is subjected to a fetish-like image: it is composed of a benevolent and intimate core sustained by e.g. pure food that is constantly threatened by external impurity in the outer domain. While the pragmatic group claims that the externality of the material is only secondary to one's inner, deeper worship, dedication and commitment, their purist other in this instance is more preoccupied with Islam as consumption – especially with regard to protecting the body from what is seen as external impurities. In other words, bodies in Malaysia are ambiguously signified as an object of discursive conflict between Islam and fashion for the purist group and Islam as fashion for those performing pragmatism. Purism is incompatible with excessive and immoral display of the body. Conversely, pragmatic Malays often see *dakwah* attire as excessive and material without being a sign or proof of inner dedication. Both groups find the ways of the other regressive, unfamiliar and excessive. The visibility and phantasmagorical qualities of the body come into being as what I have called a new ontology of consumption tightly linked to the advertising, promotion and marketing of an ever-growing range of commodities and services. In all of this, bodies in Malaysia have been subjected to a number of moral, political and religious discourses. In halalisation, these discourses seem to both meet and conflict.

In the course of the fieldwork, I realised that it would perhaps be difficult to find a country in which the contemporary study of religious consumption, or, more precisely, the fusing of religious revivalism and consumer culture in an urban perspective would be more rewarding. The recognition that religious consumption takes on increased significance both challenges and actualises some fundamental assumptions and theories within social science. In other words, we can say that after having substantiated the significance of religious consumption as a field of study in the everyday lives of middle-class Malays, it is challenging to explore the wider implications of religious consumption in more abstract terms.

I have shown how the emergence of a modern Malay consumer ontology is both shaped by and shapes the wider nationalisation of Islam and halalisation. A number of social and religious tensions linked to proper Islamic consumption arise in this market for identities. Of particular importance is the question of strategically attaining balance and moderation against excessive materialism, or allowing pleasure and sexuality to provide the meaning and content of commodities. Removing the material excess of the commodity form has everything to do with properly cleansing and re-signifying commodities. In essence, this whole endeavour to transmute commodities is part of a wider fascination with purity and authentication. In doing so, these processes involve controlling the compelling nature of the fetish. The second coming of capitalism or millennial capitalism in Malaysia has given rise to ideas of a new form of Islamic capitalist reasoning. These ideas and the constant attempts to translate them into workable everyday practices, however, are continuously being contested. In all this, the suburban homes of middle-class Malays are primary sites for exploring the ideas, practices and contestations of Islamic consumption.

Any kind of commodity improperly handled can be signified as excessive in the Malay middle-class world. Several informants, for example, classify excess as the practice of 'flashing the card'. This idea of excess is precisely tied to the excessive handling of the credit card rather than the card in itself, as the vast majority of Malays hold one or more credit cards. Understandings of commodities hinge on the context of their everyday handling rather than their intrinsic properties. The point is that the effects of the commodity on people and contexts depend on how the tension between its imputed properties and its handling (either mitigating or amplifying these) are played out. In this respect, ideas and practices of halal and haram are essential. In other words, the nature (intrinsic qualities), processing (production method and context), and manner of acquisition (the morality/immorality of handling and origin) of commodities all determine whether they are classified as halal, haram, or indeterminable. These criteria are, obviously, open to endless speculation and interpretation. In the end, the ultimate meaning of these rules follows divine order.

Not only large objects such as houses or cars can be seen as excessive. Several informants held that to them excess was concentrated in buying pricey coffee in Starbucks or Coffee Bean instead of a plain and inexpensive cup of coffee in a modest local café. However, it is not the expensive 'branded' cup of coffee *per se* that is seen as excessive. Rather, it is the whole range of connotations linked to practice that evokes ideas of excess: enjoyment of 'foreign' products displacing Malaysian originals in an increasingly globalised market; unpatriotic consumption; suspicions about the haramness of products and their handling; the selling of alcohol together with otherwise halal products in shops and restaurants; immoderate display of status in terms of generation and class (yuppie New Malays showing-off), gender (Malay women frequenting what are seen as improper establishments), ethnicity (the Chinese are seen by many Malays to be more morally uninhibited and overly aware of performing in public life).

When excessive consumption is denounced as materialism, the implication is that it has subversive effects such as hedonism, pleasure and expressive lifestyles. Moreover, personal excess can be seen to be a socially unacceptable investment in individualism at the expense of altruism and social welfare (Ger and Belk 1999: 184). Proper Islamic practices of consumption are ideally socially acceptable, balanced and negotiated in moral terms (ibid.: 201).

The quest for balanced consumption against that which is seen as excessive is exemplified in Mahathir's statement in his speech held on 29 April 1997 at the *National Congress Vision 2020: The Way Forward*. Mahathir explained that 'at this particular moment in time what seems particularly pressing is the need to ensure the correct balance between material and spiritual development' (http://www.pmo.gov.my). Mahathir's ideas build on the contention that the actions of Muslims must be balanced between the present and the spiritual world, and that these worlds should be given equal importance (Mahathir 1993: 4). This type of pragmatic juxtaposition has been subjected to massive critiques from PAS, PUM (Malaysian Ulama Association) and *dakwah* groups. Some Malays are more articulate about this kind of critique than others. Mahathir's ideas should be seen as a strategic attempt at appeasing and pre-empting these critical voices. Helpfully, Mahathir provides us with his famous and infamous list of the where and what of essential excess. Relegating excess to the realm and body of the Western other, Mahathir (2001: 230) writes that

> Hedonism, the love of pleasure and the gratification of the senses, has gradually displaced religion and made it more and more irrelevant. [...] The relation between members of western society is now largely based on material gains and sexual gratification. Selfishness dominates in the search for these objectives. The community has given way to the individual and his desires. Inevitably, the result is the breakdown of institutions. Marriages, family, respect for elders, for conventions, for customs and traditions have all but disappeared. In their place emerged new values based largely on rejection of all that relates to faith. And so there are single-parent families which breed future incests, homosexuality, cohabitation, unlimited and

unrestrained materialism and avarice, irreverence, disrespect for all and sundry and, of course, rejection of religion and religious values.

In fact, all this evokes the whole connotative range of meanings of excess. In situating enjoyment and materialism in excessive consumption through the senses that produce the ultimate Western hedonist body with a nihilist mind, Mahathir crafts the ultimate object of otherness. These ideas are not, however, limited to Malaysian discourses of Islam, but seem to be fundamental to transnational Islam, which associates Western and especially US culture with excess of every kind. The paradox, nevertheless, is that while Islamic networks intensify through global communication technologies, and today particularly the Internet, the potential of this technology also confronts Islam with massive and baffling cultures of consumption. This, to some Muslims, is felt to be an unbearable pluralisation of lifestyles most visible in the field of consumption (Turner 1994). For example, the following article on the Internet 'Consumed consumers' attacks the perils of consumer culture:

> What is most striking about consumer culture, aside from its unprecedented ubiquity, is its celebration of consumption. The economy is our religious faith, consumption our orthodoxy. This becomes even more frightening when we discover that the targets are innocent children. This article attempts to reclaim our kids from a toxic commercial culture that has spun completely out of control. Children are innately innocent regardless of their belief system. Muslim children have a dual challenge – to knowingly miss the bandwagon of their peers and also to uphold their Islamic values. (http://islamicity.com/articles/Articles.asp?ref=IC0108-331)

More specifically, these critiques react against what is conceptualised as un-Islamic or haram consumption.

One theme permeates the whole of Mahathir's invocation of the range of Western excess and displacement of religious energy as energy surplus to the world of matter. Removing religious energy from the world of ideas has produced an overpowering spiritual lack or imbalance in the West. Mahathir points out that this imbalance is a product of the withdrawal of religious faith in guiding social conduct. These ideas reflect a particular reading of excess as being intrinsically material. In effect, Western material-ism unavoidably produces improper handling of commodities. The drive behind these notions may lie in deep-rooted fears of mass-produced commodities that are both 'empty' and plentiful, and therefore open to excessive pleasure. In fact, these assumptions about the empty core of commodities may provide the impetus for the entire process of halalisation. Central to these ideas is the urge to make Islam control and fill these empty vessels properly. If it escapes Islamic control, the empty vessel may become a vessel of evil in the way this has happened in the West. Thus, commodities in the West will always remain commodities and cannot function as things, artefacts or anti-commodities.

In Georges Bataille's weird and wonderful monograph *The Accursed Share* (1991) excess occupies a quite unique position. Bataille states that 'it is not necessity but its contrary "luxury" that presents living matter and mankind with their fundamental problems' (ibid.: 12). Initially, excess energy as a supreme impetus or overdetermination of all life processes radiates from the sun and must then be expended on earth. Especially in the field of consumption, excess is a crucial term for Bataille as 'we use the excess to multiply "services" that make life smoother, and we are led to reabsorb part of it by increasing leisure time' (ibid.: 24). Furthermore,

> ... there is generally no growth but only a luxurious squandering of energy in every form! The history of life on earth is mainly the effect of a wild exuberance; the dominant event is the development of luxury, the production of increasingly burdensome forms of life. (Ibid.: 33)

Bataille's central critique is of radical materialism and the utilitarian reduction of individuals to individualists in modern capitalism. Counter to the destructive processes of commodification in a profane world, Bataille sees religion and sacrifice as a field of resistance and opportunity. He writes that 'Sacrifice restores to the sacred world that which servile use has degraded, rendered profane' (ibid.: 55). The deepest purpose of sacrifice is always to 'give destruction its due, to save the rest from mortal danger of contagion' (ibid.: 59). Here, Bataille develops a central idea for my argumentation, namely that

> [o]nce the world of things was posited, man himself became one of the things of this world, at least for the time in which he labored. It is this degradation that man has always tried to escape. In his strange myths, in his cruel rites, man is in search of a lost intimacy from the first. Religion is this long effort and this anguished quest: It is always a matter of detaching from the real order, from the poverty of things, and of restoring divine order. (Ibid.: 57)

By restoring divine order in production and handling, commodities are re-signified as non-commodities. This sacralisation of commodities fulfils the need for the authenticity that has evaporated in mass production. Obviously, halalisation is all about mass-producing authentic things as non-commodities. The purist group promoting and imaging an Islamic way of life persistently made reference to authenticity in the form of the traditional and pure lifestyle at the time of the Prophet. In craving this type of relived authenticity, mass production must necessarily be re-thought from an Islamic perspective.

The local example below provided by a former civil servant in the Malaysian government is striking in its effort to identify and establish 'the proper' and non-excessive in Malay Muslim consumption:

> One of the means of circulation of wealth by the rich is through generous consumption. This is why Allah has prohibited monasticism and allowed good food, beautiful clothing, spacious houses, etc. for those who could afford it. It is also for this reason that reasonable and proper adornments and beautification are regarded as mubah (allowed). Islam however strongly forbids conspicuous show of wealth by having luxuries and further flaunting them to the public. Any kind of lifestyle involving overconsumption of unnecessary goods which have minimal benefits, or which do more harm than good is considered as wasteful. (Nik 2001: 117–8)

Obviously, the problem is the understanding and definition of luxuries and excess central to balanced consumption. Nik states that

> [e]xtravagance means exceeding the limits of what is beneficial in the use of what is allowed in Islam. The definition of goods considered overly luxurious depends on the overall standard of living in a country. In a very poor country, expensive sports cars can already be considered as too luxurious. In a very rich country, chartering a big aircraft to bring the whole family for shopping in London or Paris is obviously excessively luxurious. (Ibid.: 132)

Under the heading 'Luxury test', the Islamicity.com website argues:

> The luxuries of life open their arms for them. This perception is not true. The Almighty has created this world as a trial and test for all of us. Every one of us undergoes this trial in some form or the other. It is not that only the poor and the needy are put through this test. Affluence also is a form of trial. Here the trial is to test a person regarding his attitude towards the Almighty. He is tested on whether he shows gratitude to the Almighty on His favors and blessings. As such, since a person generally tends to forget his Lord if he is blessed with an affluent life, this trial is perhaps tougher

than that of a person who is put through the trial of poverty and adverse circumstances; in such circumstances, a person tends to remember the Lord more – or at least, has more opportunities for this remembrance. (http:// www. islamicity. com/ articles/Articles.asp?ref=RI0402-2211)

Walter Benjamin's contention, not unlike that of Bataille, is that the originality of works of art has been polluted and disfigured by modern forms of reproduction. Benjamin writes that 'Even the most perfect reproduction of a work of art is lacking in one element: its presence in time and space, its unique existence at the place where it happens to be' (1999: 214). However, the reproducibility of authenticity in mass produced objects, in effect, produces a differentiation and grading of authenticity. Benjamin's most vivid idea for my further argument is that 'To be sure, at the time of its origin a medieval picture of the Madonna could not be said to be "authentic". It became "authentic" only during the succeeding centuries and perhaps most strikingly so during the last one' (ibid.: 236). Instead of functioning as forgeries or imitations, reproductions feed on the surplus authenticity of the distant original.

In fact, halalisation thrives only on the surplus authenticity craved by some Malays while others see this quest as excessive, shallow, demonstrative and materialistic. These types of understandings powerfully echo wider debates in contemporary Malaysia over the nature of excessive consumption in the context of the nationalisation of Islam. Moreover, state monopoly certification of that which is considered halal is a concentration of symbolic power that flourishes only by institutionalising and standardising the surplus value of authenticity. Without this authentic surplus value, surplus is signified as what I would call 'a matter' of excess.

Revisiting Bataille, religion is simply the pleasure a society invests in the use or destruction of excess resources:

> This is what gives religions their rich material aspect, which only ceases to be conspicuous when an emaciated spiritual life withdraws from labor a time that could have been employed in producing. [...] Religious activities – sacrifices, festivals, luxurious amenities – absorb the excess energy of a society, but secondary efficacy is usually attributed to a thing whose primary meaning was in breaking the chain of efficacious actions. (Bataille 1991: 120)

Religion's fundamental claim to intimacy is, however, quite unsuccessful as religions erroneously 'give man a contradictory answer: *an external form of intimacy.* So the successive solutions only exacerbate the problem: intimacy is never separated from external elements, without which it could not be *signified*' (ibid.: 129–30). The point is that the domestication of Islam reclaiming this intimacy operates so that intimacy can exclusively be expressed as a thing if this thing is 'essentially the opposite of a *thing*, the opposite of a product, of a commodity – a consumption and a sacrifice. Since intimate feeling is a consumption, it is consumption that expresses it, not a thing, which is its negation' (ibid.: 132). Hence, halalisation is all about standardising the re-signification of commodities as things or anti-commodities.

Bataille acknowledges this dialectic in consumption in that man is constantly driven to waste the excess, and yet 'he remains eager to acquire even when he does the opposite, and so he makes waste itself an object of acquisition. Once the resources are dissipated, there remains the prestige acquired by the one who wastes' (ibid.: 72–3). In one of his subsequent works, *Theory of Religion*, Bataille is more elaborate on the ambiguous nature of the material in religion: he recognises the struggle in the world of matter between the beneficent/apprehensible on the one hand and malefic/unstable/dangerous on the other (Bataille 1992: 72).

In *The Accursed Share*, Bataille argues that historically resources in early Islam were invested in conquests and expansion very similar to the development of industry through capitalist accumulation (Bataille 1991: 89). The pious Muslim renounced any expenditure that was not turned against infidel enemies. But because of Islam's foundation and conquests, its meaning was lost in the constituted Muslim empire which 'quickly opened itself to the influence of the conquered lands whose riches it inherited'. Bataille sees this as a regression to the pre-Islamic and material tribal world opposed by the Prophet in the Koran. These ideas are strikingly similar to the discussion of the demonisation of the pre-Islamic past in Malaysia. Consequently, piety and moderation in Islam materialise only in the context of conquest or missionary work, without which it appears to be 'a tradition of chivalrous values in which violence was combined with prodigality, and love with poetry', Bataille states in a sweeping Orientalist manner (ibid.: 90). In essence, this was a culture of excess and enjoyment. Modernist Islam may be seen as a desire for returning to the authenticity of the deeds and life of the Prophet. Hence, the enormous fascination with the Hadith that can function as a guide to the authentication of everyday practices. Often, this desire for a return to tradition is evoked through ideas of the simple life – balanced consumption performed by moderate consumers.

Understandings of excess in Malaysia encompass a wide range of moral and social connotations. Malays often covertly believe other Malays to be driven by 'greed, envy, and malice and are forever trying to get the better of one another through displays of status and prestige and by attempting to gain control over one another's resources, loyalties and affections' (Peletz 2002: 121). These suspicions are intimately tied to the material and emotional excess of the other.

I have reflected upon the idea of the fetish in relation to Siegel's (1997) conceptualisation of this fetish as a 'fetish of appearance'. The fetish signified forms of power that cannot be appropriated, but are nevertheless felt to be possessed. In its power as a magical instrument the fetish is claiming a false relation to origin. It compels personal recognition of new and unfamiliar forms of identities forged in the perplexing excess of modernity. Commodities can be seen as 'things with a particular type of social potential' (Appadurai 1999: 6). In the following I examine how this social potential is translated into ambiguous conceptualisations of commodities as fetishes in Malaysia. In Marx's classic account of the nature of commodities it is argued that within commodities wider social contradictions are concentrated: 'The mysterious character of the commodity-form consists therefore simply in the fact that the commodity reflects the social characteristics of men's own labour as objective characteristics of the products of labour themselves, as the socio-natural properties of these things' (Marx 1976: 163).

In capitalist societies such as Malaysia, the fundamental rupture between production and consumption deprives consumers of knowledge of the true capitalist process behind the production of commodities. This rupture leaves commodities open to fetishisation as sacred objects 'in the misty realm of religion. There the products of the human brain appear as autonomous figures endowed by a life of their own, which enter into relations both with each other and with the human race' (ibid.). Hence, the malevolent transmutation of commodities into fetishes compels uncontrollable feelings and practices.

The changing symbolism of the devil among Bolivian tin miners after Spanish colonisation explains how the figure of the devil came to embody all the strange forces of the new capitalist economy (Taussig 1980). Contrasting earlier forms of the reciprocal economy, the capitalist system evolved as the object of miners' hate, fear and economic dependency. Taussig (ibid.: 26) writes that 'The market established basis of livelihood becomes in effect a constantly lived out daily ritual, which, like all rites, joins otherwise unconnected links of meaning into a coherent and apparently natural network of associations.' The new type of ritual worked out by miners 'reflects the ambiguities and contradictions of an economic practice that straddles two incompatible worlds' (Appadurai 1999: 53).

Clearly, there are parallels between the way in which the contradictions of the market and capitalism in Taussig's understanding is ritually worked out and internalised in the cosmology of the workers, and how particular forms of consumer behaviour among urban Malay middle-class families are ritualised. While Taussig assumes that capitalism and traditional culture are fundamentally incompatible, Malays performing purism in Malaysia work hard to argue, firstly, that Islam and capitalism are indeed compatible, and, secondly, that any incompatibilities precisely can be overcome by halalisation. In effect, the purist group's claims about this type of compatibility fit the intangible and shadowy nature of Malaysian capitalism. Islamic banking in modern Malaysia is a prime example of the fusing of religious revivalism, state involvement and consumer culture.

Fetishes in Malaysia materialise as commodities/things that are ambiguously signified and open to the inscription of both material and religious surpluses. As noted above, fetishes compel modes of feelings and actions. Evoking the thinking of Durkheim (1995) and Eliade (1987) in their seminal monographs on the sociology of religion, the sacred emerges singularly in binary opposition to its opposite, the profane. The constancy of this struggle actively produces the sacred as a dynamic and negotiable category. The sacralisation of certain consumer objects and actions that is taking place in the Islamic field in Malaysia comes into being as an antithesis to the profane, as discussed by Durkheim. For Durkheim the sacred is generated when lifted out of the context of ordinary, functional human use (1995: 38). Sacred things are protected and isolated by prohibitions and must be separated from the profane. Kopytoff's notion of 'singularisation' accurately captures this mechanism (1999: 73). With reference to Durkheim, singularisation works to mark certain fields of society as sacred and thus resistant to any commoditised pollution. In this sense, singularisation takes on the effect of the transmutation of commodities into mere things or artefacts.

More specifically, sacralisation works as a 'labelling' or 'tagging' of various objects and services as being halal or approved. Consuming these items may in the end produce a sacred effect or feeling of purity or morality against that which is haram and impure. Halal is a signifier that one adds in order to control content and impure connotations. Of major importance is the formal certification of these products guaranteed by the state and consumers' trust in the halalness of products. This arena of conceptualising and authenticating halal and haram is wide open to all sorts of contestation, exploitation, rumours and speculations. As halalisation intensifies, the standardisation and moral significance of legitimacy of Islamic consumption deepens and widens. The halal logo also fills the commodity with a content and makes it available for performance of identity – not unlike the way the label 'organic' also makes commodities available for identity construction and display.

The origin of the fetish as an idea and a problem has been traced to the 'cross-cultural spaces' of the West African coast in the sixteenth and seventeenth centuries (Pietz 1985: 5). More specifically, fetishes emerge in processes of triangulation between 'Christian feudal, African lineage, and merchant capitalist social systems. It was within this situation that there emerged a new problem concerning the capacity of the material object to embody – simultaneously and sequentially – religious, commercial, aesthetic, and sexual values' (ibid.: 6–7). Fetishes materialised in conjunction with 'the emergent articulation of the commodity form that defined itself within and against the social values and religious ideologies of two radically different types of non-capitalist society, as they encountered each other in an ongoing cross-cultural situation' (ibid.: 7). Hence, the fetish is signified only as a product of 'the problematic of social value of material objects as revealed in situations formed by the encounter of radically heterogeneous social systems' (ibid.). This deeply ambiguous image of fetishes brings to mind the emergence of how the whole process of halalisation was a way of coming to terms with, or Malaysianising, the influx of increasingly more commodities.

Pietz points out that 'The fetish has an ordering power derived from its status as the fixation or inscription of a unique originating event that has brought together previously heterogeneous elements into a novel identity.' This form of ordering is also evident in the fixation in the form of 'desires and beliefs and narrative structures establishing practice are also fixed (or fixated) by the fetish, whose power is precisely the power to repeat its originating act of forging an identity of articulated relations between certain otherwise heterogeneous things' (ibid.: 7–8). This invocation of ritually repeated practices is intimately linked to bodily functions and performances in everyday life. Halalisation is deeply rooted in the social, moral and religious context of commodities as fetishes. What is more, there is a tension between fetishisation (based on imputed properties) and performance (based on the malleability of meaning according to context).

The compelling nature of the fetish lies in its inherent worship of a false god/demonic spirit and in that it simultaneously was 'practised to achieve certain tangible effects (such as healing) upon or in the service of the user' (ibid.: 10). Thus, the benevolent part of fetishes can work as objects or formulas endowed with the power to produce sacred effects or averting and dispelling danger. The fetish may be inscribed with impersonal forces that should intentionally be inherent properties of the object, i.e. the power in the Arabic scripture emanating from the holy Koran. Even the powers of a plaque with Islamic calligraphy placed above the entrance of a door to a Malay middle-class house can be questioned and contested.

My informant Ahmad provided a brilliant example of such malevolent residues in a commodity. He explained that if he wanted to buy a watch he would have to be sure there was no cross on the face of this, as Christian symbols are not allowed in Islam. He brought out this example because he once bought a watch of the well-known Swiss brand Victorinox with a version of the Swiss flag in its logo. Ahmad's mother then told him that he could not have a watch with such a symbol in it so he had to dispose of it.

I have argued that any object could be perceived as excessive or improperly handled or displayed. Naturally, the basics of everyday necessities are relatively more unlikely to be conceptualised as excessive compared to more expensive or publicly visible commodities such as houses, cars or fashion. That which can easily be understood as illegitimate or excessive consumption is more likely to be marked or embedded in various forms of ritualisation in order to appear legitimate or balanced.

The performance aspects in all this are obvious, and staging excess as balance is intimately linked to distinctions between the semi-regions. Informants were alert to their physical appearance in public whereas practice in the home followed much more relaxed patterns. For example, all female informants wore the *tudung* in public as well as loose fitting clothes. Conversely, these items did not seem to acquire any special moral importance in the homes of informants. Performance takes on meaning as an essential 'practice strategy' in balancing the public display of status/

wealth with moderation/piety. Thus, the pre-emption of likely critiques of excessive consumption occupies a central position in performances.

Of special importance is the way in which the family takes on meaning as legitimating forms of consumption that may be particularly subjected to these types of critiques. Going to McDonald's, for example, was seen by the purist group as highly problematic ideologically, but was legitimised as pressure from children that could not be resisted. The same was the case with American movies or television programmes in the home. These were relatively uncritically watched in spite of parental awareness of the problematic aspects in this.

Comparing the purist and pragmatic Malays, the former are more concerned with the search for more and more commodities and practices to be subsumed by halalisation. In this respect, ritualisation is a way of ordering and classifying practices. Ritual practice thus works as that which possesses or has the potential of becoming halal. That which is seen as clearly haram, e.g. alcohol, is then exorcised as impure. Against this, Malays exhibiting pragmatism are much more relaxed and uninterested in these halal/haram distinctions, which are seen to be the moralistic trademark of the purist group. For this group, public ritualisation as sets of ordered and reiterated actions are crucial. These performances aim at generating a 'sacred' effect through the evocation of potential forms of authenticity. The pragmatists practise bricolages of choices, styles and tastes embodying individual and deep authenticity against the conformity of purism.

Ritual and ritualisation are strategies rooted in the body. Thus, the expressiveness of the body is deeply involved in performances of the self. The bodily distinctions produced by ritual come into being as social roles, which represent one or more parts presented by the performer. Deep knowledge of legitimate taste is crucial for the argument that middle class is a practised set of values rather than an objective category. The understanding and practice of Malay consumption is more and more focused on proper Islamic practice generating and generated by the nationalisation of Islam. The question of 'getting consumption right' in Malay middle-class families has everything to do with this understanding and practice of legitimate Islamic taste, formative of distinctions.

Distinction can refer to a difference, or the recognition of a difference, between objects or people on the one hand. On the other hand, it may signify excellence in quality, talent, honour or respect – that which singles someone or something out. These dual meanings evoke the previous discussion of excess or surplus. Excess in one form or the other (e.g. material, spiritual, religious or honorary titles) is embedded in structures and processes of distinctions. For Bourdieu (1984: 2) 'Consumption is (...) a stage in a process of communication, that is, an act of deciphering, decoding, which presupposes practical or explicit mastery of a cipher or code.' This culture of knowledge and practice works as a 'principle of pertinence' enabling consumers 'to identify, among the elements offered to the gaze, all the distinctive features and only these, by referring them, consciously or unconsciously, to the universe of possible alternatives' (ibid.: 4). Most importantly, my informants reflected on class and Islamic consumption through the construction of a wide range of material and mental distinctions.

To my mind, however, the trouble with Bourdieu's argument is his somewhat one-dimensional interest in class and class fractions. This overdetermination seems to prevent any analytical focus on religion or ethnicity, which would not have been insignificant for his wider study in its social, spatial, and historical context. It has been demonstrated that intrinsic properties may evoke elaborate ideas and requirements about proper context and handling. Therefore, Islamic consumption cannot merely be explored as a process of communication. Instead, distinctions materialise far more as intangible sentiments that are not exclusively extrinsic to the nature of the commodity form.

NOTE

1   *Tabung Haji* is a savings fund for the *haj* institutionalised and formalised within Islamic banking in cooperation with the state.

7

Consuming the Hand That Feeds You

CONSUMPTION AS THE PREDICAMENT OF STATE POLITICS

In this chapter I explore ways in which 'the political' in contemporary Malaysia endeavours to condition certain understandings and practices of proper Islamic consumption among Malay middle-class families. I contend that 'the political' in Malaysia is 'played out in the *moral register*' or in moral terms as struggles between 'right' and 'wrong' (Mouffe 2005: 5). In the last section I will show how modern rituals of the state may conflict with more traditional and personal forms of ritual in Islam, and examine the way in which these divergences represent different imaginings of the Malaysian nation.

Throughout this monograph, I have hinted at the effects of the state, politics and Islam filtering down to shape or contest certain forms of consumption in the private sphere. The ongoing discursive tension between UMNO and PAS in particular overshadows any other single issue in the censured media in Malaysia. Symbolic consumption in all its forms is indispensable in state nationalist discourses of elite and middle-class privileges and rights. Against this image, PAS, PUM and *dakwah* groups officially position themselves as true guardians of the faith, often propagating some form of Islamic state. This is an attempt at performing pious and spiritual Malay identities against materialistic infidels. The central question, however, is how Malays more generally understand these claims as models of practice. These issues are sensitive in the Malaysian context, and I addressed them not so much in terms of voter behaviour among informants, but rather in terms of how meaning was created in this discursive struggle.

Human existence is preconditioned on the interaction of living in both a private and a public sphere. The private realm can be said to have become the site for self-disclosure, intimacy and the sharing of feelings (Sennett 1977: xvii). In this way, the public realm has been destroyed by the way we overcharge the private realm with feelings of authenticity and sincerity. As a consequence, the city has become an impersonal stage for human interaction. The fall of politics is due to our own desire to transfer intimate metaphors such as warmth and trust to questions of power and allocation of resources. This is an accurate description of the severe feeling of political mistrust found in my empirical data, contrasted to the authenticity of domesticated and intimised Islam. These ideas seem to be of particular relevance in a suburban middle-class context and in ambiguous dealings with state politics.

In the home we reflect over our psyches and the authenticity of our feelings (ibid.: 4). Naturally, this has a strong bearing on the family; as it turned into a 'refuge from the terrors of society, it gradually became also a moral yardstick with which to measure the public realm of the capital city'. Thus, public life deteriorated and became morally inferior so that privacy and stability were only found within the united family (ibid.: 20). The anxieties and uneasiness with public life emerge in two forms in the ethnographic material. They appear in the form of anxieties, firstly, about the immoral city and the suburban world of seclusion against a threatening and divisive outside, and secondly, about shopping malls as essentialised realms of consumption and material excess. Sennett, however, seems to me to overemphasise the way in which capitalism has spurred the moral withdrawal from public exposure. In the Malaysian context, for example, it should be added that state authoritarianism is immensely powerfully represented in public architecture, planning and the control and censorship of ideas and practices.

To my informants, debates between UMNO and PAS in contemporary Malaysia were seen as merely the discursive staging of pragmatic power games rather than deeper theological or ideological differences. Several informants pointed out that PAS's performance of piety was not only false, but also unconvincing, dated and naïve. Jeti formulated this critique as follows:

> The image of PAS is not very sensible – their houses do not have any kind of furniture. The image is given they sit on the floor and don't have chairs. But most of the PAS people that I know actually live quite normal lives. It's a political game that people play. In Terengganu, they may be less materialistic because they are poor, but in KL I don't see this sort of difference.

These points are significant in several respects. Jeti's ideas point to a crucial tendency, namely that striving for wealth and material possessions is indicative of normalcy. It follows from this that piety and moderation are not preferences or choices, but instead effects of underdevelopment, thrift and necessity. Ultimately, Malayness and Malay identity emerge not as the rejection of consumption *per se*, but in and through Islam as certain registers of Islamically and socially acceptable consumption.

It is no coincidence that the Northern PAS-controlled state of Terengganu is mentioned in the example above. Terengganu works as a closely inspected laboratory for the practice of PAS discourse. Within state discourses in the media, the problematic implementation of Islamic law (sharia) is emblematic of the inherent contradictions in fundamentalist Islam. Above, we have seen how malls evoke different forms of moral panic. One specific narrative concerning quintessential materialism in the form of malls in Terengganu shapes Yasir's view of PAS. His point is that PAS cannot really be against malls and materialism as long as more and more malls are being constructed there – precisely as in Kuala Lumpur, where the government is constructing more and more monuments to attract tourists, he argued. Once again, political discourse is seen as shallow posturing that is not in any consistent way put into practice. Hazan was content with the government's ability to balance spiritual and material values. This feeling materialised in distinction to his painful childhood memories in Terengganu:

> I still remember how the PAS people treated my family there as government supporters. That's why I never agree with the way they behave in this country. When we invited *kampung* people, they said we were non-Muslim and we should be more Muslim. They isolated you from the *kampung* like you didn't exist.

This pressure on those who are seen as lesser Muslims is congruent with ideas concerning *dakwah* as the imposition of discursive conformity. Siti argued that PAS's crusade against materialism and their refocus on the next world appears to be fundamentally illogical: 'But if you're so poor, you don't have time to pray.' Material frugality is, in effect, anti-ritualistic from a middle-class position at the centre of which worship is exactly materially conceptualised and practised. These ideas parallel Mahathir's contention that Islamic prayer must be accompanied by other and more worldly values and practices.

Conversely, to some informants, UMNO and state nationalism is criticised for its overemphasis on mega-projects such as the Petronas Towers and Menara KL – rumoured to be favourite venues for state elite cronies. Azmi, supporting the Parti Keadilan Nasional (National Justice Party), an opposition party headed by Anwar Ibrahim's wife, felt that the state wrongly prioritised these symbolic spectacles: 'We don't oppose development, but we don't need mega-projects, the abuse of funds.' From 1974 to 1982, Anwar was leader of ABIM. In the 1970s, ABIM, together with PAS, critiqued policies of the government led by UMNO for being 'un-Islamic colonial traditions and secular practices which separated religion from political, social and economic issues' (Jomo and Cheek 1992: 85). When the PAS–ABIM relationship deteriorated in the late 1970s and early 1980s, Mahathir invited Anwar to become an UMNO member and on 29 March 1982 Anwar resigned as President of ABIM and joined UMNO. Anwar rapidly ascended within UMNO to become Minister of Finance in 1991 and Mahathir's Deputy Prime Minister in 1993. It came as a shock to most Malaysians when Mahathir removed Anwar from his post as Deputy Prime Minister on 2 September 1998.

This sacking caused one of the most severe political crises in Malaysia since the riots in 1969. A large number of Malaysians saw Anwar as Mahathir's natural heir, and he enjoyed widespread popularity. Anwar was accused of sodomy, adultery, bribery and corruption. This whole incident was politically motivated and staged (Peletz 2002: 258–61). Particularly incriminating were the implications of immoderate and excessive misuse of power by an elected official such as Anwar. During the trial, extreme cultural transgressions in the form of sex slavery, group sex and incest surfaced in the media in a hitherto unseen manner. The Anwar case seemed to reinforce my informants' critique of the lack of authenticity in Malaysian politics, UMNO and Mahathir in particular.

In the wake of the political crisis caused by the Anwar case of 1998–9, a new form of Malay vernacular political literature emerged (Noor 2001: 407). This type of *Reformasi* discourse attacked what it saw as the moral decline of politics, secular elites, religion and nation (ibid.: 408). This body of literature constantly feeds into and is fed by gossip and rumour, mapping movements of political elite factions (ibid.: 412). In this popularised genre of literature

> ... we see how a political, economic and structural crisis has been radically
> recontextualised and reconstructed from an Islamist viewpoint as a deeper

crisis that strikes right at the heart of the social and cultural fabric of contemporary Malay society. Here we can also see the politics of memory at work where images, motifs, characters and a vocabulary from an Islamic past are brought into play to serve as a backdrop to the conflict at present. (Ibid.: 413)

A deep-rooted lack of confidence in the public politics of Islam has brought the family as a metaphor of sincerity and authenticity to the forefront in modern Malay imaginings. The recurrent phrase 'It's just politics' signified shallowness, so markedly different from the world of the private sphere. The informants Irfan and Murni accurately captured the distrust of political life. They argued that PAS as well as UMNO misunderstood the teachings of the Prophet and the Holy Book and thus the oneness and *umma* of Malay Muslims. The main concern expressed by Murni was this:

What saddens me is it breaks the family. We have families, PAS and UMNO, and they conflict. Brothers should have a close talk, but because of politics, they just break. They are not fighting about religion, actually. They're fighting about politics.

The logic in this is that the impurity of politics pollutes the purity of Islam, and the national itself. These ideas are in themselves a driving force behind the processes I have described as the domestication of Islam or cultural intimacy. At the same time, the national family has now become a powerful metaphor that signifies the natural core of the Malaysian nation. This cultural and historical type of nation is far more resilient and naturalised in its folk-imagined version than any political nationalism. A clear tendency in the above discussion is that informants indirectly articulated loyalties through a critique of the political, far more than expressing direct support of one party or ideology. To informants, politics in Malaysia remains impure power struggles that strategically make reference to certain inauthentic interpretations of Islam. Distinguishing between the two Malay registers of consumption, there was surprisingly little divergence, as they both seemed disappointed with the pragmatics of power politics.

One month after the 9/11 bombings in the US and my arrival in Kuala Lumpur, I was in the PAS-influenced Al-Mujahideen mosque, situated between TTDI and One Utama mall, looking at an announcement that encouraged boycotting American goods because of the war in Afghanistan and American support of Israeli/US oppression of the Palestinians. The global economic downturn and insecurity following 9/11 moderated consumer sentiments in Malaysia and the government launched a campaign in the media aimed at boosting the consumption of domestically produced goods especially. My fieldwork allowed me to examine this question in depth among the informants. The purists were, not surprisingly, more inclined to support the call to boycott, and simultaneously discursively rejected the state's encouragement to increase spending. For example, Binsar made clear that boycotting was morally imperative because of

> ... what the Americans have done to the Afghans. Personally, I boycott American goods, but it's hard for me to ask my family to follow what I do. Because, you know, the children they love to go to McDonald's or Kentucky Fried Chicken. I try to tell them about Coca-Cola. It's not good, but it's very hard to boycott because our government is dependent on more and more investments from America.

In this purist group, however, the performance of individual identities of boycotting and consumption stands in contrast to actual family practices. Their idealisation of a non-materialistic lifestyle is not directly reflected in clear-cut practices of boycotting and modest consumption. Thus, while these Malays articulate or stage a fascination with and a modelling of the pious lifestyle of the Prophet as described in the Hadith, the embodiment of the Islamic way of life is unattainable and almost impossible to put into practice.

Turning to the pragmatic group of informants, I can say that regarding boycotting the discursive aspects are downplayed and this is reflected in a much more relaxed and individualised attitude towards boycotting and consumption. As in the case of the encouragement to spend, informants evoke their individual consumer choices, pragmatism and issues of national identity in debates over consumption and boycotting. In sum, divergences between these two groups of middle-class Malays are products of performed distinctions rather than actual practice.

These tendencies are reflected in the media consumption of the informants. State nationalist ideology is at work in newspapers and television, and the Internet has emerged as a major source of alternative information. Newspapers in Malaysia have been primary vehicles of UMNO political discourse and control. Newspapers are cultural texts in which the state and 'the public' are represented (Gupta 1995: 377). With respect to major newspapers in Malaysia, these were all owned or dominated by BN interest groups. Moreover, newspapers comprise a major market for advertisement.

Statistically, I found that the English-language papers *The Star* (27 per cent) and the *NST* (20 per cent) were favourites with Malay respondents, followed by *Utusan Malaysia* (18 per cent) and *Berita Harian* (14 per cent) in Bahasa Malaysia. 7 per cent listed that they read the printed version of the PAS-supported *Harakah* newspaper on a regular basis.

The controversial question of whether Malaysia should become an Islamic state was a favourite state nationalist topic in these newspapers. This issue was particularly suitable for portraying PAS as a party of waning traditionalists. For pragmatic and purist informants alike, this topic caused confusion rather than clear-cut ideology. Unsurprisingly, Malays in the purist group were friendlier to the idea of setting up an Islamic state in Malaysia, but regrettably knew of no workable formula that could be adapted to Malaysia. To Siti, the ongoing struggle between the government and the opposition has produced radical doubt. Reflecting the view of the entire group of informants, she explained that 'If the government says A, the other side will surely say B. Why buy the paper then?' In the eyes of Siti, *Harakah* was nonsense because it was an unreliable source with the singular purpose to undermine and destabilise state authority.

Most informants, however, would turn to *Harakah* as a source of alternative and 'unbiased' information. Azmi pointed to the fact that the *NST*, *Berita Harian* and *The Sun* all were government-dominated newspapers, which the government had shares in whereas *Harakah* was considered more 'neutral' and 'independent'.

Likewise, Yasir bought *Harakah* because it was a more 'political' newspaper, the sole main paper voicing their thoughts openly. Compared to all other papers, *Harakah* and its Internet version HarakahDaily.net stood out as credible alternatives. Hazan felt that there was no actual choice ideology-wise because of government control. In this way, the reading of newspapers, informants explained, is a practice that requires selectivity, critical sense and empathy. Hazan argued that you should know how to interpret the content. When they say 'no' it's probably 'yes'. And 'yes' is probably 'no'. Consequently, you have to interpret by yourself and discuss with friends. Hazan was strongly opposed to PAS and *Harakah*:

> I don't really read or know about *Harakah*. Don't really follow *Harakah*. But sometimes I do read *Harakah*. It was good, actually. It gives you another perception of news. Different in the sense of content and how you tell a story, an untold story, it is often exaggerated.

Even though Hazan supported the government, he found some of the rumours and gossip in *Harakah* interesting, and maybe even more credible compared to what can be read in the other papers. During the Anwar Ibrahim trial, Hazan, like many other Malaysians, turned to *Harakah*. Jeti explained that the journalistic approach determined her choice in newspaper. Her favourite paper was *NST*, and she especially liked the world section. In Jeti's opinion *NST* had started only quoting certain people and replacing it with the 'other side of the story' when the Anwar Ibrahim trial unfolded. So she stopped buying *NST*: 'It was constantly justifying what the government is doing even though any person who doesn't have to study law would know that the case is not going on correctly.' Conversely, *Harakah* appeared to be 'more clear even though they don't deal with all subjects and they can be quite conservative as in the debate over an Islamic state. What I really like is that everybody can write in and they print it even if we disagree.'

In general, there is a high level of mistrust involved in newspaper reading. The credibility crisis animates most informants to read several newspapers in order to minutely compare how different issues are presented or misrepresented. Little ideology is involved in newspaper preferences. In its massive critique of the state and censorship, *Harakah* stands out as a pragmatic alternative appealing to the majority of informants.

Many of the above tendencies are similarly involved in television viewing. I contend that the pervasive state presence in national television has a quite unintended effect: a deep-rooted mistrust in the way in which the state stages and performs politics in the local media. Indeed, the state's presence in the local media has backfired so that the state itself, instead of the targeted Western other, has become the object of intense critique by the Malaysian middle class. On national television in Malaysia, praying for prosperity has actively linked Islam, wealth and national progress, all hopefully concentrated in the New Malay (Ong 1999: 204–5). In television programming, the effects of the nationalisation of Islam are strongly felt. Malaysian television programmes have been flavoured by Middle Eastern influences through statements in a number of programmes attempting to identify local viewers with the wider Muslim world (Riddell 2001: 310).

Only in 1996 was Malaysia's first communication satellite, Astro, set in orbit, meaning that the population nationally could access international television and radio stations, the Internet and multimedia technology. In 2001, Astro had more than one million Malaysian subscribers, presumably because of its wide selection of national and international channels. My TTDI survey showed that on average the Malay families had 1.6 television sets per household. In spite of the purists' elaborate critique of the dangers involved in subscribing to Astro, there was no general evidence that these Malays, compared to the pragmatists, would be less inclined to subscribe.

Malay traditionalism and national censorship were the major causes of a critique of local television programming in the lives of the informants. When discussing her preferences in television channels, Jeti was particularly serene about what to avoid: 'I don't watch Malay drama because it's Malay, the quality is bad, and it doesn't fulfil Malay life. Love stories, marriages where the woman always suffers. I think it's also chauvinistic.' Instead, her preference was Chinese movies. Jeti chose CNN and BBC, and 'underground circulation' on the Internet, as I shall return to shortly, to avoid media censorship. Likewise, Azmi felt that restrictions in the media were severe to an extent that even the selection on *Astro* was too narrow, repetitive and expensive. When Astro was first introduced, Azmi recollected, everybody was excited, but soon the family realised that Astro spoiled the children, who would be watching excessively. Nevertheless, the family had two television sets and two decoders. In comparison with BBC and CNN, the local channels were seen as appalling: 'We shift the channel when Mahathir appears.' This disgust with Mahathir, however, had to be contained in the home as Azmi was 'lobbying' for government jobs and pretended to be neutral.

Television as a medium for communicating about Islam was an issue touched upon by several informants. 'Question and answer' formats on television were popular and in these programmes questions addressing everyday-life problems of conduct, appearance and morality were brought forward. Informants, however, were divided on the question of the educational value of these programmes. As expected, the younger generation preferred more trendy channels. Gender-wise, male informants were fixed on sports, which strongly guided their selection of Astro.

Through the concentration of 'informational capital', the state tries to impose mental structures and 'common principles of vision and division' (Bourdieu 1999: 61). This attempt is obvious in the censorship of newspapers and national television, but not necessarily successful or pervasive.

Against this concentration of informational capital with the state, heavily critiqued by all informants alike, my quantitative and qualitative data show that today the Internet has become an immensely popular alternative. The survey data showed that the average Malay family in TTDI owned at least one computer. Informants would all use the Internet on a daily basis for different purposes. While one group of informants merely use the Internet to acquire general information in relation to work, entertainment, religion or studies, the second group is also oriented towards using the Internet to acquire what they call unbiased and alternative information in the Malaysian censorship context of Islam, politics and oppositional views.

The Internet may enable Muslims to plug into cosmopolitan networks of Islam, which reproduce the properly Islamic as invocations or as sets of signifiers of religion as culture. As a consequence, Islam in cyberspace materialises as a global Muslim property open to a diverse global audience – especially after 9/11, which put an emphasis on Islamic ethics at a global level. Sites such as HarakahDaily.net and a multitude of transnational ones are accessed on a daily basis, and often because they can provide straightforward answers to a multitude of everyday questions and confusions. Informants expressed that it was a quite different feeling to access sites on which they were not compelled to continuously interpret and read between the lines as in the national media context.

Interestingly, there were no significant divergences in terms of the accessibility of various middle class, ethnic, gender and generation groups to the Internet. Moreover, both registers of Malay consumers understood and practised the Internet in similar ways. By now, the computer and Internet access have become standard equipment in Malaysian middle-class homes. Obviously, the intimacy of these homes provides a safe context for accessing information that in official discourses is considered unpatriotic and subversive. This fact opens up a whole range of new modes of cultural intimacy as that which can be kept out of the public gaze with regard to entertainment, politics and religion. I have tried to show that to informants no workable political ideology is in existence. In general, there was heartfelt mistrust in what was seen as the shallowness, pragmatism and immorality of Malaysian politics.

In conclusion, neither state nationalism nor globalism in Malaysia has in any way erased other and competing forms of nationness or national identity. Rather, multiple mass-mediated nationalisms coexist with other types of nationalist identities. Consequently, 'mass media are a potent force in educating people about different nationalities and nationalisms' (Wilk 1993: 295). The ongoing struggle between UMNO, PAS and various *dakwah* groups did not take on an ideological character with informants, but rather these struggles were seen as discursive stagings of pragmatic power games. PAS's performance of piety, for example, was, in effect, understood as nothing but sheer performance to reach political ends – political disputes that polluted religion and caused Malay middle-class families to legitimate a personalised and domesticated form of Islam.

THE POWER OF RITUAL

I now deal with the question of how forms of Islamic ritualisation in domesticity or 'community spaces' can challenge the public spectacles of the state. The influx of new Islamic ideas and practices seems to be particularly appealing to the Malay middle class. As these new forms of religious practice are fundamentally private, they are out of the gaze of the state, and thus seen by the state as deviationist in nature. I argue that nation-building processes in Malaysia are strongly informed by distinct types of modern ritualisation. In the eyes of state nationalism, the excess of certain forms of traditional Islamic rituals is depriving 'the national' of its energy or surplus. Halalisation has proved to be a new field of dominance in which the state tries to concentrate its power. In effect, Islamic consumption emerges as a kind of invocation of a 'national Islam' or as a sign or logo of the nation in everyday life. The discussion of Islamic ritualisation below should be seen against the backdrop of previous discussions of suburbanisation, cultural intimacy and overspills between the parallel semi-domains of front and back – thus, suburbia is a perfect stage for performing religious or ritual scripts subjected to careful preparation in privacy.

When interviewing Hamza, a member of the Jamaat who helped publish the At-taqwa mosque's newsletter, I learned that he distinguished two distinct groups of Malays partaking in mosque life: firstly, the more pragmatically inclined group to which he himself felt he belonged; secondly, a group characterised by their fixation on promoting commendable acts as morally obligatory. The most awe-inspiring quality of this group, Hamza explained, was their ritualisation of all aspects of everyday life: 'They will enter the mosque and make sure to enter with the right leg first. Everything is considered to be a prayer.' The expression of power as ritualistic control of existence and body is intimately tied to this group's performance of the disavowal of material goods and worldly pleasures and desires.

What I have called the purist register of Malays signifies the latter of these groups. More pragmatic Malays were not entirely convinced about the authenticity of the performance of purism through ritual, which they saw as a moralistic demonstration. Against this image, the purist register tends to feel that the pragmatic group of Malays were excessively materialistic, un-Islamic, uncritical or indifferent in their consumption. Following a recent trend within the nationalisation of Islam in Malaysia, to some Malays fundamentalism has been re-signified as an expression of proper dedication rather than extremism. Hamza explained to me that this type of fundamentalism essentially was about simplicity: 'They would like to live a simple life. They would like to do a simple life although most of them are professionals. They are brain surgeons, CEOs of a bank or a company. But they would like to live a life outside of this world.'

Another and more recent trend that comes to mind is the notion and practice of 'simple living', which is obviously impossible to attain fully so that a whole industry has sprung up in order to advise and guide consumers about simplicity in family life, e.g. food and decoration.[1] The attraction in all this seems to be a striving for a kind of modernity stripped of complexity and adornment and laid bare for display. Simplification functions as sets of ideas and practices focused on weeding out the excess of complexity and disorientation. Against these images of confusion, simplicity in taste, handling and context are organised and elaborated. In fact, halalisation is a sentiment that necessitates the employment of modern technology, design, control and power. Without these technologies, the quest for reinscribing industrialised commodities with purity, simplicity and authenticity would be meaningless.

Consequently, as I learned from purist informants such as Yasir and Binsar, some Malay men have seemingly become more involved in the interior decoration of the home, as this practice has virtually merged with that of Islamic piety before God. Interestingly, Yasir and Binsar were fascinated with appropriating and domesticating simple Islamic living. In this way, simplicity can be an expression of halalisation. Binsar explained that 'In magazines, I am interested in simple interior decoration, especially of the kitchen.' Not surprisingly, IKEA was Binsar's favourite store in terms of taste and selection. However, Binsar's quest to achieve simplicity did not seem to be an uncomplicated one as he felt the need for the legitimation of his choices and distinctions.

This fascination with simplicity mirrors the wider tendencies in the magazines discussed above. Juxtaposition, composition, balance and subtlety much more than single objects of material status inform the knowledge of legitimate modes of decoration. Most significantly, these elaborate ideas and practices fundamentally exorcised feelings and suspicions of being excessive. Consequently, conceptualisations and practices of material excess were mended. The element of performance seems relevant to bring in here. Even though purist informants insisted on simplifying the decoration of the house, there is no clear evidence that these ideas were translated into actual practices in their homes.

Moreover, in my reading of Malaysian magazines, encouraging men to participate more in a number of domestic activities was a recurrent theme. Increased male involvement echoed the forging of modern (New Malay) masculine identities that were less traditional, fixed and concerned with clear-cut gender distinctions. Against these images, new forms of identities are idealised as more flexible and engaged. Moreover, and in a vein rather similar to halalisation, the quest for simplicity is an ongoing project and will eventually involve and question more and more ideas and practices that need moral elaboration and valorisation.

Again, all these ideals are virtually unattainable in everyday life and repeatedly necessitate attention and mental development. Therefore, the consumer behaviour of purist Malays is more ritualistic in that it persistently requires the boundaries between sacred and profane qualities and handling to be maintained. To Binsar, this urge to contain consumption took the form of strategising about what and what not to buy. Regarding family and children in particular it was crucial to have a detailed master plan before going shopping so that excess could be avoided. In reality, of course, this pious ideal rarely worked, Binsar admitted, as the entire family had different preferences that could not be contained in one master plan. Conversely, the more pragmatically inclined Malay register of consumption pre-empts attempts by the other register at standardising halalisation as legitimate taste in two ways: they either directly criticise what they see as excessive fetishisation of commodities that should not be a measure of one's inner spiritual dedication, or they simply neglect the matter or refuse to discuss it openly.

In this respect, the accounts of Udzir/Nur, and Siti stand out as the most individualised by informants. Siti did not really feel that she had goods that she clearly preferred or avoided: 'If I like a thing, I just buy it, no consideration. Except for food of course.' Therefore, typical consumer behaviour could not be essentialised. Siti: 'If I like this thing and I want it, that's why I buy.' To the more pragmatically orientated, commodities are not so much understood according to fixed intrinsic qualities that have to be subjected to forms of ritualisation or handling in order to appear Islamically acceptable. Commodities are rather seen as relatively unproblematic in religious terms. Most importantly, this register reserves the right to individualised ideas and practices that escape conformity of any kind.

One major field of tension between the registers is the purist Malays' drive to deepen and widen halalisation to cover more and more ideas and practices. Time and again, the fundamentalists approached the Jamaat member Hamza, e.g. to participate in a *Tabligh Itjima*[2] in Australia where about two million Muslims were said to attend: 'Everybody was wearing turban, Pakistani pants, all the black things. They're very religious. Very dogmatic also. Out of curiosity, I followed them.' This event signified the forcefulness of revivalist Islam as a global network or brotherhood with unlimited financial resources. In the economy of excess, this type of brotherhood is seen to thrive on material frugality invested in global conquest against shopping for the state. In fact, in the eyes of the state, mass consumption is constitutive of a modern type of re-ritualisation.[3]

Mahathir strongly critiques the ritual excess of Malays as utterly displaced national surplus invested in personal mystically inclined orders, Sufi *tareqat*, and the global projects of conquest and salvation of the Tabligh brotherhoods. He argues that 'Clearly rituals of worship cannot be properly carried out without "wealth" which comes from other forms of knowledge' (Mahathir 1986: 33). The effects of Islamic ritual practice will remain unseen without 'secular knowledge', which 'is not only related to religion but helps Muslims to do their Islamic duties more effectively and satisfactorily'. The historical glory of Islam was conditioned 'not only in devotion to Allah but also in mastering various forms of useful [sic] knowledge' (ibid.: 34). Elsewhere, Mahathir rages against

> ... ulamas with their rigidity, their belief that this world is not for Muslims, that the most important expression of iman is continuous rituals of obeisance to Allah s.w.t.,[4] that what is sunnat and therefore is optional must be considered as wajib and compulsory; it is these people who have reduced Islam and the Muslims to the inferior status that they are now. (Mahathir 2001: 261)

The consequence of excessive energy unprofitably invested in ritualisation is the underdevelopment of the Muslim world. Against this undesired type of ritualisation, shopping for the state is a sign of the grand-scale incursion of state and nation in Malaysian bodies. I now turn to the two forms of ritual, *wajib* and *sunnat*, in the lives of Malays.

Firstly, the compulsory daily five *salat* prayers. This type of prayer is subjected to both religious and political contestation. In narratives of informants, I learned that their mosque of preference was determined both by convenience in terms of location and the impact of political and Islamic discourse. There are three mosques in TTDI. The largest and most directly government-controlled is At-Taqwa, whereas Balai Islam presumably is independent and thus requires private funding for its operation and activities. Then, the Al-Mujahideen is influenced by PAS. The majority of informants normally preferred At-Taqwa. Azmi and Henny as well as Yasir frequently went to At-Taqwa, but mostly to Balai Islam because there was less government 'politicising' there. Mascud was the sole informant who normally went to Al-Mujahideen. In spite of informants' claims that Muslims could unproblematically go to any mosque of their personal choice, Islamic discourse apparently imprints on daily practices.

In respect of commendable acts such as *solat tahajud* and *solat tasbih*, the performance of these was divided along the lines of the two registers. Yasir would argue that most Malays were quite unaware of the deeper Islamic meaning of these acts. All Malays in the purist group claimed to perform commendable acts regularly. Among the pragmatically inclined Malays, some performed these acts on a regular basis while others expressed indifference in this respect. Jeti felt guilty about not performing them as consistently as her father required and only performed them when her father was present. Siti argued that *sunnat* should only be performed according to your individual ability and choice and not be imposed on you by moralistic others. Lastly, Ahmad had his personal motivation for performing *solat tasbih*: 'Let's say I want to get rich, you have to pray to God. Then you pray a lot. If, say, you want to get something that you know is very difficult, you do what you can to get it, but you can't. So, you have to pray.'

The informant Ahmad in many ways embodied the New Malay spirit, but he felt that he was still 'not quite there' in terms of affluence and social status. Thus, he hoped that performing commendable acts such as *solat tasbih* together with hard work would be the ticket to proper middle-classness. There is a distinct feel of Malaysian millennial capitalism in this example – the presence of an invisible hand. It is this invisibility and intangibility that is repulsive in the eyes of the state, i.e. beliefs in the magical or superstitious as avenues for personal wealth accumulation.

Within the last decade, the state in Malaysia has become more and more concerned with the influx of mystically inclined Islamic ideas from especially Sumatra and Java in Indonesia. These groups are often labelled deviationist and excessively secretive, as was the case with Arqam. Sufi *tareqat* in Malaysia are underground formations and enclave representations of isolated potential to rethink mystical Islam rather than mass movements (Sirriyeh 1999: 175). The appeal of Sufi mysticism to the Malay middle class may arise from the extreme asceticism of these ideas and groups. In a way, Sufism can be seen to work as an inspiration that can actively counter or balance material excess. I cannot think of two more contradictory figures or images of the body than that of the Sufi saint versus the middle-class Malay shopping for the state. This conflict is all about the quest for authenticity. Sufism is deep-rooted in Islamic thinking, but first and foremost it is a mystical tradition grounded in practices aiming at reaching ecstasy and an elevated state of mind in a specific ritualised context. In essence, Sufism is esoteric and for the most part practised by religious specialists.

In state imaginings in Malaysia, these secretive and esoteric practices are considered deviationist and unwanted, but they are nevertheless enjoying popularity in the new Malay middle class. The state is fearful of what it sees as uncontrollable, subversive and regressive ritual practices that may displace modern and patriotic national energy. Moreover, piety and moderation are seen as unproductive and un-patriotic. Most informants were aware of real, imagined or rumoured Sufi activities in or around TTDI, but these séances were as a rule confined to the privacy of the middle-class homes. In a way, these activities can be seen as quintessential practices of cultural intimacy to be kept out of the public gaze. Unsurprisingly, in the narratives of the purist register, support and participation in such activities were most pronounced. Binsar explained that he would attend meetings of a *tareqat* of which he knew the leader. Yasir was more reluctant in his acceptance of Sufi *tareqat* because he felt that a charismatic leader generally influenced these, which was quite un-Sufi. Nonetheless, his primary objection to Malay Sufi practice was that it was infused with material excess:

> I don't believe that if you want to become Sufi you have to dress in a certain way. You have to wear a big turban, you have to wear Uzbekistan kind of pants, which I know some people are doing. And they have to have a beard,

they have to be present down there at certain hours. I think that the real essence of Sufi is in a pure state.

Interestingly, Yasir's idea here is an exact replay of standard critiques articulated by pragmatic Malays of the purist registers' preoccupation with halalisation as shallow material display. For Jeti and Mascud, Sufism was seen as an expressive Islamic tradition in the field of art and poetry, or as the ultimate stage of enlightenment. Mascud explained that Sufis were fearless of anything or anyone except God. In this fascination, there was obviously an element of admiration for the purity of the Sufi tradition. The majority of informants, however, said that extremism was a trademark of *tareqat* and that they were excessively ritualistic and individualistic. Siti, for one, felt that 'Sometimes Sufis, *tareqat*, they think they're a higher class of Muslims. In Islam, it shouldn't be like this. Everybody should have a personal relationship with God.'

Intimately linked to informants' ideas about Sufism and *tareqat* was the distinction between openness and secretiveness in Islam. In the accounts of informants, it was a generally held idea that Muslims should always be open about their faith as there was 'nothing to hide'. This may, however, not always be the case concerning Sufism and *tareqat*. Jeti argued that one of the problems in Islam was its seclusion and sectarianism, which prevented open discussion and rather furthered dogmatism and extremism – a central idea in modernist Islam. Against this, Yasir said that there are mystical aspects of Islam that some people are just not prepared for and that Islam teaches you to cultivate faith within your home before you start going elsewhere. Conversely, Yasir in his position as head of his own *dakwah* organisation rejected the type of domestication of Islam taking the form of arranging *kelas agama* in the home: 'The problem is that the affluent think that when they have the money they don't want to visit the *ustaz*, the *ustaz* has to visit them. The *ustaz* must make time for me.' In effect, this is an expression of the crisis of Islamic authority that materialises in the wake of the domestication of Islam. There was a clear tendency to see that *kelas agama* was a phenomenon most popular among informants high in economic and cultural capital, such as Izura. Having a prayer room in your house was another point of tension where the purist register felt that Islamic authority might be undermined by the domestication of Islam. Ideally, as the puristically orientated Irfan put it 'Of course Muslims are best off praying in the mosque because you get twenty-seven times more rewarded.'

I have tried to show how Islamic practice in Malaysia is undergoing processes of ritualised domestication. This domestication can be seen as a response to or an effect of the wider nationalisation of Islam as a hegemonic state project. Growing authoritarianism from the 1970s onwards has produced a crisis of not only authority, but also authenticity for the Malaysian state and UMNO in particular. This crisis has taken on new forms in the era of an emergent ontology of consumption in the Malay middle class.

*****

Shopping for the state and patriotic consumption naturally come to mind as forms of re-ritualisation that work as the performance of Malay identities through proper Islamic consumption. The physical and symbolic violence of the state may possess a capability to 'produce and impose [...] categories of thought that we spontaneously apply to all things of the social world including the state itself' (Bourdieu 1999: 53). The argument here is that the performance of physical authority is unthinkable without symbolic capital. More specifically,

> Symbolic capital is any property (any form of capital whether physical, economic, cultural or social) when it is perceived by social agents endowed with categories of perception which cause them to know it and to recognize it, to give it value. (Ibid.: 62)

The state 'is the site par excellence of the concentration and exercise of symbolic power' (ibid.: 63). And ultimately so when symbolic capital is transferred as 'objectified symbolic capital, codified, delegated and guaranteed by the state, in a word bureaucratised' (ibid.: 66). To my mind, the power concentrated with the state in the form of symbolic capital to bureaucratise, standardise and certify ideas and practices of halalisation may be the ultimate state effect so that the modern state is materialising out of 'the powerful, apparently, metaphysical effect of practices' (Mitchell 1999: 89). This allegiance to the state is preconditioned on trust in its capability to certify and authenticate proper Islamic consumption. My informant Maslina explained that even though one may suspect that Kentucky Fried Chicken is not entirely halal, 'You have to trust the logo and the certification because you like it.'

221

Ritualisation is intimately linked to what I have called the domestication of Islam. In the Malay middle class, traditional forms of allegiance to the state have apparently been translated into distrust of excessive political practices. Against this, shopping for the state can be seen as new symbolic ideas and practices – state effects that bring the state back in. In terms of food in particular, the state in Malaysia is now effectively certifying and standardising this field of consumption most susceptible to ideas of purity/ impurity and the body. In all this, Malay consumer trust in state practices is essential. Thus, shopping for the state can work to pre-empt the divergent critiques of both registers of middle-class Malays and retransfer new modes of loyalty to the state. At the same time, patriotic consumption may be seen to counter underground Islamic deviationism. Nation-building itself more than ever seems to rely on inventions of novel national practices and symbolisations.

In spite of the ubiquity of state nationalist ideology in contemporary Malaysia and its successful attempt at curbing challenging positions, informants were highly critical of the immoral ways in which the political game polluted the purity of Islam, e.g. how PAS tried to perform a particular version of ascetic Islamic consumption. The extensive media consumption, e.g. of the Internet, in the Malay middle class has helped forge multiple mass-mediated nationalisms that coexist with other types of nationalist identities. Closely related to these divergent nationalisms, Islamic practice in Malaysia is undergoing processes of ritualised domestication that work as a response to or effect of the wider nationalisation of Islam as a hegemonic state project.

However, I recognise that ways to express transcendence through proliferating materiality is much older than mass consumption. Throughout history, material culture, e.g. mosques such as Masjid Negara (Figure 29), has been expressive of a particular kind of materiality and monumentality. (Miller 2005)

Throughout this monograph, I have employed dramaturgical metaphors, and Clifford Geertz[5] makes use of a similar conceptual grammar in analysing what he calls the theatre state in nineteenth-century Bali. The expressive nature of the Balinese state was enacted through spectacle and ceremony that dramatised cultures of inequality and status pride (Geertz 1980: 13). In Malaysia, these ubiquitous state rituals are performed in a number of fields: monumental architectural modernity as in the case of the Masjid Negara and numerous other constructions, and as state effects in

Figure 29: Masjid Negara. The state in Malaysia translates Masjid Negara as National Mosque in spite of the fact that literally its name means State Mosque – a staging of state nationalist Islam as 'national' Islam in public urban space.

the certification of halal products as a symbolic language of authority in the nationalisation of Islam. All these state effects are immensely functional rituals. Nationalism may even most forcefully be concentrated in this excess of the state (Aretxaga 2000). Geertz shows that the type of polity *negara* 'designates is one in which the interplay of status, pomp, and governance not only remains visible, but is, in fact, blazoned' (Geertz 1980: 121).

The *negara* in Malaysia incites and is incited by two forms of powerful images. The modern state as effect emerges through its language and practice of wealth, science and technology, and then only second in how this type of modernity can most fruitfully be invested in Islam. Political symbolisations (myth, insignia, etiquette, palaces, titles, ceremonies) are all merely instruments of social domination (ibid.: 122). Most important, however, for the overall argument, is the deeply material nature of the state ceremony as motor. The excess of state rituals was, in fact, 'the measure of the realm's well-being. More important, it was a demonstration that they were the same thing' (ibid.: 129).

Ironically, the whole process of nation-building in Malaysia and elsewhere in the post-colonial world encompasses a de-emphasis on ritual practice as argued, whereas nation-building itself is unimaginable without the invention of new national practices and symbolisations. Keyes et al. (1994: 6–7) point out that 'politics of ritual displacement have faltered because no civic order promoted by any state has proven capable of meeting all fundamental existential problems as a consequence of the social dislocations and restructuring that modernizing and nation-building policies have generated'. Authoritarian and repressive measures to counter underground religious ritual practices (deviationism) in Malaysia have been complemented with state-led ethnic Malay responsiveness.

The nation-building process, in fact, can be seen as the invention of new forms of mental and material Malay nationness. Invented traditions function as tacitly accepted ritual or symbolic practices that 'seek to inculcate certain values and norms of behaviour by repetition, which automatically implies continuity with the past' (Hobsbawm 1992: 1). The spectacle of the state in Malaysia is an obvious example of this type of staging. Another is the way in which the pre-Islamic past has been demonised as a revisionist nationalist project: 'Inventing traditions [...] is essentially a process of formalization and ritualization, characterized by reference to the past, if only by imposing repetition' (ibid.: 4). Spectacles are by nature material and functional and in Malaysia monuments and 'national' urban architecture refer to the reservoir of meaning and continuity in the Islamic past.

In a way, nation-state bureaucracies are an analogue to ritual systems of a religion, as both are founded on the principle of identity among elects as an exclusive community (Herzfeld 1992: 10). Dissatisfied with public ritual alone, the state and bureaucracy in Malaysia desire 'rituals of personal commitment – practices that are sometimes less obviously ritualistic' (ibid.: 37). As we have seen, the state tries to exorcise deviationist ritualism, but the central question is how this state in Malaysia tackles the existential problems that arise as a consequence of the politics of ritual displacement. Understandings and practices of ritual, however, tend to circle around different ideals of consumption as halalisation. The emergence of a ritual economy seems to be a prominent example of the blurring of the boundaries between the religious and the secular in the Malaysian ritual context (Moore and Meyerhoff 1977).

NOTES

1   See for example the magazine 'RealSimple – the Magazine about simplifying your life '(http://www.realsimple.com/realsimple/).

2   Literally, the *tabligh* is the work done by Muslims to call others to Allah.

3   For a more detailed discussion of this debate, see Fischer (forthcoming 2008).

4   S.W.T is an acronym in Arabic that in English translates into 'Allah is pure of having partners and He is exalted from having a son.'

5   According to Geertz, *'Negara (nagara, nagari, negeri)*, a Sanskrit loanword originally meaning "town", is used in Indonesian languages to mean, more or less simultaneously and interchangeably, "palace", "capital", "state", or "realm", and again "town". It is, in its broadest sense, the word for (classical) civilization, for the world of the traditional city, the high culture that city supported, and the city of superordinate political authority centered here. The opposite of *Negara* is *desa*, which can be flexibly signified as "countryside", "region", "village", "place", and sometimes even "dependency" or "governed area".'

   Desa is the rural world of peasants, tenants, political subjects, and the people, and it was in between *negara* and *desa* that the classical polity emerged (Geertz 1980: 4).

8

Consumptions, Conclusions and the Wider Picture

Before finishing the fieldwork in TTDI, I crossed over from TTDI to Sungai Pencala and Arqam once more. The workshops and the entire commune that were once a bustling centre for halal production were now quiet. The state had effectively curbed Arqam as the vanguard of halalisation. Moreover, that same state had consumed Arqam's halal entrepreneurship to form what I have explored as halalisation, the nationalisation of Islam, and the emergence of a unique Malay Muslim ontology of consumption. In other words, what was to become state institutionalised halalisation had been removed from its micro-social base in Arqam into mass consumption. Arqam's mystical and heterodox form of millennialism had been erased and replaced by a particular version and vision of modern Malaysianised millennialism through halalisation. In this conclusion, I shall on the one hand summarise the main findings of the monograph and, on the other, discuss the wider perspectives that arise from these findings.

No single theory was able to capture the immense complexity involved in modern religious consumption. Bourdieu's seminal book *Distinction* was invaluable and is probably the most qualified and complex study so far of classing and consumption. At the same time, this work misrecognises all that is transcendental or intangible. Paradoxically enough, this intrinsic misrecognition gives rise to a clear-cut distinction between the tangible (rational) and intangible (irrational). I have demonstrated that such a distinction is problematic and that it is unable to address a whole range of questions.

Before discussing the main findings of the monograph, it would have been desirable to outline a neat, smooth or functional scheme for ordering informants according to class fraction and practice of proper Islamic consumption. Alas, such an endeavour is unworkable as informants

226

constantly wove in and out of, firstly, economic, cultural and social capital and, secondly, 'the religious' in terms of performing piety and placing oneself in or being placed in the religious field. This study showed that Malay Muslim class fractions most of all emerge from ideas and practices of proper Islamic consumption in cultural intimacy. In other words, consumption links micro-social actions and wider structural processes and transformations such as halalisation, the nationalisation of Islam, and the expansion of global markets.

The mosques and the market comprise immensely powerful fields of force in Malay middle-class identity formation. What I found was that these two fields of force together with a ubiquitous Malaysian state is releasing a tremendous amount of social energy in contemporary Malaysia. Indeed, modern Malay Muslim identity in Malaysia is unimaginable, even incomprehensible, without taking divergent understandings and practices of Islamic consumption into consideration. Central to this new form of ontology of proper Islamic consumption is the idea of excess (surplus/energy) versus balance. Hard work was put into overcoming this and other everyday difficulties. This problem has permeated and informed a wide range of discussions throughout the monograph.

The Malay middle class is by now consolidated as a class *für sich*. This Malay middle class has developed into an emic and performative category. Above all, informants articulated excessive consumption of the other as that which modelled class distinctions in suburbia. Against these images, more traditional class parameters such as income and education were secondary. Of particular concern to informants were the strategies the other employed to invest social and financial resources as forms of surplus in consumption. Interestingly, there were no discernible differences between the two groups of Malays in this respect – they were both acutely aware of classing as strategic ideas and practices.

In other words, this class is both shaped by and actively shaping state and market in Malaysia. The Malay middle-class's material stake in the social order enabled what I have called shopping for the state. The state now demands patriotic consumption of subjects in return for the steady delivery of Malay privileges. This modern form of governmentality was part of a neoliberal paradigm within the framework of a Malaysianised mode of millennial capitalism. These privileges were, however, accompanied by the deepening of authoritarian powers from the 1970s onwards. In all this there was a delicate balance between shopping for the state and intensifying authoritarianism. The ethnicisation of the state that accompanied its authoritarian measures should be seen as a response to the *dakwah* challenge of state nationalist authority. Ironically, the *dakwah* challenge provided the state with its most subtle mode of domination – the certification and standardisation of ever more halalised products.

The Malaysian state's involvement in a large number of *bumiputera* businesses and commodities that were open to halalisation coincided with an expansion and openness of global markets and the emergence of a new consumerist ontology. For individuals and groups, the Malaysian nation was reconceptualised as an aesthetic community in which shopping for the state was intrinsic to novel forms of proper Islamic consumption. Moreover, this ontology of Islamic consumption was inseparable from the transformation of Islam into an ethnic and political signifier of Malayness. Halalisation set the standard for legitimate taste preferences and at the same time worked as Malaysianising, legitimising or purifying the intensified flow of foreign commodities and brands into nation and home.

There is an apparent complexity and confusion in Malay middle-class identity formation in these interfaces between Islam, nation, state and market. Siegel captured these ambiguities, possibilities and confusions in the idea that the fetish is a magical instrument claiming false relation to origin. At the same time, this fetish is a fetish of appearance and modernity. Malaysianising all the contradictory imports and impulses above is inseparable from what I have called the nationalisation of Islam. In essence, the nationalisation of Islam is concerned with the streamlining of Islamic ideas and practices into manageable national imaginings.

From the detailed exploration of consumer choices in the everyday lives of middle-class Malays, the moral expansion of halal requirements stands out as the most significant, and the most contested. From halal requirements concerning food, these ideas have deepened and widened to cover a whole range of commodities and practices. Halalisation and its constant elaboration actively fuses myths of state, Islam and nation. In other words, halalisation gives rise to new ways of inventing and imagining the post-colonial state in Malaysia. In the wake of halalisation, the purist Malays, who claim to be perfect at practising proper Islamic consumption, are subjecting the pragmatic group to moral and religious pressure.

I have shown how the two Malay registers of modern lifestyles perform quite divergent and distinctive understandings and practices of Islamic consumption. At the same time, there were continuous overlaps, overspills and confusion involved in the consumption of these groups. Hence, proper Islamic consumption is understood and to a lesser extent practised differently by purist and pragmatic Malays. Distinctions between these two registers in Malay Muslim consumption arise primarily as products of performance as an everyday strategy for 'getting consumption right'. Moreover, performance is an essential tool in staging modern identities in an urban/suburban setting, and especially with respect to the semi-domains. These two Malay groups appear to be split between individual consumer desires and the social and moral anxieties of new forms of consumption. At the same time, working out this tension and another linked to excess and balance in halalisation necessitates constant attention and the performance of legitimating rituals.

Through performance of proper handling, ritualisation and contextual-isation, fetish-like commodities are subjected to the cleansing of any malevolent intrinsic qualities or residues. This cleansing aims at bringing out the authenticity that can transmute commodities into non-commodities. These ideas and practices are mainly focused on essentialising purity of, in or on the body, especially in the case of food and dress. These understandings of proper Malay consumption of commodities can be seen to fit into wider historical and structural transformations such as the second coming of capitalism. Thus, there seem to be subtle and intimate connections between micro-social ideas and practices in the everyday life of middle-class Malays and these more generalised tendencies in the globalised market for identities. In other words, the idealisation of Islamic consumption in Malaysia can be seen as an attempt at forging an alternative halalised capitalism, as I have shown in the case of Islamic banking and credit systems. In this sense, halalisation thrives on styles of surplus authenticity yearned for by the more puristically orientated. Deprived of this authenticity, the commodity form is merely 'a matter' of excess or malevolent surplus energy.

Halalisation and the mass availability of commodities have had strong effects on Malay middle-class families. Families work hard to explain why and how some commodities are demonising. Another job is working out how family rituals may legitimise and cleanse commodities for import into cultural intimacy. Again, these ideas and practices are constantly subjected to diverse critiques. Purist Malays' constant attempts at deepening and widening proper Islamic consumption have produced a number of distinctions, suspicions and anxieties in the everyday lives of urban Malays. Paradoxically, halalisation has worked as the disciplining of bodies as well as having expanded the availability of a new range of Islamically legitimate tastes and fashions. In respect of bodies, demarcations between the front and back regions are vital but fuzzy. Hence, the realm of intimacy in Malay middle-class families can best be understood as that which is semi-private or semi-public. Into this sphere, commodities are imported, appropriated and consumed on a daily basis. Against this intimate and shared form of Malay Muslim consumption, a number of real or imaginary 'excessive' others emerge. It is these outside others that figure prominently in the ethnographic material, but are surprisingly insignificant in the sample data.

Purity in the form of halalisation is not a fixed symbol or a complete process, but rather something lived and dynamic in the everyday lives of Malays. Consequently, the realm of halalisation must constantly be expanded and elaborated by consumers, capitalists and the state in order to retain its impetus. In this battle for purity as legitimate taste, pragmatic Malays play the part of a 'supporting cast' in the performance of individualised consumption. Against what is seen as a purist taste hegemony, pragmatic Malays evoke authenticity as that which is inseparable from individual and sovereign choices and preferences. In the end, these choices are seen to produce Malay middle-class identities that are effects of these individualised choices.

Suburban expansion is probably the most substantial product of the expanding middle class in a country such as Malaysia. TTDI is the quintessential middle-class suburb, distinctly different from the *kampung* and Kuala Lumpur. Suburbia is thus a concentration of mythical middle-classness, which may be both monumental, and intimately private. The suburb is a parameter of achievement, order, privileges and state/market entrepreneurial capitalism. At the same time, suburbia seems to embody excessive materialism, social seclusion and the craving for community. Moreover, class consciousness was intimately tied to the domesticity of Malay middle-class homes in which class also took a generational and gendering form. The rising Malay middle class embodied economic, national and social cohesion and progress. All these qualities were concentrated in the New Malay.

The widespread mistrust of politics and the state among informants had the effect that religious and political ideologies were not directly translated into everyday practices. In this respect, divergences between purist and pragmatic Malays were products of performed distinctions rather than actual practices.

The emergence of the national family was evident through my reading of newspapers, and especially magazines. The Malay middle-class family has taken on meaning as a national project crucial to the ethnicised state and nation. Within the last three decades, these families have been subjected to a multitude of moral, political and religious calls. At the same time, family life has become the primary target of the advertising industry and expansion of the market.

Increased authoritarianism in Malaysia may have caused a revitalisation of a number of Islamic rituals that work as underground phenomena. In spite of the state's insistence on seeing these ritual practices as deviationist, this type of domesticated ritual escapes direct state control. In Islamic consumption and halalisation, however, the state has discovered an enormously powerful field in which it reserves the right to certify, standardise, control and expand the demarcations of halal versus haram. Therefore, the state becomes a site of the concentration and exercise of symbolic power.

*****

In TTDI, there was a Chinese restaurant selling pricey but delicious food with inspiration from the Island of Penang. On one of my visits there, I noticed that quite unusually no Malays were among the guests even though the establishment had been certified as halal by JAKIM. The next day I was in the 'independent' Balai Islam mosque. On the notice board outside the mosque, I noticed a decree issued by the Balai Islam stating that in this restaurant the food is not halal (*makanan ini tidak halal*). Rumours among informants had it that JAKIM and Balai Islam were now 'looking into the matter'. Until the dispute was settled, Malays were best off frequenting the Malay-owned restaurant across the street. This restaurant boldly displayed the JAKIM logo of state certification. In this incident, the whole problem of Islamic consumption seems to be concentrated: the excess of material Chineseness in the eyes of Malays, the challenges to state authority, and the everyday power of halalisation intrinsic to the halal logo. Ultimately, the distinction between logo (state) and brand (trademark) has been erased, and thus halalisation emerges as that which is legitimate in the preferences and tastes of Malays.

THE LOCAL AND THE GLOBAL ISLAMIC THING

In this section, Malaysian Islamic experiences are discussed in a wider perspective. Obviously, as we have seen throughout the monograph, there is no intrinsic contradiction between globalised capitalism in the new millennium and Malaysianised Islamic modernity. In fact, the two do not in any way seem to be seriously incompatible. In spite of any resistance or uneasiness expressed by the purist register of informants in particular, each informant recognised that Malaysia is part of a highly integrated and globalised world system in which flows of commodities, people, finance and ideas are intensifying.

Islam in Malaysia and other parts of Southeast Asia such as Indonesia would seem to have a syncretic tinge to it compared to, for instance, the Middle East. Today, more than ever, the incorporation of a distinct materiality or 'thingness' into this syncretic stream of Islam seems to be pervasive. In fact, discursive Islam is driven by a constant charging and recharging of the 'religious' as materially or spiritually excessive.

The nationalisation of Islam and halalisation may be all about creating, fixing and maintaining the religious as a material base, the thingness in enjoyment: 'The element which holds together a given community cannot be reduced to the point of symbolic identification: the bond linking together its members always implies a shared relationship toward a Thing, toward Enjoyment incarnated' (Zizek 1993: 201). The emergence of an ontology of Islamic consumption has infused discursive Islam in Malaysia with an immensely powerful ability to syncretise politics, state, authority and morality. In spite of state nationalist insistence on exorcising the excessively magical, deviationist, ritualistic and *adat*, these repressions seemingly reappear in the commodity form as fetishes and adornments indispensable to modern forms of state power on the one hand, and individual claims of piety on the other. For purist Malays, halalisation has caused a deep concern with halalised piety.

Contrary to the commonly held notion that 'Islamists' in general endeavour to transform the state itself, my study demonstrates that this idea is a simplification. As in Egypt, with regard to the cultural politics of a women's grassroots piety movement, Islamic revivalism is much more focused on personal forms of piety, freedom and agency – and escaping nationalist politics altogether (Mahmood 2004). This contention is supported by the argument that in Egypt 'the concerns, loyalties, sentiments, and practices that da'wa has given rise to presuppose a form of community for which the nation is a contingent, but not essential component' (Hirschkind 2001: 26). Moreover, this tendency has been reinforced post-9/11 with the stress on Islamic ethics at a global level. Among my informants, 9/11 seemed to give a more global and ethical dimension to the above processes, i.e. sentiments that in proper Islamic consumption the local, national and global converged in the 'contingent relations of the global marketplace' (Devji 2005:11).

On 16 August 2004, Malaysia's Prime Minister Abdullah Haji Ahmad Badawi officially launched the Malaysia International Halal Showcase (MIHAS) 2004 in Kuala Lumpur. The title of the Prime Minister's speech was 'Window to the Global Halal Network' (www.pmo.gov.my). He argued that establishing Malaysia as a 'global halal hub' was a major priority of the government, and that MIHAS was not only Malaysia's, but 'the largest integrated halal trade expo to be held anywhere in the world'. In the wider context, Badawi asserted that halal produce is increasingly being recognised by Muslims as well as non-Muslims globally as 'a new benchmark' for safety, quality and purity not only for Muslims, but for all. Consequently, *Halal™* is emerging as a new global state-certified brand and/or logo envisioned to standardise the market. While the concept of halal embracing what is good, fair and ethical in business practices is nothing new, Badawi maintained that the concept seems to have taken on protective forms of religious signification. He argued that

> At a time when consumers have been shaken by news of diseases affecting basic food that we eat, it is incumbent on all of us to make every effort to ensure that such health disasters, often borne of unhealthy practices by growers and producers, no longer occur.

In essence, halal modernity reflects a universally held desire for a return to purity. Consequently, the proliferation of halal standards should be globally accessible. In the ubiquity and grandeur of these visions there seems to be a desire for proliferating the 'thingness' or material core of model Southeast Asian capitalist Islam.

Historically, real and symbolic 'Middle Eastern Islam' for instance has impacted on its Southeast Asian counterpart: 'Southeast Asian Muslims borrow abstract ideas as well as concrete examples from the Middle East to strengthen their faith and Islamise their often pragmatic and Westernised cultural bearings' (Abaza 1996: 139). Ambivalently, many Southeast Asian Muslims view the Middle East as the home of high culture and knowledge while criticising its feudal traditions, violence and undemocratic rulers.

At the same time, the Middle East signifies traditional and rather un-sophisticated cities with regard to taste and modern architectural symbols of modernity – quite unlike Southeast Asian metropolises such as Kuala Lumpur or Jakarta. Arguably, Muslims of Southeast Asia are using 'Arabic and Islam against Western and other hegemonies, but at the same time resort to Western ideologies as a bulwark against Middle Eastern cultural hegemony' (ibid.: 139). With specific regard to Malays in peninsular Malaysia, these have traditionally been seen by Middle Eastern Muslims as 'lax', and

> ... with the advent of modernity and mass culture as a global phenomenon, and the constant need of self-definition vis-à-vis Western culture as well as towards the other ethnic and religious groups in the region, the Muslim communities and, in particular, the literate middle classes, might find themselves being challenged to prove that, as Muslims of the periphery, they are better than any Middle Eastern Muslim (ibid.:148).

Middle Eastern influences played a major role in the way Malaysian Islam was shaped. Modernist movements in Malaysia were highly informed by these streams of knowledge in the struggle against British colonialism, criticism of religious bureaucracies, and the authority of the sultans over religious affairs (Zaina 1987: 3). Notions of pan-Islamism and reformism from the Middle East filtered down to village level in the Malay world to establish an opposition between Melayu and the British colonial power (Andaya and Andaya 1982: 202). Most importantly maybe, it was after all Arab traders who spread Islam in peninsular Malaysia in the thirteenth century.

In Badawi's visions, there seems to be an inherent quest for reversing the historically material and spiritual dominance of Islamic centres in the Middle East, Pakistan or South Asia. Moreover, halalisation on a global scale could be an avenue for curbing what is seen as unlimited and immoral (haram) Chinese/Western capitalist expansion. In this perspective, the proliferation of halalisation on a global scale may compensate for the mysticism, syncretism, impurity or imperfection that historically have been imputed to Southeast Asian Islam. Promoting halalisation as a conceptually more wholesome or modern system may at the same time curb claims of Southeast Asian Islamic materialism vis-à-vis challenging discourses and thus situate Malaysia comfortably in a social geography of excess.

Naturally, 'the material' is not insignificant in Middle Eastern Islam or Turkey, as evidenced by Navaro-Yashin's study of Islamists and secularists. Similarly, in modern Iran a public Islamic space or 'bourgeois civil society' has been produced by religious practice. This space has merged with the processes of 'commercialisation, privatisation and building of a middle class whose way of life is tending to acquire hegemony on the national scale' (Adelkhah 1999: 127). Moreover, there is a growing 'money orientation' in all walks of life in Islamic Iran and disputes and disagreements among clerics, for instance, are primarily 'conflicts over material interests, or more basically about different ideas of government, society, the nation, the faith of believers, daily religious practice, the family, business or the state' (ibid.: 136).

A comparative study of Islam in Indonesia and Morocco shows that for both countries there seems to be a steadily growing gap between Sunni perceptions of Koranic revelations and actual belief (Geertz 1968). This disjunction is, above all, produced by the rise of individually diversified experiences, 'multiformity', and, most of all, Islam's growing inability 'to inform the faith of particular men and to be informed by it' (ibid.: 15). Apparently, a 'progressive increase in doubt' is deepening. Geertz distinguishes between 'religiousness' (being held by religious convictions) and 'religious-mindedness' (celebrating belief rather than what belief asserts) (ibid.: 61). The contention in this monograph has been that the material or proper Islamic consumption in the context of halalisation in essence endeavours to drive back the inescapable slide from religiousness to religious-mindedness.

The effects of these processes are by no means universal in the Muslim world. Geertz discerns differences between Morocco and Indonesia, which obviously shares much of its history, language and religious traditions with Malaysia. The power of Islam in Indonesia, and other parts of Southeast Asia more generally, Geertz writes, is based on an inclination towards absorbing all styles of thought into one broad stream. This tradition is generally receptive to the argument that 'Islamic doctrine and scientific discovery are really not conflicting but complementary forms of belief' (Geertz 1968: 106). At the same time, in the Indonesian version of Islam, and strikingly consonant with what we have seen in Malaysia,

> ... almost everything is tinged, if lightly, with metaphysical meaning, the whole of ordinary life has a faintly transcendental quality about it, and it is rather difficult to isolate one part of it in which religious beliefs and the

attitudes derived from them play a more prominent role than any other. (Ibid.: 112)

Conversely, in Morocco there is an inclination towards 'religious perfectionism' and 'moral rigor' that has attempted to 'isolate a purified Islamic faith from contamination with everyday life' (ibid.: 106).

The everyday grappling with the understandings and practices of the proper in Malay Muslim consumption, 'getting consumption right', is all about the cultural logics of inclusion, subsumption, and syncretism, not exclusion in a rigid sense. Middle-class Malays work hard to demonstrate how the particularities of their visions are compatible with religious capitalism and modernity. In a way, this particular mode of Malay Muslim consumption endeavours to reveal how the 'secular' and the 'scientific' are merely practical and useful expressions of Islamic knowledge (ibid.: 112). Informants would continuously explain, justify, or legitimate their understanding and practice of consumption with reference to 'Islam', the Koran, Hadith or Sunna. Consequently, the quest to come to terms with new modes of consumption in halalisation can be seen to result in re-readings of the scriptures and that may again deepen the compatibility of Islam, capitalism and wealth.

THE CLASH OF FAMILISMS?

Throughout this monograph, 'the family' has permeated discussions in a number of contexts and perspectives. The title of this final section is a paraphrase of Huntington's famous and infamous book *The Clash of Civilizations* (1993) that some observers in the post-9/11 context consider to posses almost prophetic qualities. I contend that in the wake of the last two US elections in which religious, civilisational and family values became ultimately decisive factors, what seems to be emerging is a kind of 'globalised moralistic familism'. These ideas were further developed in Huntington's most recent book *Who Are We? The Challenges to America's National Identity* (2004). In this book, the argument is presented that 'ordinary' Americans are more nationalistic than cosmopolitan liberal. Consequently, these ordinary citizens possess a natural and instinctive mistrust of the unpatriotic activities of political elites similar to what we have seen in Malaysia. In all this, there is a desire for defining and locating the national core of the nation in everyday life. Modern politics is more and more aimed at capturing and exploiting this type of intimacy in populist rhetoric. Inevitably, this core is situated in what I have called the national family. It is from xenophobic, defensive and moralistic panic over the social and moral integrity of families that the clash of familisms emerges.

In other words, what we are witnessing in the US, Southeast Asia and elsewhere is the universalisation of the particular with specific reference to familism. The particularistic values of families clash with and against an outside that is increasingly perceived as threatening, immoral, disjunctive and divisive. This outside is precisely seen from within families to be tainted with state driven politicisations of religion, values and idealised families as the core of modern nations. Huntington's argument and vision of neatly organised and bounded civilisations that clash against an isolated West is driven by what he calls the re-Islamisation of the Middle East. After presenting families with images of a threatening and disjunctive world (global terrorism as civilisational struggle provides the best example), the state in return demands patriotism of these families. Together, civilisational and familial metaphors are crucial elements in modern populist politics.

The more familial metaphors of intimacy and authenticity are exploited in political discourse the more families withdraw into cultural intimacy. I have shown how the public realm has been damaged by the overcharging of such displaced metaphors of intimacy. Paradoxically, desires to transfer intimate metaphors such as warmth and trust to questions of power and allocation of resources have been captured by the state. In the eyes of many families, this exploitation further stresses the immorality and insincerity of modern forms of power politics. It seems that familial loyalty can best be regained in and through modern forms of consumption.

Bibliography

Abaza, Mona (1996) 'Islam in south-east Asia: varying impact and images of the Middle East'. In Hussin Mutalib and Taj Ul-Islam Hashmi (eds), *Islam, Muslims and the Modern State. Case-Studies in Thirteen Countries*. Houndmills, Basingstoke, Hampshire: Macmillan Press, pp. 139–51.

Abdul Rahman Embong (1998) 'Social transformation, the state and the middle classes in post independence Malaysia'. In Ibrahim Zawawi (ed.), *Cultural Contestations. Mediating Identities in a Changing Malaysian Society*. London: Asean Academic Press, pp. 83–116.

— (2001) 'Beyond the crisis: the paradox of the Malaysian middle class'. In Abdul Rahman Embong (ed.), *Southeast Asian Middle Classes. Prospects for Social Change and Democratisation*. Bangi: Penerbit Universiti Kebangsaan Malaysia, pp. 80–102.

— (2002) *State-led Modernization and the New Middle Class in Malaysia*. Houndmills and New York: Palgrave.

Abu-Lughod, Lila (1999) *Veiled Sentiments. Honor and Poetry in a Bedouin Society*. Berkeley and Los Angeles: University of California Press.

Ackerman, Susan E. and Raymond L. M. Lee (1997) *Sacred Tensions: Modernity and Religious Transformation in Malaysia*. Columbia: University of South Carolina Press.

Adelkhah, Fariba (1999) *Being modern in Iran*. London: Hurst & Co. in association with the Centre d'Etudes et de Recherches Internationales Paris.

Andaya, Barbara Watson and Leonard Y. Andaya (1982) *A History of Malaysia*. Hong Kong: Macmillan.

Anderson, Benedict R. O'G (1991) *Imagined Communities: Reflections on the Origin and Spread of Nationalism*. London: Verso.

Appadurai, Arjun (1999) 'Introduction: commodities and the politics of value'. In Arjun Appadurai (ed.), *The Social Life of Things. Commodities in Cultural Perspective*. Cambridge: Cambridge University Press, pp. 3–63.

Aretxaga, Begona (2000) 'A fictional reality: paramilitary death squads and the construction of state terror in Spain'. In James A. Sluka (ed.), *Death Squad: The Anthropology of State Terror*. Philadelphia: University of Pennsylvania Press, pp. 46–9.

Asad, Talal (1986) *The Idea of an Anthropology of Islam*. Washington DC: Georgetown University Center for Contemporary Arab Studies.

— (1997) 'Remarks on the anthropology of the body'. In Sarah Coakley (ed.), *Religion and the Body. Comparative Perspectives on Devotional Practices*. Cambridge: Cambridge University Press, pp. 42–52.

Azimabadi, Badr (1994) *The Permitted and the Prohibited in Islam*. New Delhi: Kitab Bhavan.

Azmi, Jumaatun (2003a) *Halal Food: A Guide to Good Eating – Kuala Lumpur*. Kuala Lumpur: KasehDia Sdn. Bhd.

— (2003b) *Halal Food: A Guide to Good Eating – London*. Kuala Lumpur: KasehDia Sdn. Bhd.

Bachelard, Gaston (1994) *The Poetics of Space. The Classic Look at How We Experience Intimate Places*. Boston: Beacon Press.

Balibar, Etienne (1991) 'The nation form: history and ideology'. In Etienne Balibar and Immanuel Wallerstein: *Race, Nation, Class. Ambiguous Identities*. London: Verso, pp. 86–106.

— (1994) *Masses, Classes, Ideas: Studies on Politics and Philosophy Before and After Marx*. London: Routledge.

Bataille, Georges (1991) *The Accursed Share. An Essay on General Economy. Volume 1: Consumption*. New York: Zone Books.

— (1992) *Theory of Religion*. New York: Zone Books.

Bell, Catherine (1992) *Ritual Theory. Ritual Practice*. Oxford: Oxford University Press.

Benjamin, Walter (1999) *Illuminations*. London: Pimlico.

Bourdieu, Pierre (1977) *An Outline of a Theory of Practice*. Cambridge: Cambridge University Press.

— (1984) *Distinction. A Social Critique of the Judgement of Taste*. London: Routledge.

— (1990) *The Logic of Practice*. Cambridge: Polity.

— (1999) 'Rethinking the state: genesis and structure of the bureaucratic field'. In George Steinmetz (ed.), *State/Culture: New Approaches to the State After the Cultural Turn*. New York: Cornell University Press, pp. 53–75.

Bowen, John R. (1993) *Muslims Through Discourse. Religion and Ritual in Gayo Society*. Princeton: Princeton University Press.

Brookfield, Harold, Abdul Samad Hadi and Zaharah Mahmud (1991) *The City in The Village. The In-Situ Urbanization of Villages, Villagers and Their Land around Kuala Lumpur, Malaysia*. Singapore: Oxford University Press.

Bruner, Edward M. (1986) 'Ethnography as narrative'. In Victor Turner (ed.), *The Anthropology of Experience*. Champaign: University of Illinois Press, pp. 139–55.

Bruner, Jerome (1986) *Actual Minds, Possible Worlds*. Cambridge, Mass.: Harvard University Press.

— (1990) *Acts of Meaning*. Cambridge, Mass.: Harvard University Press.

Bunnell, Tim. 2003. *Malaysia, Modernity and the Multimedia Super Corridor.* London and New York: Routledge Curzon.

Caldeira, Teresa P. R. (2000) *City of Walls: Crime, Segregation and Citizenship in Saõ Paulo.* Berkeley: University of California Press.

Carsten, Janet (1997) *The Heat of the Hearth. The Process of Kinship in a Malay Fishing Community.* Oxford: Clarendon Press.

Carsten, Janet and Stephen Hugh-Jones (1995) 'Introduction: about the house. Lévi-Strauss and beyond'. In Janet Carsten and Stephen Hugh-Jones (eds), *About the House. Lévi-Strauss and Beyond.* Cambridge: Cambridge University Press, pp. 1–46.

de Certeau, Michel (1984) *The Practice of Everyday Life.* Berkeley: University of California Press.

Chin, Elizabeth (2001) *Purchasing Power. Black Kids and American Consumer Culture.* Minneapolis: University of Minnesota Press.

Chua, Beng-Huat (2000a) 'Consuming Asians: ideas and issues'. In Beng-Huat Chua (ed.), *Consumption in Asia. Lifestyles and Identities.* London: Routledge, pp. 1–34.

— (ed.) (2000b) *Consumption in Asia. Lifestyles and Identities.* London: Routledge.

Cohen, Lizabeth (2004) *A Consumers' Republic. The Politics of Mass Consumption in Postwar America.* New York: Vintage Books.

Comaroff, Jean and John L. Comaroff (2000) 'Millennial capitalism: first thoughts on a second coming'. *Public Culture* vol. 12 (2), pp. 291–343.

Crouch, Harold (1996) *Government and Society in Malaysia.* Ithaca: Cornell University Press.

D'Alisera, Joann (2001) 'I love Islam. Popular religious commodities, sites of inscription, and transnational Sierra Leonean identity'. *Journal of Material Culture,* vol. 6 (1), pp. 91–110.

Davidoff, Leonore and Catherine Hall (1987) *Family Fortunes: Men and Women of the English Middle Class 1780–1850.* London: Hutchinson.

Denny, Frederick M. (1985) 'Islamic ritual: perspectives and theories'. In Richard C. Martin (ed.), *Approaches to Islam in Religious Studies.* Tucson: University of Arizona Press, pp. 63–77.

— (2006) *An Introduction to Islam. Third Edition.* Upper Saddle River: Pearson Prentice Hall.

Department of Malaysian Islamic Development (JAKIM) (n.d.) *Application for a Halal Certificate and Logo.*

Devji, Faisal (2005) *Landscapes of the Jihad. Militancy, Morality, Modernity.* London: C. Hurst & Company.

Douglas, Mary (1996) *Thought Styles: Critical Essays on Good Taste.* London: Sage.

— (2004) *Purity and Danger. An Analysis of the Concepts of Pollution and Taboo.* London: Routledge.

Dovey, Kimberley (1985) 'Home and homelessness'. In Erwing Altman and Carol Werner (eds), *Home Environments*. New York: Plenum, pp. 33–64.

Durkheim, Emile (1995) *The Elementary Forms of Religious Life*. New York: The Free Press.

Eagleton, Terry (1994) 'Ideology and its vicissitudes in western marxism'. In Slavoj Zizek (ed.), *Mapping Ideology*. London and New York: Verso.

Economic Planning Unit (2001) *Eighth Malaysia Plan*. Putrajaya: Prime Minister's Department.

Eliade, Mircea (1987) *The Sacred and the Profane. The Nature of Religion. The Significance of Religious Myth, Symbolism, and Ritual within Life and Culture*. San Diego and New York: Harcourt Brace and Company.

Featherstone, Mike (1991) 'The body in consumer culture'. In Mike Featherstone, Mike Hepworth and Bryan S. Turner (eds), *The Body. Social Process and Cultural Theory*. London: Sage.

Fischer, Johan (2007) 'Boycott or buycott? Malay middle-class consumption post-9/11'. *Ethnos* vol. 72 (1): 129–50.

— (forthcoming 2008) 'Nationalizing rituals? the ritual economy in Malaysia'. *Journal of Ritual Studies* vol. 22 (2).

Fishman, Robert (1987) *Bourgeois Utopias. The Rise and Fall of Suburbia*. New York: Basic Books.

Forbes, Dean (1996) *Asian Metropolis. Urbanisation and the Southeast Asian City*. Oxford: Oxford University Press.

Geertz, Clifford (1968) *Islam Observed. Religious Development in Morocco and Indonesia*. Chicago: The University of Chicago Press.

— (1980) *Negara: The Theatre State in 19th Century Bali*. Princeton: Princeton University Press.

— (1983) *Knowledge: Further Essays in Interpretive Anthropology*. New York: Basic Books.

— (1993) *The Interpretation of Cultures*. London: Fontana Press.

Ger, Güliz and Russell W. Belk (1999) 'Accounting for materialism in four cultures'. *Journal of Material Culture*, vol. 4 (2), pp. 183–204.

Gibson-Graham, J. K. (1997) *The End of Capitalism (as We Knew It). A Feminist Critique of Political Economy*. Oxford: Blackwell.

Giddens, Anthony (1991) *Modernity and Self-identity*. Cambridge: Polity Press.

Gillette, Maris Boyd (2000) *Between Mecca and Beijing. Modernization and Consumption among Urban Chinese Muslims*. Stanford: Stanford University Press.

Gillis, John R. (1996) *A World of Their Own Making. Myth, Ritual, and the Quest for Family Values*. Cambridge: BasicBooks.

Gilsenan, Michael (2000) *Recognizing Islam. Religion and Society in the Modern Middle East*. London: I. B. Tauris.

Goffman, Erving (1971) *The Presentation of Self in Everyday Life.* London: Penguin Books.

Goh Beng Lan (1999): 'Modern dreams. an inquiry into power, cityscape transformations and cultural difference in contemporary Malaysia'. In Joel S. Kahn (ed.), *Southeast Asian Identities. Culture and the Politics of representation in Indonesia, Malaysia, Singapore, and Thailand.* Singapore: I. B. Taurus.

— (2001) 'Rethinking urbanism in Malaysia: power, space and identity'. In Maznah Mohamad and Wong Soak Koon (eds), *Risking Malaysia. Culture, Politics and Identity.* Bangi: Penerbit UKM in Association with Malaysian Social Science Association.

— (2002) *Modern Dreams. An Inquiry into Power, Cultural Production, and the Cityscape in Contemporary Urban Penang, Malaysia.* Ithaca: Southeast Asia Program Publications at Cornell University.

Gomez, Edmund Terence (1994) *Political Business. Corporate Involvement of Malaysian Political Parties.* Townsville: Centre for South-East Asian Studies, James Cook University of North Queensland.

Gullick, J. M. (1994) *Old Kuala Lumpur.* Oxford: Oxford University Press.

Gupta, Akhil (1995) 'Blurred boundaries: the discourse of corruption, the culture of politics, and the imagined state'. *American Ethnologist*, vol. 22 (2), pp. 375–402.

Hansen, Thomas and Finn Stepputat (2001) 'Introduction: states of imagination'. In Thomas Hansen and Finn Stepputat (eds), *States of Imagination. Ethnographic Explorations of the Postcolonial State.* Durham and London: Duke University Press, pp. 1–40.

Haron, Sudin (1997) *Islamic Banking. Rules and Regulations.* Petaling Jaya: Pelanduk Publications.

Harris, Marvin (1997): 'The Abominable Pig'. In Carole Counihan and Penny Van Esterik (eds), *Food and Culture. A Reader.* New York and London: Routledge.

Herzfeld, Michael (1992) *The Social Production of Indifference. Exploring the Symbolic Roots of Western Bureaucracy.* Chicago and London: The University of Chicago Press.

— (1997) *Cultural Intimacy. Social Poetics in the Nation-State.* London: Routledge.

Hirschkind, Charles (2001) 'Civic virtue and religious reason'. *Cultural Anthropology*, 16 (1), pp. 3–34.

Hirschman, Charles (1987) 'The meaning and measurement of ethnicity in Malaysia: an analysis of census classification'. *Journal of Asian Studies*, vol. 46 (3), pp. 555–82.

Hobsbawm, Eric J. (1992) 'Introduction: inventing traditions'. In Eric J. Hobsbawm and Terence Ranger (eds), *Invention of Tradition.* Cambridge: Cambridge University Press, pp. 1–14.

Hogan, Trevor and Christopher Houston (2002) 'Corporate cities – urban gateways or gated communities against the city?: The case of Lippo, Jakarta'. In Tim Bunnell, Lisa B. W. Drummond and Ho Kong Chong (eds), *Critical Reflections on Cities in Southeast Asia.* Leiden: Brill Academic Publishers.

Huntington, Samuel (1993) *The Clash of Civilizations: And the Remaking of World Order.* New York: Free Press.

— (2004) *Who Are We? The Challenges to America's National Identity*. New York: Simon and Schuster.

Jacobs, Jane M. (1996) *Edge of Empire. Postcolonialism and the City*. New York: Routledge.

Jomo K. S. (1986) *A Question of Class. Capital, the State, and Uneven Development in Malaya*. Singapore: Oxford University Press.

Jomo, K. S. and Ahmad Shabery Cheek (1992) 'Malaysia's Islamic movements'. In Joel S. Kahn and Francis Loh Kok Wah (eds), *Fragmented Vision. Culture and Politics in Contemporary Malaysia*. North Sydney: Asian Studies Association of Australia in association with Allen & Unwin, pp. 79–106.

Kahn, Joel L. (1996) 'The middle classes as a field of ethnological study'. In Muhammad Ikmal Said and Zahid Emby (eds), *Malaysia: Critical Perspectives. Essays in Honour of Syed Husin Ali*. Kuala Lumpur: Persatuan Sains Social Malaysia, pp. 12–33.

Kassim, Mohd Sheriff Mohd (1995) 'Vision 2020's linkages with the sixth Malaysia plan and the second outline perspective plan'. In Ahmad Sarji Abdul Hamid (ed.), *Malaysia's Vision 2020*. Kelana Jaya: Pelanduk Publications, pp. 67–87.

Kessler, Clive S. (2001) 'Alternative approaches, divided consciousness: dualities in studying the contemporary Southeast Asian middle class'. In Abdul Rahman Embong (ed.), *Southeast Asian Middle Classes. Prospects for Social Change and Democratisation*. Bangi: Penerbit Universiti Kebangsaan Malaysia, pp. 31–45.

Keyes, Charles F., Laurel Kendall and Helen Hardacre (1994) 'Introduction: contested visions of community in east and Southeast Asia'. In Charles F. Keyes, Laurel Kendall and Helen Hardacre (eds), *Asian Visions of Authority. Religion and the Modern States of East and Southeast Asia*. Honolulu: University of Hawaii Press, pp. 1–18.

Khoo Boo Teik (1995) *Paradoxes of Mahathirism: An Intellectual Biography of Mahathir Mohamad*. Kuala Lumpur: Oxford University Press.

Khuri, Fuad I. (2001) *The Body in Islamic Culture*. London: Saqi Books.

Kolig, Erich (2001) 'Modernisation without secularisation? civil pluralism, democratisation, and re-islamisation in Indonesia'. *New Zealand Journal of Asian Studies*, vol. 3 (2), pp. 17–41.

Kopytoff, Igor (1999) 'The cultural biography of things'. In Arjun Appadurai (ed.), *The Social Life of Things. Commodities in Cultural Perspective*. Cambridge: Cambridge University Press, pp. 64–91.

Kusno, Abidin (2000) *Behind the Postcolonial. Architecture, Urban Space and Political Cultures in Indonesia*. New York: Routledge.

— (2002) 'Architecture after Nationalism: Political Imaginings of Southeast Asian Architects'. In Tim Bunnell, Lisa B. W. Drummond and Ho Kong Chong (eds), *Critical Reflections on Cities in Southeast Asia*. Leiden: Brill Academic Publishers, pp. 124–52.

Lasch, Christopher (1979) *Haven in a Heartless World. The Family Besieged*. New York: W. W. Norton and Company.

Leaman, Oliver (2004) *Islamic Aesthetics. An Introduction*. Edinburgh: Edinburgh University Press.

Lee, Boon Thong (1976) 'Patterns of urban residential segregation: The case of Kuala Lumpur'. *Journal of Tropical Geography* vol. 43, pp. 41–8.

— (1983) 'Planning and the Kuala Lumpur metropolis'. *Asian Journal of Public Administration*, vol. 5 (1), pp. 76–86.

— (1987) 'New towns in Malaysia: development and planning policies'. In David R. Phillips and Anthony G. O. Yeh (eds), *New Towns in East and South-east Asia. Planning and Development*. Hong Kong, Oxford and New York: Oxford University Press.

— (1989) 'Reexamining the ethos of urban development strategies in Malaysia'. *Jurnal Fakulti Satera & Sains Sosial Universiti Malaya*, vol. 5, pp. 155–65.

Lee, Martyn J. (2000) 'Introduction'. In Martyn J. Lee (ed.), *The Consumer Society Reader*. Oxford: Blackwell, pp. viiii–xxvi.

Lee, Raymond L.M. (1993) 'The globalization of religious markets: international innovations, malaysian consumption'. *Sojourn*, vol. 8 (1), pp. 35–61.

Liechty, Mark (2002) *Suitably Modern. Making Middle-Class Culture in a New Consumer Society*. Princeton: Princeton University Press.

Loeffler, Reinholdt (1988) *Islam in Practice. Religious Beliefs in a Persian Village*. New York: State University of New York Press.

Mahmood, Saba (2004) *Politics of Piety: The Islamic Revival and the Feminist Subject*. Princeton: Princeton University Press.

Marx, Karl (1976) *Capital Vol. 1*. London: Verso.

Maurer, Bill (2005) *Mutual Life, Limited. Islamic Banking, Alternative Currencies, Lateral Reason*. Princeton: Princeton University Press.

Mauss, Marcel (1979) 'Body techniques'. *Sociology and Psychology,* vol 2 (1), pp. 70–87.

Mazzarella, William (2003) *Shoveling Smoke. Advertising and Globalization in Contemporary India*. Durham and London: Duke University Press.

Miller, Daniel (1994) *Modernity. An Ethnographic Approach. Dualism and Mass Consumption in Trinidad*. Oxford and New York: Berg.

— (1997) *Capitalism: An Ethnographic Approach*. Oxford and New York: Berg.

— (1998) *A Theory of Shopping*. Cambridge: Polity Press.

— (2000) 'Object domains, ideology and interests'. In Martyn J. Lee (ed.), *The Consumer Society Reader*. Oxford: Blackwell, pp. 106–24.

— (2001a) 'Driven societies'. In Daniel Miller (ed.), *Car Cultures*. Oxford and New York: Berg, pp. 1–33.

— (2001b) 'Behind closed doors'. In Daniel Miller (ed.), *Home Possessions. Material Culture Behind Closed Doors*. Oxford and New York: Berg, pp. 1–19.

— (2001c) 'Possessions' in Daniel Miller (ed.), *Home Possessions. Material Culture Behind Closed Doors*. Oxford and New York: Berg, pp. 107–21.

— (2005) 'Materiality: an introduction'. In Daniel Miller (ed.), *Materiality*. Durham and London: Duke University Press, pp. 1–50.

Milne, R. S. and Diane K. Mauzy (1999) *Malaysian Politics under Mahathir*. London: Routledge.

Milner, Anthony (1998) 'Constructing the Malay majority'. In Dru C. Gladney (ed.), *Making Majorities: Constituting the Nation in Japan, Korea, China, Malaysia, Fiji, Turkey, and the United States*. Stanford: Stanford University Press, pp. 151–69.

Mitchell, Timothy (1999) 'Society, economy, and the state effect'. In George Steinmetz (ed.), *State/Culture: New Approaches to the State After the Cultural Turn*. New York: Cornell University Press.

Moeran, Brian (1996) *A Japanese Advertising Agency: An Anthropology of Media and Markets*. London: RoutledgeCurzon.

Mohamad, Mahathir (1970) *The Malay Dilemma*. Singapore: Times Books International.

— (1986) *The Challenge*. Kelana Jaya: Pelanduk Publications.

— (1993) *Perspectives on Islam and the Future of Muslims*. Kuala Lumpur: Institute of Islamic Understanding.

— (2001) *Islam and the Muslim Ummah. Selected Speeches of Dr. Mahathir Mohamad, Prime Minister of Malaysia*. Kelana Jaya: Pelanduk Publications.

— (2002) *Reflections on Asia*. Kelana Jaya: Pelanduk Publications.

Moore, Sally F. and Barbara G. Myerhoff (1977) 'Introduction: secular ritual: forms and meanings'. In Sally F. Moore and Barbara G. Myerhoff (eds), *Secular Ritual*. Assen/ Amsterdam: Van Gorcum, pp. 3–24.

Mouffe, Chantal (2005) *On the Political*. Abingdon and New York: Routledge.

Muzaffar, Chandra (1979) *Protector? An Analysis of the Concept and Practice of Loyalty in Leader-led Relationships within Malay Society*. Pulau Penang: Aliran Press Publications.

Nagata, Judith (1984) *The Reflowering of Malaysian Islam. Modern Religious Radicals and their Roots*. Vancouver: University of British Columbia Press.

— (1994) 'How to be Islamic without being an Islamic state'. In Akbar S. Ahmed and Hastings Donnan (eds), *Islam, Globalization and Postmodernity*. London: Routledge, pp. 63–90.

— (1995) 'Modern malay women and the message of the veil'. In Wazir Jahan Karim (ed.), *'Male' and 'Female' in Developing Southeast Asia*. Oxford: Berg, pp. 101–20.

Nairn, Tom (1977) *The Break-up of Britain*. London: New Left Books.

Navaro-Yashin, Yael (2002) *Faces of the State. Secularism and Public Life in Turkey*. Princeton: Princeton University Press.

Nik Mohamad Affindi Bin Nik Yusuff (2001) *Islam and Wealth. The Balanced Approach to Wealth Creation, Accumulation and Distribution*. Kelana Jaya: Pelanduk Publications.

Noor, Farish A. (2001) 'Constructing kafirs. The formation of political frontiers between the government and the Islamic opposition during the 1998–1999 political crisis of Malaysia'. In Angelika Neuwirth and Andreas Pflitsch (eds), *Crisis and Memory in*

Islamic Societies. Proceedings of the third Summer Academy of the Working Group Modernity and Islam held at the Orient Institute of the German Oriental Society in Beirut. Beirut: Orient Institute of Beirut, pp. 403–16.

O'Connor, Richard A. (1995) 'Indigenous urbanism: class, city and society in Southeast Asia'. *Journal of Southeast Asian Studies*, vol. 26 (1), pp. 30–45.

O'Dougherty, Maureen (2002) *Consumption Intensified: The Politics of Middle-class Daily Life in Brazil.* Durham and London: Duke University Press.

Ong, Aihwa (1995) 'State versus islam: malay families, women's bodies, and the body politic in Malaysia'. In Aihwa Ong and Michael G. Peletz (eds), *Bewitching Women, Pious Men. Gender and Body Politics in Southeast Asia.* Berkeley: University of California Press, pp. 159–94.

— (1999) *Flexible Citizenship. The Cultural Logics of Transnationality.* Durham and London: Duke University Press.

Ong, Aihwa and Michael G. Peletz (1995) 'Introduction'. In Aihwa Ong and Michael G. Peletz (eds), *Bewitching Women, Pious Men. Gender and Body Politics in Southeast Asia.* Berkeley: University of California Press, pp. 1–18.

Peletz, Michael G. (2002) *Islamic Modern. Religious Courts and Cultural Politics in Malaysia.* Princeton: Princeton University Press.

Pietz, William (1985) 'The Problem of the Fetish', *Res*, vol. 9, pp. 5–17.

PuruShotam, Nirmala (1998) 'Between compliance and resistance. Women and the middle-class way of life in Singapore'. In Krishna Sen and Maila Stivens (eds), *Gender and Power in Affluent Asia.* London: Routledge, pp. 127–66.

Riaz, Mian N. and Muhammad M. Chaudry (2004) *Halal Food Production.* Boca Raton: CRC Press.

Riddell, Peter (2001) *Islam and the Malay-Indonesian World. Transmission and Responses.* Singapore: Horizon Books.

Riese, Astrid, Lasse Koefoed and Johan Fischer (1997) *The End of the Western World: Modernitet og Identitetsdannelse i Malaysia* [The end of the western World. modernity and identity formation in Malaysia]. Roskilde University: Unpublished MA Dissertation.

Robertson, Roland (1992) *Globalization. Social theory and Global Culture.* London: Sage.

Robison, Richard and David S. G. Goodman (eds) (1996) *The New Rich in Asia. Mobile Phones, McDonald's and Middle-Class Revolution.* London and New York: Routledge.

Roff, William R. (1994) *The Origins of Malay Nationalism. Second Edition.* Singapore: Oxford University Press.

Said, Kamaruddin M. (1993) *The Despairing and the Hopeful. A Malay Fishing Community in Kuala Kedah.* Bangi: Penerbitan Universiti Kebangsaan Malaysia.

Sardar, Ziauddin (2000) *The Consumption of Kuala Lumpur.* London: Reaktion Books.

Schimmel, Annemarie (1992) *Islam. An Introduction.* New York: State University of New York Press.

Sennett, Richard (1977) *The Fall of Public Man*. London: Penguin Books.

Shamsul, A. B. (1994) 'Religion and ethnic politics in Malaysia – the significance of the islamic resurgence phenomenon'. In Charles F. Keyes, Laurel Kendall and Helen Hardacre (eds), *Asian Visions of Authority. Religion and the Modern States of East and Southeast Asia*. Honolulu: University of Hawai'i Press, pp. 99–116.

— (1997) 'Identity construction, nation formation, and Islamic revivalism in Malaysia'. In Robert W. Hefner, and Patricia Horvatich (eds), *Islam in an Era of Nation-States. Politics and Religious Rivival in Muslim Southeast Asia*. Honolulu: University of Hawai'i Press, pp. 207–27.

— (1998a) 'Bureaucratic management of identity in a modern state: 'Malayness' in postwar Malaysia'. In Dru C. Gladney (ed.), *Making Majorities: Constituting the Nation in Japan, Korea, China, Malaysia, Fiji, Turkey, and the United States*. Stanford: Stanford University Press, pp. 135–50.

— (1998b) 'Nations-of-intent in Malaysia'. In Stein Tønnesson and Hans Antlöv (eds), *Asian Forms of the Nation*. Richmond: Curzon Press, pp. 323–47.

— (1998c) 'Contextualizing "reproductive technology" in non-western societies: The "body" in Malay society'. Paper presented at the conference *Genes over the World: Reproductive Technologies, The Moral and Cultural Dimension* organised by Evangelische Akademie Locum in association with the International Steering Committee EXPO 2000, Hanover held at Loccum-Rehburg, Germany 23–6 October, pp. 1–17.

— (1999a) 'From *orang kaya baru* to *melayu baru*. cultural constructions of the malay "new rich"'. In Michael Pinches (ed.), *Culture and Privilege in Capitalist Asia*. London: Routledge, pp. 86–110.

— (1999b) 'Consuming Islam and containing the crisis. Religion, ethnicity, and the economy in Malaysia'. In Mason Hoadley (ed.), *Economies or Economics*. Copenhagen: Nordic Institute of Asian Studies, pp. 43–61.

— (2000) 'Colonial knowledge and identity formation: literature and the construction of Malay and Malayness'. *Asian Culture Quaterly*, vol. xxvii (1), pp. 49–64.

Shiraishi, Saya (1997) *Young Heroes. The Indonesian Family in Politics*. New York: Cornell Southeast Asia Program.

Siegel, James (1997) *Fetish, Recognition, Revolution*. Princeton: Princeton University Press.

— (1998) *A New Criminal Type in Jakarta. Counter-Revolution Today*. Durham and London: Duke University Press.

Simoons, Frederick J. (1994) *Eat Not This Flesh. Food Avoidances from Prehistory to the Present*. Madison and London: The University of Wisconsin Press.

Sirriyeh, Elisabeth (1998) *Sufis and Anti-Sufis: The Defence, Rethinking and Rejection of Sufism in the Modern World*. Richmond: Curzon Press.

Sloane, Patricia (1999) *Islam, Modernity and Entrepreneurship among the Malays*. Houndmills, Basingstoke, Hampshire: Macmillan Press.

Starrett, Gregory (1995) 'The political economy of religious commodities in Cairo'. *American Anthropologist*, vol. 97 (1), pp. 51–68.

Stivens, Maila (1998a) 'Modernizing the Malay mother'. In Kalpana Ram and Margaret Jolly (eds), *Maternities and Modernities. Colonial and Postcolonial Experiences in Asia and the Pacific*. Cambridge: Cambridge University Press, pp. 50–80.

— (1998b) 'Sex, gender and the making of the new Malay middle classes'. In Krishna Sen and Maila Stivens (eds), *Gender and Power in Affluent Asia*. London: Routledge, pp. 87–126.

Talib, Rokiah (2000) 'Malaysia: power shifts and the matrix of consumption'. In Chua Beng-Huat (ed.), *Consumption in Asia. Lifestyles and Identities*. London: Routledge, pp. 35–60.

Taussig, Michael (1980) *The Devil and Commodity Fetishism in South America*. Chapel Hill: The University of North Carolina Press.

— (1992) 'Maleficium: state fetishism'. In *The Nervous System*. New York and London: Routledge, pp. 111–40.

— (1999) *Defacement. Public Secrecy and the Labor of the Negative*. Stanford: Stanford University Press.

Thompson, E. P. (1963) *The Making of the English Working Class*. New York: A. A. Knopf.

Thompson, Kenneth (1998) *Moral Panics*. London: Routledge.

Turner, Bryan S. (1994) *Orientalism, Postmodernism and Globalism*. London: Routledge.

Wallerstein, Immanuel (1991) 'The bourgeois(ie) as concept and reality'. In Etienne Balibar and Immanuel Wallerstein, *Race, Nation, Class. Ambiguous Identities*. London: Verso, pp. 135–52.

Wilk, Richard R. (1993) 'Beauty and the feast: official and visceral nationalism in Belize'. *Ethnos*, vol. 58 (3–4), pp. 294–317.

Yanagisako, Sylvia Junko and Jane Fishburne Collier (1987) 'Introduction'. In Sylvia Junko Yanagisako and Jane Fishburne Collier (eds), *Gender and Kinship. Essays Toward a Unified Analysis*. Stanford: Stanford University Press, pp. 1–13.

Yao Souchou (2000) '*Xiao ye*: food, alterity and the pleasure of Chineseness in Malaysia'. *New Formations*, nr. 40, pp. 64–79.

— (2002) *Confucian Capitalism. Discourse, Practice and the Myth of Chinese Enterprise*. London: RoutledgeCurzon.

Zainah, Anwar (1987) *Islamic Revivalism in Malaysia. Dakwah among the Students*. Kelana Jaya: Pelanduk Publications.

Zizek, Slavoj (1993) *Tarrying with the Negative*. Durham and London: Duke University Press.

Zukin, Sharon (2004) *Point of Purchase. How Shopping Changed American Culture*. New York: Routledge.

NEWSPAPERS

NST 8 December 2001.

NST 9 January 2002.

NST 18 January 2002.

NST 7 March 2002.

NST 1 April 2002.

The Star 9 October 2001.

The Star 27 October 2001.

The Star 30 October 2001.

The Star 5 November 2001.

The Star 13 November 2001.

The Star 4 December 2001.

The Star 8 January 2002.

The Star 30 March 2002.

The Star 15 April 2002.

The Star 2 May 2002.

The Sun 30 March 2002.

MAGAZINES AND PERIODICALS

Asiaweek 16 June 2000.

Female March 2002.

Ibu September 1992.

Ibu May 1993.

Ibu October 1994.

Ibu December 1994.

Ibu January 1995.

Ibu September 1995.

Ibu February 1996.

Ibu February 1997.

Ibu April 1997.

Masyarakat TTDI No. 2 October 1992.

Masyarakat TTDI No. 3 December 1992.

Masyarakat TTDI No. 1 March 1993.

Masyarakat TTDI No. 2 July 1993.

Masyarakat TTDI No. 3 September 1994.

Masyarakat TTDI No. 1 March 1995.

Masyarakat TTDI No. 2 September 1995.

Masyarakat TTDI No. 2 September 1996.

Masyarakat TTDI No. 1 August 1997.

Masyarakat TTDI No. 2 October 1998.

Masyarakat TTDI No. 1 March 2001.

Masyarakat TTDI No. 2 June 2001.

Masyarakat TTDI No. 4 December 2004.

Muslimah May 1988.

Muslimah April 1995.

Muslimah July 1997.

Wanita March 1971.

Wanita June 1971.

Wanita July 1979.

Wanita April 1983.

Wanita June 1983.

Wanita July 1983.

Wanita December 1989.

Wanita January 1991.

Wanita January 1992.

Wanita March 1992.

Wanita May 1992.

Wanita November 1992.

Index

NIAS Press is the autonomous publishing arm of
NIAS – Nordic Institute of Asian Studies, a research institute
located at the University of Copenhagen. NIAS is partially funded by the
governments of Denmark, Finland, Iceland, Norway and Sweden
via the Nordic Council of Ministers, and works to encourage and
support Asian studies in the Nordic countries. In so doing, NIAS
has been publishing books since 1969, with more than two
hundred titles produced in the past few years.

COPENHAGEN UNIVERSITY

Nordic Council of Ministers